Political Sociology in a Global Era

Political Sociology in a Global Era

An Introduction to the State and Society

Berch Berberoglu

Paradigm Publishers

Boulder • London

Copyright © 2013 by Paradigm Publishers

Published in the United States by Paradigm Publishers, 5589 Arapahoe Avenue, Boulder, CO 80303 USA.

Paradigm Publishers is the trade name of Birkenkamp & Company, LLC, Dean Birkenkamp, President and Publisher.

Library of Congress Cataloging-in-Publication Data

Berberoglu, Berch.
  Political sociology in a global era : an introduction to the state and society / Berch Berberoglu, University of Nevada, Reno.
     pages cm
  Includes bibliographical references and index.
  ISBN 978-1-61205-173-4 (pbk. : alk. paper)
  1. Political sociology. 2. State, The. 3. Social classes. 4. Social movements. 5. Globalization—Social aspects. I. Title.
  JA76.B47 2012
  306.2—dc23

                                                                        2012047990

Printed and bound in the United States of America on acid-free paper that meets the standards of the American National Standard for Permanence of Paper for Printed Library Materials.

Designed and Typeset by Straight Creek Bookmakers.

17 16 15 14 13   2 3 4 5

Dedicated to the Memory of
Albert J. Szymanski

Contents

Preface

OVER THE COURSE OF THE PAST CENTURY, the state has come to play a central role in modern society. And with this role, there has emerged a renewed interest among scholars in the study of politics and the state. Discussions and debates on the nature and role of the modern state have grown and spread across many disciplines. Together with the analysis of class structure, the state has taken center stage in social analysis in such disciplines as political economy, history, anthropology, and comparative politics, as well as sociology.

Although political sociologists have long tackled the question of the state and its role in society, interest in the state has now become a central feature in the study of politics and society. As a result, the relationship between class and state has become more obvious than before, and some important conclusions have been reached regarding the class nature of the state and politics in contemporary capitalist society.

I hope that this book will make a significant contribution to the field of political sociology and will help clarify the relationship between the state and society in general and the class basis of the state, power, and politics in particular.

Despite all the political turmoil and upheavals of the recent past, societies around the world have shown remarkable resilience in their resistance to change. The Soviet Union is no more, yet the old Soviet republics function much the same as before under a new national identity. The former Eastern European socialist states have over the past two decades moved in a capitalist direction, yet communists have won important victories in elections in Poland, Hungary, and other countries in Eastern Europe during this period. Some have declared the death of socialism and communism in the East and the decline of class politics in the West, yet China has been making great progress under the banner of "socialism" and "communism" that it claims to uphold and is now poised to become the strongest economy in the world, while class struggles have been intensifying in Greece, Spain, Portugal, Italy, France, Germany, and other advanced capitalist states in the West, including the United States. Socialist and communist forces are vying for power through the electoral process in some of these countries, while mass protests against capitalism through the Occupy Wall Street Movement have spread from the United States to many countries around the world. In South Africa, apartheid has been officially abolished, yet the white power structure and Afrikaner capital has flourished under the leadership of Nelson Mandela and the African National Congress (ANC). The "Evil Empire" has been defeated, some have happily proclaimed, yet a substitute has taken its place as the sole superpower as we move onward in the new twenty-first century. Some have declared "the end of history" with capitalism triumphant, but the contradictions of capitalism are surfacing everywhere once again and are bound to intensify with the economic and political crises that have been unfolding across the globe.

The world is rapidly changing, as centers of power shift from one region to another, but the unfolding contradictions of global capitalism are forcing its chief protagonists to build new alliances to maintain their power in response to these changes. We have seen the fierce competition and rivalry between the leading capitalist powers in the economic sphere over the past few decades. The political-military rivalry and confrontation between the competing poles of capital that are in turn bound to develop in the next period will be a reflection of changes in the economic base of global capitalism that the capitalist states will inevitably face on a worldwide basis. Thus, the cyclical fluctuations that have threatened the stability of the capitalist system from within its economic conditions to this day will now lead the system to a new plane where gradual quantitative changes will of necessity lead to the resolution of its fundamental contradictions in a qualitative way, such that the continuing rivalries between the chief capitalist powers will soon evoke open conflict between the main antagonistic classes—labor and capital—within each capitalist society and lend themselves to new (revolutionary) political and social transformations in the coming period. This is already occurring in vast areas of the world, from Latin America to North Africa and the Middle East, and is fast spreading to Greece, Spain, Italy, and other European states, with prospects for further expansion to the rest of Europe and, ultimately, North America, as we are beginning to see.

As we move forward in the twenty-first century, class conflict will emerge as a primary feature of struggles within and between the major capitalist powers as they attempt to further dominate the global political economy in the post-Soviet world order. As we leave behind the Cold War rivalry between the United States and the USSR—a rivalry which kept the U.S. labor movement in check for decades—the rapidly developing contradictions of global capitalism will soon prompt the working class in the United States and elsewhere to take charge of its own agenda and interests and confront the power of capital and the capitalist state head on, and put up a determined fight in the ensuing class struggles bound to come. Thus, the twenty-first century promises to be an exciting century that will affect all aspects of life in a new and most decisive way. The next big fight between labor and capital, between the forces of progress and reaction, may be upon us sooner than many have been led to believe, as the all-round contradictions of capital and the entire capitalist system unravel in front of our eyes in the period ahead.

As in any human activity involving social thought or action, the ideas expressed here are the result of a collective process. Thus, the assumptions made, the concepts utilized, and the approach adopted in this book have been developed over many years of reflection and analysis, involving many people who have addressed the pressing issues concerning the state, and politics in general, and the centrality of *class* in analyzing political institutions and affairs within a comparative-historical framework—a process that is enriched with the highest level of cumulative scholarship embodied in this work.

Much of the intellectual debt I owe ultimately goes to working people and their struggles throughout modern history; together with the giants of social thought in the late nineteenth and early twentieth century, who have helped interpret *and change* the world, it is the common working people who have provided the framework of analysis presented in this book.

Within the academic community, mentors and colleagues have played an important role in the formation and transformation of my thinking during the course of my intellectual development. First and foremost, I am grateful to Larry T. Reynolds for introducing me to the tools and framework of social analysis that I have come to adopt in my studies on politics and society. His teaching and seminars have played an important role in influencing my thinking on critical questions of our time. I would also like to thank Blain Stevenson for his part in setting me on a most valuable political and intellectual journey during my early college years and through my graduate studies, for without his guidance, my work would not have taken the direction it has today. Similarly, I thank James Petras for making a powerful impact on my thinking through his writings and during my graduate studies at the State University of New York at Binghamton in the early 1970s. His intellectual and political influence on me continues to enrich my thinking after four decades.

The consolidation of my ideas on society, especially political sociology, began to take place at the University of Oregon, where I studied for my doctorate under Albert Szymanski in the mid 1970s. During his provocative seminars on social theory, class analysis, and political sociology, I began to formulate many of the ideas I had wrestled with in my earlier studies. My intellectual development came to a head and began to bear fruit at the conclusion of my studies at Oregon in 1977. And an important book that has influenced my thinking in political sociology ever since is Szymanski's *The Capitalist State and the Politics of Class* (Cambridge, MA: Winthrop, 1978). For all I learned from Al, and for his role as friend and mentor, I express my deep appreciation and gratitude. This book is dedicated to his memory.

I would also like to thank Walda Katz Fishman, Alan Spector, Marty Orr, James Petras, Michael Parenti, Dave Harvey, Karl Kreplin, Johnson Makoba, Clayton Peoples, and Levin Welch for their collaboration or participation in discussions and commentary on some of the major political issues addressed in this book.

I would like to thank my students in my undergraduate and graduate political sociology classes and seminars who have discussed and debated the class nature of politics and the state in capitalist society. Their valuable insights and input have helped shape this book.

Finally, I would like to thank my wife, Suzan, for her unwavering intellectual support, without which this book could not have been written.

Needless to say, the ideas expressed in this book—dependent as they are on those of countless others—are nevertheless mine; any errors in facts or interpretation thus remain mine alone.

Introduction

TODAY, AS WE ENTER THE SECOND DECADE of the twenty-first century, and as the state continues to play an increasingly central role in modern society and takes center stage under advanced capitalism, scholars and observers across the political spectrum have developed an interest in the current structure and future direction of the state and its role in society. Thus, while conservative analysts have intensified their anti-state rhetoric, combined with "free market" advocacy against state intervention in the economy and society, and liberal academics have focused on the question of bureaucracy and attempted to develop a "state centered" theory of the state, those on the left have continued their discussion and debate around the class nature of the state, its structural imperatives, and its role in the age of globalization.[1]

Central to the study of the state and its role in society is an analysis of its nature and structure, as perceived by observers from different perspectives. Thus to the question "What is the state?" conventional and Marxist theories of the state have provided competing views and have reconceptualized the relationship between the state and society in various ways. These alternative views of the state are discussed and criticized at length in Chapters 1 and 2.

It should be pointed out at the outset that this book is not a text in conventional political sociology, as the field is traditionally defined, for it does not deal with established mainstream political parties or electoral politics; nor is it a book of political theory as such, though various theories of the state and politics are discussed at length. Instead, this book goes to the heart of the nature and role of the state in society and examines the *linkages between class and state* in different comparative and historical settings, for as the state has increasingly taken center stage in social life, these linkages, taken together, constitute the very foundation of the modern state as the central political institution of our time.[2]

"When talking about the state in any society," writes R. B. Sutcliffe, "we have to ask several questions: firstly, who (what social class, group or alliance of classes) controls or wrestles for the power of the state? Secondly, we must ask how great is the power of the state? This depends upon how powerful are the groups or classes which control it."[3] In discussing the state, "the first question must always be which class is dominant in a given social formation," argues Leys; "since this dominance must be enforced by the state, the class character of the state is given by this relationship."[4] The central question regarding the nature of the state, then, is the character of its relationship with the prevailing dominant social forces in society.

In examining the origins and development of the state, it becomes clear that this question can be answered only through a historically specific analysis of the laws of motion of different modes of production lodged in a particular social formation. The failure of attempts to construct a universal, abstract model of state behavior across societal lines demonstrates the correctness of this observation. Yet, debates over the nature of the state at the general, theoretical level rage across various disciplines and within particular perspectives as well. Thus, while historians, political scientists, sociologists, and other academics ponder the boundaries of state rule in civil society, the structural imperatives of the capitalist economy on state policy continue to occupy center stage of discussion and debate on the state.

The central argument of this book is that class structure and class relations are the major determinants of political power and the state, and that class conflicts and class struggles lie at the center of social and political transformations, for it is only through such struggles that state power is attained and the will of the victorious social class(es) is imposed over society. Thus, it can be argued that the state, as the chief superstructural institution of society, is a *direct product* of the class structure, which sets the political parameters of the social formation in question.

It is argued in this book that efforts toward the conceptualization of the state outside the base-superstructure problematic are doomed to failure, as the political (or more broadly, superstructural) institutions of society (of which the state is the chief component) are a reflection of the social-economic base that the state itself subsequently legitimizes to complete its dialectic. Far from a mechanical, reductionist interpretation of state determinations as a product of the productive forces shaping the relations of production, the interpretation of the base-superstructure problematic adopted in this book is lodged in a *social* (not technical) acceptance of the *primacy of production relations* that define the nature and structure of social classes, class struggles, and struggles for state power. It is within this context of the class basis of political power that the productive forces must be understood, notwithstanding the fact that the productive forces themselves have long ago set the initial parameters of the social conditions leading to the development of social classes, class conflicts, and the formation of the state.

Chapter 3 provides an analysis of the role of the state in different types of societies in the historical process, and traces the origins and development of the state from earlier times to more recent periods. It shows that with the division of society into classes, the state arose to serve the interests of the wealthy and privileged sectors of society. Thus, the ancient, slave-owning state came to serve the interests of the slave owners, the medieval feudal state came to serve the interests of the landlords, and the modern capitalist state came to serve the interests of the capitalists.

Chapter 4 examines the development of the capitalist state in its transition from medieval feudalism, beginning in the sixteenth century. The transformation of the feudal state began with the growth of a merchant class that came to possess immense wealth through overseas trade. Gradually, with the rise to prominence of merchants and manufacturers during the subsequent mercantilist era, the state came to reflect the interests of the rising bourgeoisie, who swept aside competing class forces in the struggle for state power. This chapter takes a closer look at the state as it developed in Europe, and then shifts to the United States to trace the development of the U.S. state since its founding in the late eighteenth century. Through a careful examination of the Constitutional Convention, its participants, and proceedings, this chapter lays bare the class origins and nature of the early U.S. state, which set the stage for its subsequent transformation into a capitalist state following the Civil War, and ultimately into an advanced capitalist state in the early twentieth century.

Chapter 5 takes up the task of examining the crisis of the advanced capitalist state in the United States in the latter part of the twentieth century into the twenty-first, and provides data and analysis on some of its fundamental contradictions. Here, it is argued that the crisis of the advanced capitalist state in the United States is a product of its global expansion—that is, a consequence of the expansion of U.S. capital on a world scale.

Chapter 6 examines the nature and role of the state in the less-developed countries and discusses the nature of the capitalist state in different historic and geographic settings. In this context, the chapter discusses the origins and development of the state in Latin America, Asia, Africa, and the Middle East within the framework of the global political economy and shows that the state in the less-developed countries has historically been an organ of local landowning and capitalist interests tied to foreign capital. This neocolonial relationship explains the class nature of the state in these regions and at the same time reveals its most fundamental contradictions, which often have led to civil wars and revolutions.

An alternative path against capitalism and the capitalist state across the globe has led to the emergence of social movements that have engaged in mass protests, demonstrations, and social upheaval in a number of important regions of the world. Chapter 7 provides an analysis of the factors contributing to the emergence and development of social movements against the prevailing social order and examines the nature and evolution of social movements that have been developing in response to the impact of neoliberal capitalist globalization on societies around the world in the late twentieth and early twenty-first centuries.

Finally, Chapter 8 provides a concluding analysis of the nature, origins, development, and role of the state, and examines the relationship between class, state, and power in society, informing our inquiry into the politics of change based on the nature of class relations, class struggles, and social transformation.[5]

Notes

1. In the pages that follow, the major competing perspectives on the role of the state and politics in classical and contemporary social-political theory are discussed.

2. The relationship between class and state, as well as the state and nation and other related issues, are discussed at length in Berch Berberoglu, *Nationalism and Ethnic Conflict: Class, State, and Nation in the Age of Globalization* (Lanham, MD: Rowman & Littlefield, 2004) and *The State and Revolution in the Twentieth Century: Major Social Transformations of Our Time* (Lanham, MD: Rowman & Littlefield, 2007).

3. R. B. Sutcliffe, *Industry and Underdevelopment* (London: Addison-Wesley, 1971), 285.

4. Colin Leys, "The 'Overdeveloped' Post-Colonial State: A Re-Evaluation," *Review of African Political Economy* 5 (1976): 44.

5. For an extended analysis of the class basis of social relations and social transformation, see Berch Berberoglu, *Class Structure and Social Transformation* (Westport, CT: Praeger Publishers, 1994) and *Class and Class Conflict in the Age of Globalization* (Lanham, MD: Lexington, 2009).

Chapter 1

Conventional Theories of the State

CONVENTIONAL SOCIAL AND POLITICAL THEORIES have always served to justify and rationalize the legitimacy of the existing social, economic, and political order. In so doing, they have invariably promoted the interests of the dominant ruling class. This has been the case with the early conservative theorists of the state, such as Niccolò Machiavelli and Thomas Hobbes, who advocated the absolute power of the state, arguing that any means utilized by the state to achieve or maintain power is legitimate.[1] Jean-Jacques Rousseau, Baron Montesquieu, Georg Wilhelm Friedrich Hegel, Emile Durkheim, and other classical conventional theorists have played a similarly conservative role in defending the existing social conditions and the legitimacy of the prevailing social order by providing a host of theoretical rationalizations that have served to maintain the rule of the dominant class in society.[2] Hegel's theory of the state is a prime example of this mode of theorizing.

Classical elite theory, which has viewed the masses as apathetic, incompetent, and unable to govern themselves—and for whom, therefore, elite rule is claimed to be both necessary and desirable—has served the same purpose as its Hegelian counterpart in rationalizing elite rule in no uncertain terms. Moreover, downgrading the intelligence and ability of the masses, classical elite theorists have claimed that not only does the incompetence of the masses prevent them from taking part in the political process, but in instances when they do rise up in revolution and take control of the state, their leadership becomes corrupted, and a new ruling class, in turn, comes to dictate its terms over society.

This chapter consists of two parts. The first part examines classical conventional theories of the state, focusing on Hegel's theory and classical elite theory of politics and the state. It provides a critical analysis of both the substance and ideological bases of classical conservative theories of the state and their reactionary political implications. The second part focuses on contemporary variants of conventional theories of the state, which include pluralism, functionalism, and their neo-Weberian variants.

Classical Conventional Theories of the State

We begin our survey of classical conventional theories of the state with a brief look at Hegel's theory—one that will serve as a basis for an analysis of the classical elite theory of politics and the state that we will examine later in this section.

Hegel's Theory of the State

Hegel's views on politics and the state were heavily shaped by his idealist philosophy of history and society. In a typical idealist formulation of the problem, Hegel's concept of the state is based not on any existing state, but on the "*idea* of the state."[3]

In his rational construction of the concept, Hegel viewed the state as having the task of achieving universality (i.e., as caretaker of the "general will"). In this sense, he counterposed the state's public mission to the private sphere within which civil society functioned. With the state representing the universal community, Hegel assigned to the state the responsibility of combating the harmful effects of civil society based on the individual will. In so doing, he set out to find a moment of mediation between the public and the private spheres to achieve the desired unity.

> The essence of the modern state is that the universal be bound up with the complete freedom of its particular members and with private well being.... The universal must be furthered, but subjectivity on the other hand must attain its full and living development. It is only when both of these moments subsist in their strength that the state can be regarded as articulated and genuinely organized.[4]

To obtain this equilibrium and thus to maintain social order and stability in society, the process requires the functional integration of the individual into the prevailing sociopolitical order led by the state.

> The state is absolutely rational inasmuch as it is the actuality of the substantial will which it possesses in the particular self-consciousness once that consciousness has been raised to consciousness of its universality. This substantial unity

is an absolute unmoved end in itself, in which freedom comes into its supreme right. On the other hand, this final end has a supreme right against the individual, whose supreme duty is to be a member of the state.[5]

In this context, Frederick Copleston points out that for Hegel "the State represents the unity of the universal and the particular" such that "in the State self-consciousness has risen to the level of universal self-consciousness."[6] In this sense, Copleston continues, "The individual is conscious of himself as being a member of the totality in such a way that his selfhood is not annulled but fulfilled."[7] And the State precisely in this way becomes the instrument for the expression of collective identity. Thus, for Hegel, Copleston writes,

> The State is not an abstract universal standing over against its members: it exists in and through them. At the same time, by participation in the life of the State the members are elevated above their sheer particularity. In other words, the State is an organic unity. It is a concrete universal, existing in and through particulars which are distinct and one at the same time.[8]

Moreover, according to Copleston's further rendering of the Hegelian state, one that highlights its spiritual content, for Hegel, "The State is the actuality of the rational will when this has been raised to the plane of universal self-consciousness. It is thus the highest expression of objective Spirit. And the preceding moments of this sphere are resumed and synthesized in it."[9]

Rationalizing the primacy of the state, Hegel assigned to the state a supreme, all-powerful position that has clearly religious and metaphysical connotations: Referring to it as "this actual God,"[10] he viewed the existence of the state as part of a divine plan, one that "embodies the true, the eternal wisdom of the Spirit—of God."[11] His statement along these lines—written in the original German as "Es ist der Gang Gottes in der Welt, dass der Staat ist," and variously translated into English as "The State is the march of God through the world," "The existence of the State is the presence of God on earth," "The march of God in the world, that is what the state is," or "It is the course of God through the world that constitutes the state,"[12]—does, despite the controversy surrounding its precise meaning, convey a link between the state and divine authority that reveals not only its religious or ethically driven character, but also its absolute nature, as some critics have accused Hegel to be promoting.[13]

This sacred, religiously defined idealist conceptualization of the state and society is similar to Emile Durkheim's functionalist definition of society as the supreme entity (conceived in similarly religious terms) to which the individual must submit and conform, if the harmony between the individual and the state is to be achieved into a unity—the ideal state.

But for Hegel, the state's role and mission is more than that mandated by God; it is sacred not so much because the state represents God's will but because it involved first and foremost the maintenance of order and harmony in the prevailing feudal society threatened by the rise of private capital (i.e., civil society). "Hegel explains the breakdown of the German state by contrasting the feudal system with the new order of individualist society that succeeded it,"[14] writes Marcuse. "The rise of the latter social order," he adds, "is explained in terms of the development of private property."[15] According to Hegel, "The feudal system proper," Marcuse continues, "integrated the particular interests of the different estates into a true community. The freedom of the group or of the individual was not essentially opposed to the freedom of the whole."[16] But, "in modern times," he writes, Hegel believed "exclusive property has completely isolated the particular needs from each other"[17] such that the parts have no relation to the whole. Thus, for Hegel, the only institution that serves to hold society together is the state.

The rationalization and legitimization of the state in these terms, however, serve to justify the continued exploitation of the masses by the dominant ruling class through the harmonizing role of the state over society, notwithstanding the claim that this was done under a divine plan devised by God. In reality this took place within the context of a feudal social order in which the state was ruled by the landowning class, and the Church was among the largest landowners, under the pretext of lifting the people to a higher, spiritual level that would usher in true freedom—one based on the unity of the public and private spheres, through their mutual communion.

Suffice it to say, the Hegelian theory of the state, based, in essence, on an idealist, metaphysical conceptualization, provides us no better than the official propaganda of the dominant classes to legitimize their rule and, in the process, to rationalize the reign of a supreme authority exerting its power over the oppressed and exploited laboring masses.

Moving beyond mythical philosophical statements and rationalizations of the state, an analysis of the class nature of the Hegelian ideal state and its role in society reveals its true nature—a utopian ideal that cannot be achieved in its purest form as projected, on the one hand, and an unconditional support for the state that, however "bad" or "sick" it may be, does represent the entire society, on the other hand. It is this authoritative role that Hegel assigns the state, explained in the abstract and divorced from any fruitful understanding of the class nature of society,[18] which, in the final analysis, reinforces his conservative theory of the state as one that rationalizes and legitimizes the exploitation of the laboring masses and their overall place in society in favor of conformity and law and order, rather than helping them liberate themselves from their misery.

In this context, Hegel did not shy away from making his views known on the affinity between his thinking and that of Machiavelli, when he wrote:

> Profoundly moved by the situation of general distress, hatred, disorder, and blindness, an Italian statesman grasped with cool circumspection the necessary idea of the salvation of Italy through its unification on one state....
>
> Machiavelli's fundamental aim of erecting Italy into a state was misunderstood from the start by the blind who took his work as nothing but a foundation of tyranny or a golden mirror for an ambitious oppressor.[19]

Praising *The Prince* and its author for his brilliant work and its relevance to the nature and tasks of the state, Hegel had this to say about Machiavelli:

> You must come to the reading of *The Prince* immediately after being impressed by the history of the centuries before Machiavelli and the history of his own times. Then indeed it will appear as not merely justified but as an extremely great and true conception produced by a genuinely political head with an intellect of the highest and noblest kind.[20]

Aside from his conservative political views and inclinations toward the justification of authoritarian rule—a product of his uncritical acceptance of the prevailing social-economic and political order under both declining feudalism and emerging capitalism, which he accepted as legitimate, including the legitimacy of private property and profit—it took the Young Hegelians, who ended up rebelling against him, to liberate Hegel from the shackles of his own metaphysics and to set his theory free from the influence of conditions so well cultivated by the Church and the dominant ruling classes that Hegel himself could not (or did not want to) see for what they were. Doing so otherwise may have forced Hegel to pick up the banner of revolution (as did Marx, Engels, and Lenin) and effect change by smashing the state, not glorifying it, as Hegel did, toward its ideal perfection.

This, of course, had to wait until the mature Marx, like the Young Hegelians before him, was able to turn everything Hegelian, including Hegel himself, on its head and provide us with a materialist conception of history and the state—one that will be taken up in Chapter 2.

For now, however, we shall look at the works of several other classical conventional political theorists who, directly and without any pretense, have advocated a conception of the state and society that has lent support to the justification and legitimization of elite rule—theories that were instrumental in giving rise to and were the rationalization for a series of authoritarian fascist dictatorships in Europe in the early twentieth century.

Classical Elite Theory on Politics and the State

Classical (aristocratic) elite theory is best exemplified by the works of Gaetano Mosca, Vilfredo Pareto, and Robert Michels. Together, their work on elite formation and oligarchic rule constitutes the core of the classical bureaucratic elite theory of politics and the state.

Classical elite theory maintains that all societies are ruled by elites and that the state is the political instrument by which the vast majority is ruled. This is so, according to this view, because the masses are inherently incapable of governing themselves; therefore, society must be led by a small number of individuals (the elite) who rule on behalf of the masses.

An understanding of the historical context in which Mosca, Pareto, and Michels developed their theories is important and instructive, for they formulated their approach in reaction to socialist currents in Europe at the end of the nineteenth century and beginning of the twentieth.

Mosca on the Political Elite and the State

"In the world in which we are living," wrote Mosca quite bluntly, "socialism will be arrested only if a realistic political science succeeds in demolishing the metaphysical and optimistic methods that prevail at present in social studies."[21] Targeting in particular Karl Marx and his theory of historical materialism, Mosca argued that his book *The Ruling Class* "is a refutation of it."[22]

> Now one of the doctrines that are widely popular today, and are making a correct view of the world difficult, is the doctrine commonly called "historical materialism." ... The greatest danger that lies in the wide acceptance of the theory, and in the great intellectual and moral influence which it exerts, lies on the modicum of truth that it contains....
>
> The conclusion of the second assumption of historical materialism, and indeed of the doctrine as a whole, seems to us utterly fantastic—namely, that once collectivism is established, it will be the beginning of an era of universal equality and justice, during which the state will no longer be the organ of a

class and the exploiter and the exploited will be no more. We shall not stop to refute that utopia once again. *This whole work [The Ruling Class] is a refutation of it.*[23]

The "realistic science" that Mosca wanted to develop was in fact primarily intended to refute Marx's theory of power on two essential points:

First, to show that the Marxist conception of a "ruling *class*" is erroneous, by demonstrating the continual circulation of elites, which prevents in most societies, and especially in modern industrial societies, the formation of a stable and closed ruling class; and secondly, to show that a classless society is impossible, since in every society there is, and must be, a minority which actually rules.[24]

Let us take a closer look at the substance of Mosca's theory and attempt to understand it against this background and in relation to Pareto's and Michels's views on politics and the state.

Mosca's main objective in his major work *The Ruling Class* was to develop a *political* theory of power. He divided people in all societies into two distinct groups: "the ruling class" (the political elite) and "the class that is ruled" (the masses). The political elite always enjoy a monopoly of power over the masses and govern society according to its own interests.

In all societies ... two classes of people appear—a class that rules and a class that is ruled. The first class, always the less numerous, performs all political functions, monopolizes power and enjoys the advantages that power brings, whereas the second, the more numerous class is directed and controlled by the first, in a manner that is now more or less legal, now more or less arbitrary and violent.[25]

Mosca attempted to establish "the real superiority of the concept of the ruling, or political, class," to show that "the varying structure of ruling classes has a preponderant importance in determining the political type, and also the level of civilization, of the different peoples."[26] Hence, for Mosca, it is the political apparatus of a given society and an organized minority (i.e., the political elite) that controls this apparatus—not the class structure—that determines the nature of the state and its transformation.[27]

Claiming that the political elite is usually composed of "superior individuals" and that this superiority serves to further the legitimization of elite rule, Mosca writes:

Ruling minorities are usually so constituted that the individuals who make them up are distinguished from the mass of the governed by qualities that give them a certain material, intellectual or even moral superiority; or else they are the heirs of individuals who possessed such qualities. In other words, members of a ruling minority regularly have some attribute, real or apparent, which is highly esteemed and very influential in the society in which they live.[28]

At one point, Mosca entertains the possibility that "the discontent of the masses might succeed in deposing a ruling class," but he immediately adds, "Inevitably ... there would have to be another organized minority within the masses themselves to discharge the functions of a ruling class."[29] Hence, for Mosca, it is pointless to make a revolution since every revolution will bring to power a minority (an elite) that will become the new ruling class and exercise its power over the masses.

Pareto on the Circulation of Elites and Elite Rule

Although there are similarities between the arguments presented by Mosca and Pareto, the latter's theoretical formulation of "the governing elite" and his conceptualization of elite rule need to be clarified: "So let us make a class of the people who have the highest indices in their branch of activity, and to that class give the name of *elite*."[30] By the term *elite*, Pareto meant to stress the superior (psychological) qualities of the ruling minority.

Further elaborating on the internal composition of this group, he divided the elite into two (political and social) segments:

> A *governing elite*, comprising individuals who directly or indirectly play some considerable part in government, and a *non-governing elite*, comprising the rest....
>
> So we get two strata in a population: (1) a lower stratum, the *non-elite*, with whose possible influence on government we are not just here concerned; then (2) a higher stratum, *the elite*, which is divided into two: *(a)* a governing *elite*, *(b)* a non-governing *elite*.[31]

Within this framework, the fundamental idea set forth and developed by Pareto was that of the "circulation of elites." By this, he meant two diverse processes operative in the perpetual continuity of elite rule: one, the process in which *individuals* circulate between the elite and the nonelite; and two, the process in which a *whole elite* is replaced by a new one.

The main point of Pareto's concept of the circulation of elites is that the ongoing process of replenishment of the governing elite by superior individuals from the lower classes is a critical element securing the continuation of elite rule. "The governing class is restored not only in numbers, but—and that is the more important thing—in quality, by families rising from the lower classes and bringing with them the vigor and the proportions of residues necessary for keeping themselves in power."[32]

A breakdown in this process of circulation of elites, however, leads to such serious instability in the social equilibrium that "the governing class crashes to ruin and often sweeps the whole of a nation along with it."[33]

In Pareto's reasoning, a "potent cause of disturbance in the equilibrium is the accumulation of superior elements in the lower classes and, conversely, of inferior elements in the higher classes."[34] Hence, "every *elite* that is not ready to fight to defend its position is in full decadence; there remains nothing for it to do but to vacate its place for another *elite* having the virile qualities which it lacks."[35]

Thus, Pareto reaches an inescapable conclusion in his four-volume study: "Aristocracies do not last. Whatever the causes, it is an incontestable fact that after a certain length of time they pass away. History is a graveyard of aristocracies."[36] According to Pareto, the dynamics of societal development are such that they eventually lead to total social transformation, and no elite is immune to this law of history.

"Revolutions," Pareto writes,

> come about through accumulations in the higher strata of society ... of decadent elements no longer possessing the residues suitable for keeping them in power, and shrinking from the use of force; while meantime in the lower strata of society elements of superior quality are coming to the fore, possessing residues suitable for exercising the functions of government and willing enough to use force.[37]

Pareto's explanation of the nature and dynamics of elite rule and their circulation, therefore, rests in large part on the personal qualities of individuals in both elite and nonelite segments of society and their willingness or failure to use force to acquire and retain political power.

Pareto's concern with the decline in legitimacy of the existing order in Italy in the early decades of this century, together with the rising popularity of Marxism, which he opposed, drove him to fascism. "Fascism, for Pareto," writes Irving Zeitlin, seemed not only to confirm his theories but also to hold out hope for a "new era." That he identified with the new order is borne out by the fact that on March 23, 1923, he accepted an appointment as senator—a position he had declined to accept in the pre-fascist government. In a letter to an acquaintance at the time of acceptance, he wrote: "I am happy to see that you are favorably disposed to the new regime, which, in my opinion, is the only one capable of saving Italy from innumerable evils." And, in the same vein, "France will save herself only if she finds her own Mussolini."[38]

"In general," Zeitlin continues, "Pareto's attitude seems to have been that since the pre-fascist regime did not, or could not, save the country from 'anarchy' by legal means, fascism had to do it by force."[39] Such an attitude is similar to Hegel's, which, as we have seen earlier in our discussion, led Hegel to develop a similar admiration of Machiavelli and his role in history.

Pareto's affinity with fascism goes well with his conservative theory of elite rule that despises the masses for their incompetency, a view that is consistent with a reactionary worldview characteristic of conservative conventional theories of the state.

Michels on Bureaucratic Organization and the State

Robert Michels, the third influential classical elite theorist, stressed that the source of the problem of elite rule lies in the nature and structure of bureaucratic organization.[40] He argued that the bureaucratic organization itself, irrespective of the intentions of bureaucrats, results in the formation of an elite-dominated society. Thus, regardless of ideological ends, organizational means would inevitably lead to oligarchic rule: "It is organization which gives birth to the domination of the elected over the electors, of the mandataries over the mandators, of the delegates over the delegators. Who says organization, says oligarchy."[41]

At the heart of Michels's theoretical model lie the three basic principles of elite formation that take place within the bureaucratic structure of political organization: one, the need for specialized staff, facilities, and, above all, leaders; two, the utilization of such specialized facilities by leaders within these organizations; and three, the psychological attributes of the leaders.

Michels argued that the bureaucratic structure of modern political parties or organizations, as well as the state, gives rise to specific conditions that corrupt the leaders and bureaucrats. These leaders, in turn, consolidate power and set themselves apart from the masses.

"Even the purest of idealists who attains to power for a few years," he wrote, "is unable to escape the corruption which the exercise of power carries in its train."[42] For Michels, this pointed to the conservative basis of (any) organization, since the *organizational form* as such was the basis of the conservatism, and this conservatism was the inevitable outcome of power attained through political organization. Hence, "political organization leads to power, but power is always conservative."[43]

Based on this reasoning, one might think that Michels was an anarchist. He was not. He insisted that *any* organization, *including those of the anarchists*, was subject to the "iron law":

> Anarchism, a movement on behalf of liberty, founded on the inalienable right of the human being over his own person, succumbs, no less than the Socialist Party, to the law of authoritarianism as soon as it abandons the region of pure thought and as soon as its adherents unite to form associations aiming at any sort of political activity.[44]

This same phenomenon of elitism/authoritarianism, argued Michels, also occurs at the individual level. Hence, to close the various gaps in his theory, he resorted to human nature–based tautological arguments: Once a person ascends to the leadership level, he or she becomes a part of the new social milieu to the extent that the person would resist ever leaving that position. The argument here is that the leader consolidates power around the newly acquired condition and uses that power to serve his or her own interests by preserving the maintenance of that power. To avoid this and eliminate authoritarianism, which comes about in "associations aiming at any sort of political activity," one must not "abandon the region of pure thought." Herein lay the self-serving conservatism of Michels, who in the latter part of his life turned, like Pareto before him, to the cause of Italian fascism.

In his introduction to a recent edition of Michels's book *Political Parties*, Seymour Martin Lipset writes, "Michels, who had been barred from academic appointment in Germany for many years … left his position at the University of Basel to accept a chair at the University of Perugia offered to him personally by Benito Mussolini in 1928."[45]

Lipset goes on to point out that "Michels found his charismatic leader in Benito Mussolini. For him, Il Duce translated 'in a naked and brilliant form the aims of the multitude.'"[46] Finally, he adds, Michels "died as a supporter of fascist rule in Italy."[47]

The three major proponents of classical elite theory—Mosca, Pareto, and Michels—have provided a political theory of elites that they believed explains the nature and dynamics of power in modern society. Best exemplified in Mosca's characterization of the ruling class as the governing elite of full-time politicians in charge of the state apparatus and society in general, classical elite theory has argued in favor of a theory based on a conceptualization centered in bureaucratic organization, particularly in the sphere of politics, such that power, according to their view, resides in government and the governing elite.

Given its contempt for the masses and its acceptance of elite rule over them as an inevitable outcome of bureaucratic organization prevalent in modern politics, classical elite theory lends itself to antipopular, reactionary conclusions that have important political implications diametrically opposed to the prospects for change and social transformation in favor of the masses.

Weber's Theory of Bureaucracy, Power, and the State

Although Max Weber is generally not included among classical elite theorists of the state, his analysis of bureaucracy and political power lends itself to an affinity with elite theory (especially with Michels's "iron law of oligarchy") as he assigns a *quasi*-autonomous role to the state wherein the bureaucrats appear to be serving their own interests, and the bureaucracy appears to be a power unto itself, with more and more permanent features.[48] "Bureaucracy," writes Weber, "is a power instrument of the first order," adding that "where the bureaucratization of administration has been completely carried through, a form of power relation is established that is practically unshatterable."[49]

"Bureaucratic organizations, or the holders of power who make use of them," Weber points out, "have the tendency to increase their power still further by the knowledge growing out of experience in the service."[50] But "expertise alone does not explain the power of bureaucracy"; equally important is the bureaucrats' possession of "official information" to which they and they alone have direct access—something that Weber sees as the "supreme power instrument" of the bureaucracy.[51]

In Weber's view, bureaucracies are large-scale, impersonal organizations in which power relations are organized in a top-down hierarchical manner for purposes of efficiently attaining centrally defined goals. Thus, bureaucratic discipline "is nothing but the consistently rationalized, methodically prepared and exact execution of the received order, in which all personal criticism is unconditionally suspended and the actor is unswervingly and exclusively set for carrying out the command."[52]

The main reason for the prevalence of and expansion of bureaucratic organization for Weber is its technical superiority to all other forms of organization.[53]

> The fully developed bureaucratic apparatus compares with other organizations exactly as does the machine with the non-mechanical modes of production. Precision, speed, unambiguity, knowledge of the files, continuity, discretion, unity, strict subordination, reduction of friction and of material and personal costs—these are raised to the optimum point in the strictly bureaucratic administration, and especially in its monocratic form.[54]

Outlining Weber's description of the general characteristics of a bureaucratic administrative staff, David L. Westby provides a summary list of the structural features of bureaucratic organization and the characteristics of bureaucratic officialdom:

A. Organizational features
   1. Official jurisdictional areas ordered by rules, so that organizational activities are assigned as official duties delimited in a stable way by rules and continuously fulfilled.
   2. An established hierarchy of authority under a central authority.
   3. Separation of office from private domicile and performance of organizational duties on the basis of written documents maintained in files.
   4. Office management presupposes specialized training as the basis for employment.
   5. Organizational activities become full-time.
   6. Management proceeds according to general rules, the knowledge of which "represents a special technical expertise."
B. Characteristics of officialdom
   1. The holding of office is a vocation, meaning that incumbency is based on training and evidence of competence, and that the official is oriented to discharge of office as a "duty."
   2. There is a strong relationship between certain organizational characteristics and the extent to which office incumbency determines the status position of the official.
   3. The official is appointed.
   4. Tenure tends to be for life. This has the effect of contributing to the performance of the organization, but may affect the social status of the official and the technical efficiency of the organization negatively.

5. The official is remunerated by a money salary (and so a money economy is a presupposition of a bureaucracy).
6. The official moves through a career within the organizational hierarchy. This, along with (4) and (5), contributes to the creation of office sinecures in the form of prebends.[55]

In this context of the nature of bureaucratic administration, Weber notes the rise to prominence of the "expert" as a logical outcome of the growth of society and of bureaucracy: "The more complicated and specialized modern culture becomes, the more its external supporting apparatus demands the personally detached and strictly objective expert."[56] Through the possession of technical knowledge, the expert is able to obtain "a position of extraordinary power." Moreover, "bureaucratic organizations, or the holders of power who make use of them," Weber continues, "have the tendency to increase their power still further by the knowledge growing out of experience in the service."[57] But "expertise alone does not explain the power of bureaucracy"; equally important is the bureaucrats' possession of "official information" to which they, and they alone, have direct access—Weber sees this as the "supreme power instrument" of the bureaucracy.[58]

The bureaucratic form of social organization, Weber argues, thus lends itself to control and domination of society and the individuals within it and generates as a by-product a social alienation that puts managers and workers, bureaucrats and citizens, in opposite camps, thus leading to conflict between those who control and govern and those who are controlled and governed at all levels of society.

Given their logic and organizational structure, bureaucracies, Weber believed, often take on lives of their own, which are often beyond the control of individual bureaucrats who take part in their daily operation. Thus, according to Weber, once a bureaucracy is firmly in place, it becomes a political force that can very seldom be successfully dismantled or eliminated.

The individual bureaucrat cannot squirm out of the apparatus into which he has been harnessed.... In the great majority of cases he is only a small cog in a ceaselessly moving mechanism which prescribes to him an essentially fixed route of march....

The ruled, for their part, cannot dispense with or replace the bureaucratic apparatus once it exists.... Increasingly the material fate of the masses depends upon the continuous and correct functioning of the ever more bureaucratic organizations of private capitalism, and the idea of eliminating them becomes more and more utopian.[59]

The key question then becomes one of determining *who* controls and directs the complex bureaucratic machine. Unlike Michels, however, Weber does *not* believe bureaucracy is, in essence, an autonomous power unto itself; rather, it is a tool or instrument *of* power.

> The bureaucratic structure goes hand in hand with the concentration of the material means of management in the hands of the master. This concentration occurs, for instance, in a well-known and typical fashion in the development of big capitalist enterprises, which find their essential characteristics in this process. A corresponding process occurs in public organizations.[60]

Thus, "the consequences of bureaucracy," Weber concludes, "depend therefore upon the direction which the *powers using the apparatus* give to it."[61]

Weber's statement here could be interpreted in two possible ways: one that assigns primacy to the political process and grants a special role to the bureaucrats—as individuals and as a group—who manage the day-to-day affairs of the political apparatus, and another where the source of power is located outside the narrow confines of the political institutions in which individual bureaucrats and the bureaucracy as a whole operate—that is, the economy and class structure of society.

It is not surprising that most contemporary Weberians have separated Weber's analysis of bureaucracy from his generalized theory of class and power in society and thus have managed to give a conservative twist to his otherwise controversial analysis. Viewed within a broader societal context, however, it becomes clear that bureaucracy and political power are to Weber the manifestations of the real social forces that dominate the social-economic structure of modern society. Thus, to give primacy to the analytic strength of these secondary political concepts would mean one is dealing with surface phenomena. This is clearly evident, for example, in the works of most contemporary theorists of complex organizations, where power is located within the structure of specific bureaucratic organizations, while bureaucracies are seen as having a life of their own and are conceived in terms of their special power and dynamics. But, to Weber, to understand more fully the logic of bureaucracy and political control, one must examine the nature of property, income, status, and other dimensions of class relations, in society. It is here, in his differential conceptualization of class, status, and power based on market relations, that one finds a uniquely Weberian approach to bureaucracy, power, and the state—an approach that has had an important influence on various contemporary conventional theories of the state.

Contemporary Conventional Theories of the State

We begin our survey of contemporary conventional theories by examining the most prominent of these theories in the United States: pluralist theory.

Pluralism

Until recently, the predominant approach in mainstream American political sociology has been pluralist theory. Claiming that society is made up of a multitude of conflicting interest groups balanced by the state, pluralists see these groups as equally influential in their impact on government policy and major institutions in society.[62] "Political power or influence in the United States," writes Arnold Rose,

> is distributed over as many citizens, working through their associations, as want to take the responsibility for power.... Through the voluntary association the ordinary citizen can acquire as much power in the community or the nation as his free time, ability, and inclinations permit him to.[63]

Society, according to pluralists, consists of many diverse groups and associations (e.g., business, labor, and professional, religious, and other organizations) and constitutes a conglomeration of dissimilar and often conflicting interests—no one of which plays a singularly dominant role—that, through a process of "democratic competition," determine the nature and direction of society.[64] Hence, "It is ... multiple memberships in potential groups based on widely held and accepted interests that serve as a balance wheel in a going political system like that of the United States."[65]

State policy, which the pluralists argue flows out of the pressures of these groups, is seen as the result of bargaining and compromise among the groups in the state's pursuit of achieving equilibrium in society. In this view, the state serves neither its own interests nor those of any single group or class; instead, its primary task is to balance the interests of a multitude of competing groups. Thus, "A major preoccupation of government is the policing of conflicts of interest."[66]

"Pressure," writes Bentley, a prominent American pluralist, "is always a group phenomenon. It indicates the push and resistance between groups. The balance of the group pressures is the existing state of society."[67] Thus,

> In governments like that of the United States we see these manifold interests gaining representation through many thousands of officials in varying degrees of success ... while "special interests" make special use of officials, rising in

other spots to dominate, using one agency of the government against another, now with stealth, now with open force, and in general moving along the route of time with that organized turmoil which is life where the adjustments are much disturbed.[68]

According to pluralists, the political process is made up of social groups, and policy outcomes are a result of group processes. Being essentially "autonomous" and "democratic," and each reflecting its special social situation, these groups, claim the pluralists, play a key role in charting the course of societal development.[69] The "push and pull" and "cross pressures" resulting from the competitive struggle between "veto groups" work to ensure a mutual resolution of problems in favor of all parties concerned and thus guarantee the stability of the political system.[70] In this way, the state is able to institutionalize its rule and maintain order in society.

Functionalism

In a manner similar to pluralist reasoning, functionalist sociologists such as Talcott Parsons and Neil Smelser have also characterized the modern U.S. state as a democratic institution whose primary function is to promote harmony within the system to secure equilibrium and order.[71] Representing the interests of society as a whole, the state coordinates the other major institutions of society—the economy, education, religion, and so on—and advances both the general social welfare and that of individuals within it. Thus, for functionalists, while the state provides strong, effective leadership and represents institutionalized power and authority vis-à-vis the citizenry, its rule nevertheless reflects the widespread and diverse interests that exist in society—interests that, the functionalists claim, are well represented within the state. As the supreme guardian of representative democracy in modern society, the state thus fulfills its role in carrying out its social tasks while ensuring its democratic control by society.

Parsons views "power" as a generalized resource with multiple functions that are equitably managed and coordinated by the state. Therefore, Parsons explains,

It has to be divided or allocated, but it also has to be produced and it has collective as well as distributive functions. It has the capacity to mobilize the resources of the society for the attainment of goals for which a general "public" commitment has been made, or may be made. It is mobilization, above all, of the action of persons and groups, which is *binding* on them by virtue of their position in the society.[72]

Thus, the state maintains an autonomous role for itself as the sole public authority and at the same time assures the equal distribution of power across competing political groups in society. "This tension in functionalist thinking on the state between a view of the necessity for a strong, modernizing, central coordinator on the one hand, and a relatively equal distribution of social powers on the other," observes one critic, "reflects the cross-pulls from two allegedly functional pre-requisites: the need for autonomy and the need for integration."[73] By distributing its control among a broad range of social groups and preventing its monopoliza-tion by any one group, the state, according to the functionalists, thus paves the way for political competition and pluralist democracy.[74]

The pluralist and functionalist notion that in America power resides with many diverse and equally powerful groups reflecting the interests of the vast majority of the population—a notion advanced in the mid-nineteenth century by Tocqueville in his *Democracy in America*—has come under strong criticism in recent decades. In the late 1950s, critics, led by C. Wright Mills, began to provide a powerful critique of pluralism and Parsonian functionalism that set the stage for subsequent debates within political sociology.[75] Expanding this effort dur-ing the 1960s and early 1970s, Grant McConnell, G. William Domhoff, Richard Hamilton, and Michael Parenti, as well as numerous others, were instrumental in widening the attack on pluralism and thus breaking its decades-long monopoly over political theory.[76]

In brief, these critics pointed out that very few people in the total population belong to a multitude of voluntary associations, and those who do are often mem-bers of social, cultural, youth, church, or other groups whose primary interests are often not political. Also, most of the associations that people belong to lack any democratic control by the rank and file, such as trade unions, political parties, and religious organizations; these organizations are bureaucratically structured, which prevents direct individual participation in decision making.[77] In addition, the dis-proportionate power of different associations rules out meaningful compromise and the balancing of conflicting interests among these groups.[78] More specifically,

> Voluntary associations are asymmetrical in the amount of power they wield per member. For example, the AFL-CIO, with over 15 million members, does not have as much clout as the Council on Foreign Relations (the leading busi-ness group dealing with foreign affairs), which has only about 1300 members, because of the tremendous economic power and the political connections of the latter group. Business people and corporations are far more organized, politically conscious, politically active, and able to influence politics through money, connections, and prestige.[79]

Thus, it turns out that pluralism in American society exists among the most powerful and wealthy business interests and groups, not among broad segments of the population.[80] In this context, the policies of the state reflect the interests of the most powerful economic groups in U.S. society—owners of the means of production and distribution, or capitalists—while the structural imperatives of the capitalist system over state policy (i.e., the basic operating principles of capitalism within which policies are formulated and implemented) result in the institutionalization of capitalist class rule.[81] Thus, the pluralist claim that the modern U.S. state is an arbiter of conflicting interests of many divergent groups in American society and that this represents "pluralist democracy" has been shown to be far from reality; critics have argued that this claim is to a large degree a reflection of the preoccupation of pluralists with analyzing *formal* political institutions, and have criticized them for confusing how politics is supposed to work with how it *actually* works under capitalism. They have further pointed out that claims regarding the prevalence of "pluralist democracy" in America have served as an ideological rationale for the continuation of prevailing class divisions in American society.

Elite Pluralism

Another variant of pluralism, commonly referred to as "elite pluralism," attempts to redefine pluralist democracy in the light of the prominence of elites in modern society. Seymour Martin Lipset is the best-known proponent of this version of pluralist theory; other pluralists, such as Robert Dahl, have arrived at a similar conception of power and politics in their later writings.[82] In this elitist reformulation of the pluralist position, the meaning of democracy is changed from one of direct popular rule to that of competition among elites to control the state. Conceding that the masses do not govern themselves through popular rule, the "elite pluralists" have thus developed the idea of "competing elites" as the main contenders for political power. As Martin Marger points out, "Modern pluralists have synthesized the reality of elite rule with the view of a pluralistic elite structure, a characteristic that presumably assures a form of democracy."[83] Such pluralistic competition takes place *among elites*, however, *not* between diverse and equally powerful groups in the larger society.

Corporatism, proposed by some as a remedy for interest-group domination of the state, is viewed by its proponents as a necessary corrective to the complexities of modern industrial society where the clash of group interests now threatens the very survival of society.[84] In this reformulation of the pluralist problematic, the state enters into the political equation as the supreme organ responsible for organizing and leading society under its own directives. Defined as representing "the common good," the state is viewed here as the guardian of order and moral authority that can bring about class harmony and national unity.[85] The corporatist state thus takes on the responsibility of leading the nation by taking an active role in the major institutions of society, including the economy.[86]

But critics point out that this intervention by a strong central state in capitalist society, growing out of the state's continued control by the capitalist class, actually results, at best, in the consolidation of capital's power in the advanced capitalist polity during "normal" periods,[87] while preparing the groundwork for the rise of the authoritarian state in crisis-ridden, less-developed capitalist countries[88] and, ultimately, providing the material base for the emergence of fascism in response to economic and political crises of advanced capitalism, as was the case in Italy and Germany earlier in this century.[89] Thus, corporatism, a more sophisticated form of elite pluralism, incorporating into the power structure the direct intervention of the state, can be seen as a political form designed to protect the interests of corporate capitalism under both "normal" and crisis conditions.

Given the convergence of the two views, the elite pluralist and corporatist conceptualizations of power turn out to be much closer to the Hegelian and classical elite theory of the state than the theory of "pluralist democracy."

Critical Elite Theories

In contrast to the classical (aristocratic) version of elite theory, which views the masses as apathetic, incompetent, and unable to govern themselves, and for whom, therefore, elite rule is both necessary and desirable, the contemporary (critical) version of elite theory views the masses as manipulated and exploited by elites and takes up a position highly critical of elite rule.

The most influential proponent of the critical version of elite theory is C. Wright Mills. In his pioneering work, *The Power Elite*, written at the height of McCarthyism and the Cold War in the 1950s, and at a time when pluralism was dominant in political theory, Mills advanced the position that American society is governed by a small but influential *power elite* consisting of the top layers of the three most important institutions of modern society: the economy, the state, and the military.[90] Referring to the power elite, Mills wrote:

> They are in command of the major hierarchies and organizations of modern society. They rule the big corporations. They run the machinery of the state and claim its prerogatives. They direct the military establishment. They occupy the strategic command posts of the social structure.[91]

In a manner similar to classical elite theorists, especially Pareto, but also Mosca, Mills characterized the elite as those holding the highest positions in the key institutions of society. Broader in scope than Mosca's political elite and more restricted in size and extent than Pareto's multitude of elites across many institutions and professions, Mills's work focused on the three institutions he identified as the centers of power in modern American society. In this sense, Mills's approach is an integration and reformulation of positions advanced by classical elite theorists, informed at the same time by the bureaucratic organizational formulations of Michels and Weber, on the one hand, and Marx's class analysis approach, on the other, while rejecting the essentially conservative political implications of the classical elite model and advancing in its place a radical critique of the theory and practice of elite rule.

Mills's intellectual struggle against conservative political interpretations of classical elite theory opened the way to a new approach in political sociology, prompting scholars like Floyd Hunter to undertake studies on the national power structure and on important policy-making groups and institutions.[92] Hunter's findings supported Mills's contention regarding the existence of a power elite composed of individuals situated in the government, the military, and the business sector—the latter, representing corporate interests, emerging as the dominant institution. Extending beyond the established academic circles, Mills's pioneering work informed the thinking of a new generation of critical scholars, such as G. William Domhoff, who have contributed to the popularization of Mills's approach through "power structure research."[93]

Domhoff, going beyond Mills, reconceptualizes the power elite in class terms. He argues that there is in the United States a corporate *upper class* that owns major business assets and controls the bulk of the wealth of the country.[94] Domhoff shows that this class, by virtue of its economic power, also controls and influences important departments and agencies of the state, and in this way becomes a "governing class." For Domhoff, the governing class is

a social upper class which owns a disproportionate amount of the country's wealth, receives a disproportionate amount of a country's yearly income, and contributes a disproportionate number of its members to the controlling institutions and key decision-making groups of the country.[95]

Domhoff goes on to show that this upper class controls the major banks and corporations; major newspapers, radio, television, and other mass media; elite universities; foundations; important private advisory groups and organizations, such as the Council on Foreign Relations and the Committee for Economic Development; as well as the executive branch of government, the cabinet, the judiciary, the military, and the regulatory agencies.[96] Thus, through an analysis of the linkages between the upper class and the personnel occupying posts in major private and public institutions of American society, Domhoff confirms the prevalence of a dominant power elite, which he identifies as "the American business aristocracy."[97]

While Domhoff's detailed empirical work on the American governmental and institutional structure and linkages of the upper class to the state has contributed much to our understanding of the mechanisms of control of the U.S. state by the "corporate upper class," the fundamentally institutional focus of this stream of thought has generally turned attention away from a class analysis approach based on the social relations of production and exploitation that Marxists have argued are the foundations of class-divided societies such as the United States.

Whereas the locus of relations between elites and masses, for both the conservative and critical versions of elite theory (except for Domhoff), is political rule by elite functionaries over the masses in society, the Marxist approach focuses on economic power based on the ownership and control of the means of production and exploitation of labor as the source of political power and control of the state (a theme that will be discussed at length in Chapter 2).

Neo-Weberian Theories

Other recent approaches to state theory, adopted by authors influenced by the Weberian school, have stressed the autonomy of the state vis-à-vis the dominant and dominated classes, hence seeing the state as an independent power base free from the control of contending class forces.[98] These authors, writing in the neo-Weberian tradition, have augmented classical elite theory to redefine the role of the state and its bureaucratic apparatuses beyond pluralist conceptualizations to provide a contemporary conventional counterpart of classical elite theory, highlighting the role of the bureaucrats, and, through them, the neutrality of the state as a relatively autonomous force that provides it a privileged status to act in its own interests.

Ellen Kay Trimberger, in her book *Revolution from Above*, provides a neo-Weberian formulation of state autonomy—as distinct from its contemporary Marxist variant, "the relative autonomy of the state," which we will discuss in Chapter 2—claiming that exceptional periods occur when the state assumes an independent role and state bureaucrats become independent agents who act in their own self or positional interests. Trimberger writes:

A bureaucratic state apparatus, or a segment of it can be said to be relatively autonomous when those who hold high civil and/or military posts satisfy two conditions: (1) they are not recruited from the dominant landed, commercial or industrial classes; and (2) they do not form close personal and economic ties with these classes after their elevation to high office.[99]

Although Trimberger contends that they hold on to no particular class interests of their own (or those of other classes), it is not clear why "dynamically autonomous bureaucrats" would be "acting to destroy an existing economic and class order" in crisis situations.[100] Trimberger's general contention that "control of the governing apparatus is a source of power independent of that held by class"[101] is presented as an argument against Marxism and is, in fact, a restatement of a revised version of the Weberian position on the state and state bureaucracy.

An extension of this line of reasoning has led some analysts, such as Fred Block, to argue that the state and state officials become "autonomous" agents while still functioning within the framework of existing structures; they acquire "autonomy" from the dominant class and determine policy over the heads of this class, including the formulation of policies that sometimes go *against* the interests of the dominant class.[102]

In his controversial article "The Ruling Class Does Not Rule," Block makes a case in favor of "state managers," who, he argues, are autonomous agents functioning in their own self (or positional) interests and are *not* consciously engaged in the protection of the interests of the dominant class. Thus, Block introduces into the debate "autonomous state managers" controlled by no one and subservient to no particular class interests other than their own—although they are forced to formulate policies within the framework of an environment that includes both ruling class domination of the economy and conflict between two contending class forces, labor and capital. This becomes clear when Block states: "State managers do have an interest in expanding their own power, including their own power to manage the economy."[103] To back up this claim, Block writes: "German capitalists were reduced to being functionaries, albeit highly paid functionaries, of the Nazi state that was acting in its own profoundly irrational interests."[104]

Elsewhere, Block contends that the rationality of the state emerges out of "the three-sided relationship between state managers, capital and subordinate classes."[105] Referring to this formulation, he writes: "The virtue of this model is that it allows one to get away from the standard Marxist methodological tool of assuming that state policies always reflect the intentionality of a social class or sector of a class. It renders obsolete the procedure of looking for a specific social base for any particular state policy."[106] Block goes on to argue: "One can say that a policy objectively benefited a particular social class, but that is very different from saying that this social class, or sector of a class, subjectively wanted the policy or that its intentions were a critical element in policy development."[107]

This seemingly broader theoretical formulation, which allows "state managers" considerable independence of action turns out to be another neo-Weberian attempt at the construction of a conventional theory of the state.

Others, such as Theda Skocpol, have adopted an approach similar to that of Trimberger and Block in conceptualizing the state as an independent force, and in the process have come to embrace a more elaborate "state centered" approach. Influenced by the theories of Weber and Hintze, and utilizing the methodological approach of Barrington Moore Jr., Skocpol's book *States and Social Revolutions* attempts to counter the classical Marxist position on the relationship of the state to the mode of production and the class basis of politics and the state.[108] She writes:

> In contrast to most (especially recent) Marxist theories, this view refuses to treat states as if they were mere analytic aspects of abstractly conceived modes of production, or even political aspects of concrete class relations and struggles. Rather it insists that states are actual organizations controlling (or attempting to control) territories and people.[109]

Arguing in favor of the view that the state is an entity with "an autonomous structure—a structure with a logic and interests of its own,"[110] Skocpol examines the French, Russian, and Chinese revolutions in terms of the centrality of the state's role in "acting for itself." "State and party organizations," she argues, must be viewed "as *independent* determinants of political conflicts and outcomes."[111] Skocpol sees in the state "potential autonomy of action over ... the dominant class and existing relations of production."[112] In this formulation, the state is divorced from social classes and acts in accordance with its distinct interests in society— interests based primarily on the maintenance of internal order and competition against external forces (i.e., other states) threatening its survival. "The political crises that have launched social revolutions," writes Skocpol, "have not at all been epiphenomenal reflections of societal strains or class contradictions. Rather, they have been direct expressions of contradictions centered in the structures of old-regime states."[113] To understand better those processes where the state has taken the center stage of history, Skocpol suggests "the need for a more state-centered approach" in studying states.[114]

Conclusion

Despite the differences between various classical and contemporary conventional theories of the state and political power, they all basically agree that the state, regardless of its internal structure, is an institution that represents the interests of society as a whole, or acts to coordinate and balance the various competing interests to maintain order by using the power relegated to it by consent or by force to govern society. The overriding characteristic of the state on which nearly all classical and contemporary conventional state theories agree is the autonomy of the state to carry out its role and functions to maintain order on behalf of society. In this conceptualization of the state, the prevailing class structure or the class forces that influence and control the state are not questioned, let alone brought to bear on the state's actions to explain particular state policies that favor the dominant classes in society. It is for this reason that the state is viewed as an independent institution devoid of class content—both in terms of the class nature of the state and the class content of its actions that affect classes differentially. Countering these conservative theories, Chapter 2 provides a survey of classical and contemporary Marxist theories of the state, society, and social transformation that emerges from the contradictions and conflicts imbedded in the prevailing social, economic, and political system.

Notes

1. See Niccolò Machiavelli, *The Prince* (1513); Thomas Hobbes, *Leviathan* (1651).
2. Jean-Jacques Rousseau, *The Social Contract* (1762); Baron Montesquieu, *The Spirit of Laws* (1748); Georg Wilhelm Friedrich Hegel, *Philosophy of Right* (1821); Emile Durkheim, *The Division of Labor in Society* (1893).
3. G. W. F. Hegel, *Philosophy of Right* (Oxford: T. M. Knox, 1942), 258.
4. Ibid., 260.
5. Ibid., 258.
6. Frederick Copleston, *A History of Philosophy*, Vol. 7 (New York: Doubleday Image, 1994), 212.
7. Ibid.
8. Ibid.
9. Ibid.
10. Hegel quoted in ibid., 213.
11. Irving M. Zeitlin, *Ideology and the Development of Sociological Theory*, 6th ed. (Upper Saddle River, NJ: Prentice Hall, 1997), 52.
12. These series of translations correspond to the following sources, respectively: Hegel, *Selections*, ed. Jacob Loewenberg (New York: Charles Scribner's Sons, 1957), 443; E. F. Carritt, "Hegel and Prussianism," in Hegel's *Political Philosophy*, ed. Walter Kaufmann (New York: Atherton Press, 1970), 36; Hegel, *Philosophy of Right* (Oxford: The Clarendon Press, 1942), 279; Carl J. Friedrich, ed., *The Philosophy of Hegel* (New York: Modern Library, 1954), 283.
13. Karl R. Popper, *The Open Society and Its Enemies* (Princeton, NJ: Princeton University Press, 1950).

14. Herbert Marcuse, *Reason and Revolution: Hegel and the Rise of Social Theory* (New York: Oxford University Press, 1941), 53.

15. Ibid.

16. Ibid.

17. Hegel quoted in ibid, 53.

18. Hegel's rudimentary class model identifies three general classes in society: the agricultural class (which includes landlords and peasants alike), the commercial class (which includes the business class), and the "universal" class (made up of civil servants in the bureaucracy). Workers in this model are completely left out of the picture—they are not part of any class! See, for example, Shlomo Avineri, *Hegel's Theory of the Modern State* (Cambridge: Cambridge University Press, 1972), 98–109.

19. Hegel, *Political Writings* (Cambridge: Cambridge University Press, 1999), 219–220.

20. Ibid.

21. Gaetano Mosca, *The Ruling Class* (New York: McGraw-Hill, 1939), 327.

22. Ibid., 447.

23. Ibid., 439, 447 (emphasis added).

24. T. B. Bottomore, *Elites and Society* (Baltimore: Penguin, 1966).

25. Mosca, *The Ruling Class*, 50.

26. Ibid., 51.

27. Ibid., 329.

28. Ibid., 53.

29. Ibid., 51.

30. Vilfredo Pareto, "Elites and Their Circulation," in *Structured Social Inequality*, ed. C. S. Heller (New York: Macmillan, 1969), 35.

31. Ibid., 35 (emphasis in the original).

32. Ibid., 38.

33. Ibid.

34. Ibid.

35. Ibid., 40.

36. Ibid., Vol. 3, 1430.

37. Ibid.

38. Irving M. Zeitlin, *Ideology and the Development of Sociological Theory* (Englewood Cliffs, NJ: Prentice Hall, 1968), 194.

39. Ibid.

40. Robert Michels, *Political Parties* (New York: Free Press, 1968).

41. Ibid., 365.

42. Ibid., 355.

43. Ibid., 333.

44. Ibid., 327–328.

45. Seymour Martin Lipset, "Introduction," in Michels, *Political Parties*, 33.

46. Ibid., 32.

47. Ibid., 38.

48. Max Weber, *From Max Weber, Essays in Sociology*, trans. and eds. H. H. Gerth and C. Wright Mills (New York: Oxford University Press, 1967).

49. Ibid., 228.

50. Ibid., 225.

51. Ibid., Vol. 3, 1418.

52. Max Weber, *Economy and Society*, eds. Guenther Roth and Claus Wittich (New York: Bedminster Press, 1968), 3: 1149.

53. Weber, *Economy and Society*, 3: 973.

54. Ibid.

55. David L. Westby, *The Growth of Sociological Theory* (Englewood Cliffs, NJ: Prentice Hall, 1991), 430. For an extended discussion of the characteristics of bureaucratic administration and staff, see Weber, *Economy and Society*, 3: 956–963.

56. Weber, *Economy and Society*, 3: 975.

57. Ibid., 1: 225.

58. Ibid., 3: 1418.

59. Ibid., 987–988.

60. Ibid., 980.

61. Weber, *From Max Weber*, 230 (emphasis added).

62. See Arnold Rose, *The Power Structure* (New York: Oxford University Press, 1967); and Arthur Bentley, *The Process of Government* (Cambridge, MA: Benklap Press of Harvard University, 1967).

63. Rose, *The Power Structure*, 247.

64. Ibid.

65. David Truman, *The Government Process* (New York: Knopf, 1964), 514.

66. V. O. Key, *Public Opinion and American Democracy* (New York: Knopf, 1964), 150.

67. Bentley, *The Process of Government*, 258.

68. Ibid., 453.

69. Nelson Polsby, *Community Power and Political Theory* (New Haven: Yale University Press, 1963).

70. David Easton, *The Political System* (New York: Knopf, 1971).

71. Talcott Parsons, *Societies: An Evolutionary Approach* (Englewood Cliffs, NJ: Prentice Hall, 1966); and Parsons, "On the Concept of Political Power," in *Sociological Theory and Modern Society*, ed. Talcott Parsons (New York: Free Press, 1967); Neil Smelser, "Mechanisms of Change and Adjustment to Change," in *Industrialization and Society*, eds. B. Hoselitz and W. Moore (New York: Mouton, 1963). For an extended critical analysis of the Parsonian approach, see Berch Berberoglu, *An Introduction to Classical and Contemporary Social Theory*, 3rd ed. (Lanham, MD: Rowman & Littlefield, 2005), Chap. 10.

72. Talcott Parsons, *Structure and Process in Modern Societies* (New York: Free Press, 1960), 221.

73. Roger King, *The State in Modern Society* (Chatham, NJ: Chatham House, 1986), 15.

74. S. N. Eisenstadt, ed., *Modernization: Protest and Change* (Englewood Cliffs, NJ: Prentice Hall, 1966). Cited in King, *State in Modern Society*, 15.

75. C. Wright Mills, *The Power Elite* (New York: Oxford University Press, 1956); and Mills, *The Sociological Imagination* (New York: Oxford University Press, 1959).

76. See Grant McConnell, *Private Power and American Democracy* (New York: Knopf, 1966); G. William Domhoff, *The Higher Circles* (New York: Random House, 1970); Richard Hamilton, *Class and Politics in the United States* (New York: Wiley, 1972); Michael Parenti, "Power and Pluralism: The View from the Bottom," *Journal of Politics* 32 (August 1970); and Parenti, *Democracy for the Few*, 9th ed. (Boston: Wadsworth, 2011).

77. Mills, *The Power Elite*.

78. Martin N. Marger, *Elites and Masses: An Introduction to Political Sociology*, 2nd ed. (Belmont, CA: Wadsworth, 1987). See also George A. Kourvetaris, *Political Sociology: Structure and Process* (Boston: Allyn and Bacon, 1997).

79. Albert Szymanski, *The Capitalist State and the Politics of Class* (Cambridge, MA: Winthrop, 1978), 5.

80. Herbert H. Hyman and Charles R. Wright, "Trends in Voluntary Association Memberships of American Adults," *American Sociological Review* 36 (April 1971).

81. Szymanski, *The Capitalist State and the Politics of Class.*

82. See Seymour Martin Lipset, *Political Man* (Garden City, NY: Doubleday Anchor, 1960); Robert Dahl, *Who Governs?* (New Haven: Yale University Press, 1961). In his later book *Pluralist Democracy in the United States: Conflict and Consensus* (Chicago: Rand McNally, 1967), Dahl introduces the concept "polyarchy," by which he means numerous elites who compete for political influence within a pluralist framework.

83. Marger, *Elites and Masses*, 76.

84. See Phillippe Schmitter, "Still the Century of Corporatism?" in *The New Corporatism*, eds. Frederick Pike and Thomas Stitch (Notre Dame, IN: University of Notre Dame Press, 1974); Alfred Stepan, *The State and Society* (Princeton: Princeton University Press, 1978); Leo Panitch, "Recent Theorizations of Corporatism," *British Journal of Sociology* (June 1980).

85. Stepan, *The State and Society.* This is, in a way, similar to labor's postwar social-democratic participation in the "corporatist" state, sometimes characterized as "the welfare state," where a compromise is struck between labor and capital under the leadership of the state, which moderates the conflict and enforces the terms of this compromise. Referring to this "social-democratic compromise," Adam Przeworski writes: "This compromise consists of a trade-off between workers' militancy and capitalists' consumption. Capitalists agree to invest at a high rate and workers agree to moderate their demands with regard to profits." See "Economic Conditions of Class Compromise" (University of Chicago, 1979), 32. Mimeographed. Also see Przeworski and Michael Wallerstein, "The Structure of Class Conflict in Democratic Capitalist Societies." *American Political Science Review* 76, no. 2 (1982).

In a quite different context, it is also possible to characterize corporatism as fascism in the advanced capitalist countries and as right-wing petty bourgeois state-capitalism and bureaucratic authoritarianism in the less-developed countries.

Virtually in all cases, however, corporatism appears to emerge in response to the rise of a militant working-class movement and is instituted to preempt a socialist revolution. In the less-developed countries, however, it may also emerge as "nationalism" in response to imperialism and internal reaction (see Chap. 6).

86. Stepan, *The State and Society.*

87. See Bob Jessop, *The Capitalist State* (New York: New York University Press, 1982), Chap. 2, for a discussion of the theory of state-monopoly capitalism, which, its proponents argue, is nothing but the consolidation of big business control of the state, *presenting itself and appearing as* a "corporatist" or "welfare" state.

88. See Guillermo O'Donnell, "Tensions in the Bureaucratic-Authoritarian State and the Question of Democracy," in *The New Authoritarianism in Latin America*, ed. David Collier (Princeton: Princeton University Press, 1979).

89. See Nicos Poulantzas, *Fascism and Dictatorship* (London: New Left Books, 1974); and Poulantzas, *The Crisis of the Dictatorships* (London: New Left Books, 1976). Also see Szymanski, *The Capitalist State and the Politics of Class*, Chap. 12.

90. C. Wright Mills, *The Power Elite* (New York: Oxford University Press, 1956).

91. Ibid., 3–4.

92. See Floyd Hunter, *Top Leadership, USA* (Chapel Hill: University of North Carolina Press, 1959). For his earlier community power structure studies, focusing on Atlanta, see Hunter, *Community Power Structure* (Chapel Hill: University of North Carolina Press, 1953).

93. For an analysis of the contributions of scholars in this tradition, see John Mollenkopf, "Theories of the State and Power Structure Research," *Insurgent Sociologist* 5, no. 3 (1975).

94. G. William Domhoff, *Who Rules America?* (Englewood Cliffs, NJ: Prentice Hall, 1967).

95. Ibid., 5.

96. Ibid. Also see G. William Domhoff, *The Higher Circles* (New York: Random House, 1970); Domhoff, *The Powers That Be* (New York: Random House, 1979); and Domhoff, *The Power Elite and the State* (New York: Aldine de Gruyter, 1990).

97. Domhoff, *Who Rules America?* 62. See also the revised and updated edition of this book for further evidence and discussion on this topic: G. William Domhoff, *Who Rules America? Challenges to Corporate and Class Dominance* (New York: McGraw-Hill, 2010).

98. See E. K. Trimberger, *Revolution from Above: Military Bureaucrats and Development in Japan, Turkey, and Peru* (New Brunswick, NJ: Transaction Books, 1978); Theda Skocpol, *States and Revolutions: A Comparative Analysis of France, Russia and China* (Cambridge: Cambridge University Press, 1979); Fred Block, "The Ruling Class Does Not Rule: Notes on the Marxist Theory of the State," *Socialist Review*, no. 33 (May–June 1977).

99. Trimberger, *Revolution from Above*, 4.

100. Ibid., 4–5.

101. Ibid., 7.

102. See Block, "Ruling Class"; and Block, "Class Consciousness and Capitalist Rationalization: A Reply to Critics," *Socialist Review*, nos. 40–41 (July–October 1978).

103. Block, "Class Consciousness," nos. 40–41.

104. Ibid., 219.

105. Fred Block, "Marxist Theories of the State in World System Analysis" (Paper presented at the First Annual Political Economy of the World System Conference, American University, Washington, DC, March–April 1977), 8.

106. Ibid.

107. Ibid.

108. Skocpol, *States and Social Revolutions*. For acknowledgement of these and other influences on Skocpol's views, see ibid., 301, notes 73 and 77.

In an entirely different context, Bob Jessop also argues against the base-superstructure problematic, claiming that "both economic and class reductionism take a one-sided approach and define the state only in relation to the mode of production or to the class struggle." See Bob Jessop, *The Capitalist State* (New York: New York University Press, 1982), 24. Moreover, insisting that "it is impossible to establish a unitary and coherent theory of the state in general on the basis of the methods and principles of the Marxian critique of political economy" (28), Jessop opts for an empiricist alternative, arguing that "such abstract and restricted forms of analysis are not equivalent to a concrete analysis of specific forms of state or state power in determinate conjunctures" (24). Far from an affirmation of the historical materialist approach, such conceptualization of the problem actually denies the possibility of constructing a general theory of the state in class society through the base-superstructure relation. Rejecting this in favor of a concrete analysis of specific states, in effect, amounts to a parallel rejection of the validity of an analysis of the laws of motion of the capitalist mode of production in favor of a concrete analysis of a specific capitalist formation—thus rendering useless a general theory of the capitalist mode (e.g., Marx's *Capital*), the capitalist state (e.g., Lenin's *The State and Revolution*), and other monumental works of classical Marxism. It is one thing to opt for such an approach from outside (or in opposition to) Marxism; but, indeed, quite another to do so while claiming an affinity to Marxism. In this sense, Jessop's approach, irrespective of his intentions or claims to the contrary, yields results similar to those of Skocpol and other bourgeois empiricists, in the name of "scientific objectivity" or historical specificity—whichever may be the case.

109. Skocpol, *States and Social Revolutions*, 31.

110. Ibid., 27. In developing this view of the state, Skocpol cites the works of Trimberger and Block, among others, and states: "I have been very greatly influenced by these writings, and by personal conversations with Trimberger and Block." Ibid., 301, note 73.

111. Theda Skocpol, "Political Response to Capitalist Crisis: Neo-Marxist Theories of the State and the Case of the New Deal," *Politics and Society* 10, no. 2 (1981): 199.

112. Skocpol, *States and Social Revolutions*, 31.

113. Ibid., 29.

114. Ibid.

Chapter 2

Marxist Theories of the State

IN CONTRAST TO CONVENTIONAL THEORIES of the state discussed in the previous chapter, this chapter presents an alternative, Marxist perspective that differs from its conventional counterparts in some important ways. The central component of the Marxist approach is an analysis of the class nature of the state, and the class character of movements waging struggle for state power.

Situating the problem in class context, this chapter shows that society and the state are products of social forces that struggle to maintain or transform class relations. Class relations are thus a product of the balance of class forces that are always anchored in class struggles. In these struggles, it is always the case that the dominant ruling class strives to remain in control of the state and maintain law and order to prolong its rule over society, whereas the oppressed class attempts to rise up to overthrow the state in order to capture state power and establish its rule over society.

This chapter examines the dynamics of this process by providing an overview of classical and contemporary Marxist theories of the state. After a brief survey of the fundamentals of the classical Marxist position on the state, we examine some recent developments in Marxist theories of the state in both Europe and the United States. This, in turn, provides the theoretical framework of the analysis of the origins, development, and contradictions of the state in the world historical process, which is presented in the remainder of the book. We begin our analysis with an overview of the classical Marxist position.

The Classical Marxist Theory of the State

The classical Marxist theory of the state, based on the writings of Karl Marx, Friedrich Engels, and V. I. Lenin, focuses on the class basis of politics as the major determinant of political phenomena. It explains the nature of the superstructure (including, first and foremost, the state) as a reflection of the *mode of production,* which embodies in it social *relations of production* (or property-based class relations). Once fully developed and matured, these class relations result in open class struggles and struggles for *state power.*

The Class Nature of the State

The state is the most powerful and most pervasive social and political institution in the world, as it holds its sway over vast territories populated by millions of people and does so in proportion to its size and strength relative to other states that claim the same rights in their respective spheres of control and influence around the world.

The state is the only institution that exercises a monopoly on the use of force and violence through legally sanctioned behavior that allows it to raise armies; declare war; maintain police powers; preside over the legal system; print money; collect taxes; arrest, try, and imprison people, and impose the death penalty; and exercise other forms of official control in governing and regulating society through a vast network of a political bureaucracy where no other societal power supersedes its authority. It is for these reasons that the state, regardless of regime, is both feared and revered by the citizens of a given society who have come to accept the rule of the state over their lives and sanction the legitimacy of that rule under "normal" conditions.

While the dominant ruling class controls and uses the state as an instrument to advance its class interests, rival groups and classes struggle to wrest power from the ruling class. However, the legitimacy of the state's rule is seldom questioned, and the powers that control the state are much less scrutinized, except when the state's authority is called into question during crisis periods when it fails to resolve the fundamental social, political, and economic problems of society. A period of decline in legitimacy of the state, and of the ruling class that controls it, follows upon the heels of crisis—a period of great turmoil that sometimes leads to social revolution. Such revolutions have occurred in the past, and will continue to occur in the future, in direct relation to the state's failure to meet the needs of the people and to represent their will. It is in this sense that the state has become the scene of class struggle, where rival class forces have fought over control of this vital political organ.

The great social revolutions of the twentieth century, and of previous centuries, have always been fought for the overthrow of the dominant ruling class and the prevailing social order by capturing state power to effect change in a new direction in line with the interests of the victorious forces that have succeeded in coming to power.

The rise to power of the despotic rulers of past empires, the emergence of a slave-owning class and its reign over the state and the people under the slave system, the rule of the landed nobility over the serfs under feudalism, and the triumph of the capitalist class over the landlords and its subsequent reign over wage labor, as well as the victory of the proletariat against the landlords and the capitalists, have all occurred through revolutions waged against the dominant classes and the state throughout the course of human history.

In *The Origin of the Family, Private Property and the State,* Engels writes:

> It is, as a rule, the state of the most powerful, economically dominant class, which, through the medium of the state, becomes also the politically dominant class, and thus acquires new means of holding down and exploiting the oppressed class. Thus, the state of antiquity was above all the state of the slave owners for the purpose of holding down the slaves, as the feudal state was the organ of the nobility for holding down the peasant serfs and bondsmen, and the modern representative state is an instrument of exploitation of wage labor by capital.[1]

Thus, in all class-divided societies throughout history, write Marx and Engels, "political power is merely the organized power of one class for oppressing another."[2] Political power, they point out, grows out of economic (class) power driven by money and wealth, but to maintain and secure their wealth, dominant classes of society establish and control political institutions to hold down the masses and assure their continued domination. The supreme superstructural institution that historically has emerged to carry out this task is the state.

Outlined in its clearest and most concise form in Lenin's classic work *The State and Revolution,* which is based on an understanding of Marx's and Engels's numerous writings on the subject, the classical Marxist theory of the state stresses that in all class-divided societies, the *class essence* of the state's rule over society is rooted in domination and exploitation by a propertied ruling class of the propertyless, oppressed class. In class society, writes Lenin, the state has always been an organ or instrument of class rule. Thus, as Engels has also pointed out, "the more it [the state] becomes the organ of a particular class, the more it directly enforces the supremacy of that class,"[3] such that "the fight of the oppressed class against the ruling class becomes necessarily a political fight, a fight first of all against the political dominance of this class."[4] The centrality of the state as an instrument of *class rule,* then, takes on an added importance in the analysis of social class and class struggles, for political power contested by the warring classes takes on its real meaning in securing the rule of the victorious class when that power is ultimately exercised through the instrumentality of the state.

In our epoch, writes Lenin, "every state in which private ownership of the land and means of production exists, in which capital dominates, however democratic it may be, is a capitalist state, a machine used by the capitalists to keep the working class and the poor peasants in subjection."[5] Thus, to accomplish this subjection, the state becomes "an organ or instrument of violence exercised by one class against another."[6]

As class relations in society are based on relations of production, which together with the productive forces constitute the mode of production, the superstructural institutions, including the state, arise from the prevailing mode and reinforce the maintenance of a social order that favors the dominant class in society.[7] As Marx writes in *Preface to a Contribution to the Critique of Political Economy*:

> In the social production of their life, men enter into definite relations that are indispensable and independent of their will, relations of production which correspond to a definite stage of development of their material productive forces. The sum total of these relations of production constitutes the economic structure of society, the real foundation, on which rises a legal and political superstructure and to which correspond definite forms of social consciousness.[8]

For Marx, then, the *relations of production,* that is, the "relationship of the owners of the conditions of production to the direct producers," as he defines it, "reveals the innermost secret, the hidden basis of the entire social structure, and with it the political form of the relation of sovereignty and dependence, in short, the corresponding specific form of the state."[9]

Thus, as a reflection of the interests of the dominant class, the state in capitalist society can be identified as the *capitalist state,* for as Marx and Engels point out, this state serves as a political organ of the bourgeoisie for the "guarantee of their property and interests."[10] Hence, "the bourgeoisie has ... conquered for itself, in the modern representative State, exclusive political sway. The executive of the modern State is but a committee for managing the common affairs of the whole bourgeoisie."[11] In this sense, the struggle of the working class against capital takes on both an economic *and* a political content.[12]

Expanding on their analysis of the superstructure in relation to its class base, Marx and Engels argued that control by the dominant economic class of the major political institutions in society reveals the nature of the dominant ideas of a given epoch. "The ideas of the ruling class are in every epoch the ruling ideas:

i.e., the class, which is the ruling material force of society, is at the same time its ruling intellectual force."[13] And the state, as the supreme political organ whose legitimacy is institutionalized by law, plays a key role in the dissemination of these ideas, thus ensuring the ideological hegemony of the ruling class. In this context, Marx, commenting on the Paris Commune,[14] wrote: "The working class cannot simply lay hold of the ready-made state machinery, and wield it for its own purposes."[15] He later added, in a letter to L. Kugelmann, "The next attempt of the French Revolution will be no longer, as before, to transfer the bureaucratic-military machine from one hand to another, but *to smash* it, and this is the preliminary condition for every real people's revolution on the Continent. And this is what our heroic Party comrades in Paris are attempting."[16]

Lenin, writing in August 1917, on the eve of the Great October Socialist Revolution in Russia, points out in *The State and Revolution* both the class nature of the state *and*, more important, the necessity of its revolutionary overthrow. He writes:

If the state is the product of the irreconcilability of class antagonisms, if it is a power standing *above* society and "*alienating* itself *more and more* from it," it is clear that the liberation of the oppressed class is impossible not only without a violent revolution, *but also without the destruction* of the apparatus of state power which was created by the ruling class and which is the embodiment of this "alienation."[17]

In an important passage in *The State and Revolution,* Lenin stresses that the state in capitalist society is not only or simply the political organ of the capitalist class; it is structured in such a way that it guarantees the class rule of the capitalists, and short of a revolutionary rupture, its entrenched power is practically unshakable:

A democratic republic is the best possible political shell for capitalism, and, therefore, once capital has gained possession of this very best shell ... it establishes its power so securely, so firmly, that *no* change of persons, institutions or parties in the bourgeois-democratic republic can shake it.[18]

Seen in this way, the centrality of the state as an instrument of *class rule* takes on an added importance, and so in examining the nature of a given state, it becomes imperative to ask the decisive question: *Which class controls and dominates the state?* Moreover, with the obvious contradictions and conflicts between labor and capital, and with the ever-more visible unity of capital and the state, how is it that capital is able to convince broad segments of the laboring masses of the legitimacy of its class rule and the rule of the capitalist state over society?

The Capitalist State and Ideological Hegemony

In explaining the process by which the capitalist class disseminates its ideology through control of the state and its dominance over society, Antonio Gramsci, a prominent Marxist writing at the turn of the twentieth century, draws attention to the *ideological apparatuses* of the capitalist state and introduces the concept of bourgeois cultural and ideological *hegemony*.[19] He stresses that it is not enough for the capitalist class simply to take control of the state machine and rule society directly through force and coercion; it must also convince the oppressed classes of the legitimacy of its rule: "The state is the entire complex of practical and theoretical activities with which the ruling class not only justifies and maintains its dominance, but manages to win the active consent of those over whom it rules."[20] Through its dominance of the superstructural organs of the state, the ruling class controls and shapes the ideas, hence consciousness, of the masses. Thus:

> Hegemony involves the successful attempts of the dominant class to use its political, moral, and intellectual leadership to establish its view of the world as all-inclusive and universal, and to shape the interests and needs of subordinate groups.[21]

With the acceptance of its ideas and the legitimization of its rule, the capitalist class is able to exercise control and domination of society through its ideological hegemony at the level of the superstructure with the aid and instrumentality of the state. Gramsci, writes Martin Carnoy, "assigned to the State part of this function of promoting a single (bourgeois) concept of reality, and, therefore, gave the State a more extensive (enlarged) role in perpetuating class," hence preventing the development of working-class consciousness.[22] As such,

> It was not merely lack of understanding of their position in the economic process that kept workers from comprehending their class role, nor was it only the "private" institutions of society, such as religion, that were responsible for keeping the working class from self-realization, but it was the *State itself* that was involved in reproducing the relations of production. In other words, the State was much more than the coercive apparatus of the bourgeoisie; the State included the hegemony of the bourgeoisie in the superstructure.[23]

Although the dialectics of the accumulation process, which involves, first and foremost, the exploitation of labor, ultimately results in class struggles, civil war, and revolution to seize state power, the ideological hegemony of the ruling class, operating through the state itself, prolongs its class rule and institutionalizes and legitimizes exploitation. Gramsci argues, "The system's real strength does not lie in the violence of the ruling class or the coercive power of its state apparatus, but in the acceptance by the ruled of a 'conception of the world' which belongs to the rulers."[24] "False consciousness," or the lack of working-class consciousness and the adoption of bourgeois ideas by the laboring masses, Gramsci argues, is the result of a complex process of bourgeois ideological hegemony that, operating through the superstructural (i.e., cultural, ideological, religious, and political) institutions of capitalist society, above all the bourgeois state, has come to obtain the consent of the masses in convincing them of the correctness and superiority of the bourgeois worldview. Thus, as Carnoy points out,

> In his doctrine of "hegemony," Gramsci saw that the dominant class did not have to rely solely on the coercive power of the State or even its direct economic power to rule; rather, through its hegemony, expressed in the civil society *and* the State, the ruled could be persuaded to accept the system of beliefs of the ruling class and to share its social, cultural, and moral values.[25]

"The philosophy of the ruling class," writes Giuseppe Fiori, "passes through a whole tissue of complex vulgarizations to emerge as 'common sense': that is, the philosophy of the masses, who accept the morality, the customs, the institutionalized behavior of the society they live in."[26] This process leads the masses to internalize bourgeois values and accept them as their own. "The problem for Gramsci then," Fiori continues, "is to understand *how* the ruling class has managed to win the consent of the subordinate classes in this way; and then, to see how the latter will manage to overthrow the old order and bring about a new one of universal freedom."[27]

The increasing awareness of the working class of this process, hence the development of working-class consciousness, stresses Gramsci, helps expand the emerging class struggle from the economic and social spheres into the sphere of politics and ideology, so the struggle against the capitalist ideology promoted by the bourgeois state and other ruling-class institutions becomes just as important, perhaps more so, as the struggle against capital develops and matures in other spheres of society. Countering the ideological hegemony of the capitalist class through the active participation of workers in their own collective organizations, the class-conscious organs of workers' power—militant trade unions, workers' political parties, and so forth—come to play a decisive role in gaining the political support of the laboring masses. In turn, through their newly gained awareness of their own class interests, the workers transcend the bounds of bourgeois ideological hegemony and develop their own counter (proletarian) political outlook, a process that accelerates with the further development of a proletarian class consciousness. Thus, as the struggle against the state becomes an important part of the class struggle in general, the struggle against capitalism takes on a truly political and ideological content.

The Capitalist State, Class Struggle, and Revolution

The transformation of capitalist society, Lenin points out, involves a revolutionary process in which a class-conscious working class, led by a disciplined workers' party, comes to adopt a radical solution to its continued exploitation and oppression under the yoke of capital and exerts its organized political force in a revolutionary rupture to take state power. The victory of the working class through a socialist revolution leads to the establishment of a socialist (workers') state. The socialist state constitutes a new kind of state ruled by the working class and the laboring masses. The cornerstone of a socialist state, emerging out of capitalism, is the abolition of private property in the major means of production and an end to the exploitation of labor for private profit.

"The theory of the class struggle, applied by Marx to the question of the state and the socialist revolution," writes Lenin,

> leads as a matter of course to the recognition of the *political rule* of the proletariat, of its dictatorship, i.e., of undivided power directly backed by the armed force of the people. The overthrow of the bourgeoisie can be achieved only by the proletariat becoming the *ruling class,* capable of crushing the inevitable and desperate resistance of the bourgeoisie, and of organizing *all* the working and exploited people for the new economic system.[28]

The establishment of a revolutionary dictatorship of the proletariat (as against the dictatorship of capital) is what distinguishes the socialist state from its capitalist counterpart. Marx pointed out in *Critique of the Gotha Program* that the dictatorship of the proletariat (i.e., the class rule of the working class) is a transitional phase between capitalism and communism. "Between capitalist and communist society," Marx wrote, "lies the period of the revolutionary transformation of the one into the other. Corresponding to this is also a political transition period in which the state can be nothing but *the revolutionary dictatorship of the proletariat.*"[29]

During this period, the state represents and defends the interests of the working class against capital and all other vestiges of reactionary exploiting classes, which, overthrown and dislodged from power, attempt in a multitude of ways to recapture the state through a counterrevolution. Thus, once in power, the proletarian state has a dual role to play: to break the resistance of its class enemies (the exploiting classes) and to protect the revolution and begin the process of socialist construction.

The class character of the new state under the dictatorship of the proletariat takes on a new form and content, according to Lenin: "During this period the state must inevitably be a state that is democratic *in a new way* (for the proletariat and the propertyless in general) and dictatorial *in a new way* (against the bourgeoisie)."[30] Thus, "*simultaneously* with an immense expansion of democracy, which *for the first time* becomes democracy for the poor, democracy for the people, and not democracy for the money-bags, the dictatorship of the proletariat imposes a series of restrictions on the freedom of the oppressors, the exploiters, the capitalists."[31] Lenin stresses the necessity of suppressing the capitalist class and its allies to deny them the freedom to foment a counterrevolution, barring them from politics and isolating and defeating efforts to undermine the new worker's state.

Used primarily to suppress these forces and build the material base of a classless, egalitarian society, the socialist state begins to wither away once there is no longer any need for it. As Engels points out:

> The first act in which the state really comes forward as the representative of society as a whole—the taking possession of the means of production in the name of society—is at the same time its last independent act as a state. The interference of the state power in social relations becomes superfluous in one sphere after another, and then ceases of itself. The government of persons is replaced by the administration of things and the direction of the processes of production. The state is not "abolished," *it withers away.*[32]

In this sense, the state no longer exists in the fully matured communist stage, for there is no longer the need in a classless society for an institution that is, by definition, an instrument of class rule through force and violence. Lenin writes:

> Only in communist society, when the resistance of the capitalists has been completely crushed, when the capitalists have disappeared, when there are no classes (i.e., when there is no distinction between the members of society as regards their relation to the social means of production), *only* then "the state ... ceases to exist," and "*it becomes possible to speak of freedom.*" Only then will a truly complete democracy become possible and be realized, a democracy without any exceptions whatsoever.[33]

It is in this broader historical context that the class nature and tasks of the state in socialist society must be understood and evaluated, according to the Marxist classics.

Contemporary Marxist Theories of the State

More recently, contemporary Marxist theorists have reintroduced into Marxist discourse Gramsci's contributions to Marxist theory focused on ideology and the state. Louis Althusser has played a key role in this effort through the incorporation of the Gramscian notion of "ideological hegemony" into his own analysis of the "ideological state apparatuses."[34]

In linking the political superstructure to the social-economic base, or mode of production, Althusser builds on the classical Marxist position that the superstructure is dependent on and determined by the base: "The upper floors," writes Althusser, in reference to the superstructure, "could not 'stay up' (in the air) alone, if they did not rest precisely on their base."[35] Thus, the state, the supreme superstructural institution and repressive apparatus of society, "enables the ruling classes to ensure their domination over the working class, thus enabling the former to subject the latter to the process of surplus-value extortion."[36] This is so precisely because the state is controlled by the ruling classes. And it is such control that makes the state, and the superstructure in general, dependent on and determined by the dominant class in the base.

In his essay "Ideology and Ideological State Apparatuses," Althusser expands his analysis of the base-superstructure relationship to include such other superstructural institutions as the cultural, religious, educational, legal, and family. As the hegemony of the ruling class in these spheres becomes critical for its control over the dominated classes, and society in general, the class struggle takes on a tri-level character, consisting of the economic, political, and ideological levels. This Althusserian conception of the structural totality of the capitalist mode in its relation with the superstructure came to inform Poulantzas's analysis of classes, class struggles, and the state, and set the stage for the subsequent discussion and debate on Marxist theories of the state.

The Poulantzas-Miliband Debate on the Capitalist State

In the early 1970s, an intense debate on the nature and role of the capitalist state prompted renewed interest in Marxist theorizing on the capitalist state for the following three decades.[37] In this debate, one position emphasizes the direct and indirect control of the state by the dominant capitalist class, and another emphasizes the structural requirements of the capitalist system affecting the state and its actions. These two views correspond to the so-called instrumentalist and structuralist positions associated with Ralph Miliband and Nicos Poulantzas, respectively. Central to the debate are questions related to the class nature of the state, the relationship between different classes and the state, and the notion of "relative autonomy" in the exercise of state power.[38]

In his original formulation of the problem in *The State in Capitalist Society,* Miliband approaches the question of the state via a critique of the pluralist models still dominant in political sociology and mainstream political theory. In so doing, he provides an approach and analysis that earns his work the unwarranted label "instrumentalism." Critiques of his work, reacting to this instrumentalism, have resulted in the formulation of a counterposition labeled "structuralism."

The central question addressed in the initial formulation of the instrumentalist problematic has been a determination of the role of the state in a society dominated by capitalist social relations. In this context, Miliband's study of the capitalist state focuses on the special relationship between the state and the capitalist class, and the mechanisms of control of the state by this class that, *de facto,* transform the state into a *capitalist state.*

In contrast, Poulantzas, representing the so-called structuralist position, focuses on the structural constraints of the capitalist system that set limits to the state's autonomy and force the state to work within the framework of an order that yields results invariably favorable to the dominant capitalist class. According to this view, the state becomes a *capitalist* state by virtue of the system of production itself in capitalist society, even in the absence of direct control of the state apparatus by capitalists.

It should be pointed out, however, that the degree of lack of direct control of the state apparatus by the capitalist class determines the degree of the state's relative autonomy from this class. And this, in turn, gives the state the necessary freedom to manage the overall interests of the capitalist class and rule society on behalf of the established capitalist order.[39]

The central problem for these competing views of the state is not so much whether the state in capitalist society is a *capitalist* state—they agree that it is—but *how* that state *becomes* a capitalist state. Far more than their limited academic value, the answers to this question have immense political implications because the debates surrounding this issue originally emerged in Europe among Marxists and local communist parties in response to the pivotal political question regarding the strategy and tactics of taking state power under advanced capitalism.

Let us briefly look at the fundamentals of the instrumentalist-versus-structuralist problematic and show, in the process, that the dichotomy has been ill conceived, as, ultimately, both Miliband and Poulantzas in later reformulations of their positions basically accept the validity of their critics' conclusions.

To start with, in his initial formulation of the problem, Miliband writes,

> In the Marxist scheme, the "ruling class" of capitalist society is that class which owns and controls the means of production and which is able, by virtue of the economic power thus conferred upon it, to use the state as its instrument for the domination of society.[40]

Miliband expounded this seemingly instrumentalist statement through his focus on "patterns and consequences of personal and social ties between individuals occupying positions of power in different institutional spheres."[41] Concentrating on a study of the nature of the capitalist class, the mechanisms that tie this class to the state, and the specific relationships between state policies and class interests,[42] Miliband leaves himself open to charges of voluntarism and instrumentalism.

In contrast, Poulantzas argues that "the *direct* participation of members of the capitalist class in the state apparatus and in the government, even where it exists, is not the important side of the matter."[43] What is crucial to understand, according to Poulantzas, is this:

> The relation between the bourgeois class and the state is an *objective relation.* This means that if the *function* of the state in a determinate social formation and the *interests* of the dominant class in this formation *coincide,* it is by reason of the system itself: the direct participation of members of the ruling class in the state apparatus is not the *cause* but the *effect,* and moreover a chance and contingent one, of this objective coincidence.[44]

In this formulation, the functions of the state are broadly determined by the structural requirements of the capitalist mode of production and the constraints placed on it by the structural environment in which the state must operate. Given these parameters of operation, the state obtains relative autonomy from the various fractions of the capitalist class in order to carry out its functions as a capitalist state on behalf of the capitalist system. Thus, Poulantzas accepts the control of the state by the capitalist class through direct and indirect means but assigns to it relative autonomy vis-à-vis any one *fraction* of that class.[45] Hence, in this formulation, the capitalist state is the state of the capitalist class and serves the interests of that class as a whole; at the same time, it maintains relative autonomy from that class's various fractions.

Miliband, defending himself against vulgar instrumentalist interpretations of his argument, later concedes that the state can and must have a certain degree of autonomy from the capitalist class. Referring to Marx's and Engels's assertion that "the modern state is but a committee for managing the common affairs of the whole bourgeoisie," Miliband writes,

> This has regularly been taken to mean not only that the state acts *on behalf* of the dominant class … but that it acts *at the behest* of that class which is an altogether different assertion and, as I would argue, a vulgar deformation of the thought of Marx and Engels.… The notion of common affairs assumes the existence of particular ones; and the notion of the whole bourgeoisie implies the existence of separate elements which make up that whole. This being the case, there is an obvious need for an institution of the kind they refer to, namely the state; and the state *cannot* meet this need without enjoying a certain degree of autonomy. In other words, the notion of autonomy is embedded in the definition itself, is an intrinsic part of it.[46]

Elsewhere, Miliband addresses this question more directly: "Different forms of state have different degrees of autonomy. But all states enjoy some autonomy or independence from all classes, including the dominant classes."[47] Nevertheless,

> The relative independence of the state does not reduce its class character: on the contrary, its relative independence makes it *possible* for the state to play its class role in an appropriately flexible manner. If it really was the simple "instrument" of the "ruling class," it would be fatally inhibited in the performance of its role.[48]

He goes on to argue,

> The intervention of the state is always and necessarily partisan: as a class state, it always intervenes for the purpose of maintaining the existing system of domination, even where it intervenes to mitigate the harshness of that system of domination.[49]

Thus, Miliband takes a big step toward reconciliation with the relative autonomy thesis, while retaining the core of his argument in seeing the capitalist state as an institution controlled by the capitalist class as a whole.

Poulantzas, in his later writings, also moves in a direction away from his earlier position on relative autonomy. He admits that in the current monopoly stage of capitalism, the *monopoly fraction* of the capitalist class dominates the state and thereby secures favorable policies in its own favor over other fractions of the bourgeois power bloc.[50] This situation, he adds, poses problems to the state's traditional role as "political organizer of the general interest of the bourgeoisie" and "restrict[s] the limits of the relative autonomy of the state in relation to monopoly capital and to the field of the compromises it makes with other fractions of the bourgeoisie."[51] The political crisis resulting from this fractional domination and fragmentation, argues Poulantzas, leads to a crisis of the bourgeois state.[52]

With these later reformulations of state theory by both Poulantzas and Miliband, we see a convergence of the two positions and arrive at the general conclusion that the state in capitalist society is *both* controlled by *and,* simultaneously, relatively autonomous of the various fractions of the capitalist class, in order to perform its functions in advancing the interests of the capitalist class as a whole and, at the same time, maintain its legitimacy over society. This "relative autonomy," however, is rapidly being undermined by the hegemonic (monopoly) fraction of the capitalist class, which, as a result, is blocking the state's effectiveness in fulfilling its political role as the "executive committee" of the entire bourgeoisie.

Offe and Hirsh on the Functions of the Capitalist State

Critical of both the Poulantzas and Miliband formulations, and moving beyond the debate to another level of structural explanation influenced by the Frankfurt School, Claus Offe and Joachim Hirsh present two complementary views of the capitalist state in the German context. In contrast to Poulantzas's strong emphasis on ideological factors, both Offe and Hirsh attempt to explain the state through its economic role. For Offe, it is based on the necessity for capital accumulation, involving the extraction of surplus and the reproduction of capitalist relations; for Hirsh, it is based on the necessity to counter the tendency of the falling rate of profit and the contradictions that emerge from it.

Offe's initial formulation focuses on the internal mechanisms of the state in terms of its dependence on capital accumulation, which, he argues, is vital for its survival. Introducing the concept of *selective mechanisms,* Offe argues that these mechanisms work to serve a number of important functions that give the state its class character. These functions are

> (1) *Negative selection:* the selective mechanisms systematically exclude anti-capitalist interests from state activity; (2) *positive selection:* from the range of remaining alternatives, the policy which is in the interests of capital as a whole is selected over policies serving the parochial interests of specific capitalist groups; (3) *disguising selection:* the institutions of the state must somehow maintain

the appearance of class-neutrality while at the same time effectively excluding anti-capitalist alternatives.[53]

These mechanisms are contradictory in nature and present problems for the state in carrying out its dual role of maintaining accumulation and legitimation. Thus, the capitalist state cannot effectively fulfill its essential role as an "ideal collective capitalist," notes Offe, unless it can conceal its class bias behind the cloak of the general interest and carry out the other functions relegated to it by the logic of capital accumulation. In this way, the state's promotion of the capital accumulation process also results in the reproduction of the bureaucratic apparatus, which itself depends on the continued accumulation of capital.[54]

Offe argues that, in attempts to overcome these functional requisites, the state faces its biggest challenge and falls short in fulfilling its crucial role. Hence, the state faces an emergent "crisis of crisis management," which reveals itself in the areas of a fiscal crisis, a crisis of administrative rationality, and a crisis of mass loyalty.[55] As the "selective mechanisms" begin to break down in periods of political crisis, the state begins to rely more and more on repression in order to maintain its class character; as a result, it exposes the inner nature of the state itself.[56]

Despite the fact that he comes from the Hegelian-Marxist tradition of the Frankfurt School and was once a student of Jurgen Habermas, Offe's theoretical conclusions on the political crisis of the capitalist state are actually quite similar to Poulantzas's conclusions on the crisis of legitimacy and, more broadly, of class hegemony in late capitalist society.[57] What distinguishes Offe's analysis from that of Poulantzas is Offe's insistence on the *autonomy* of the state from both the capitalist class and society as a whole and the primacy of the state in maintaining its special bureaucratic interests. Nevertheless, the structural imperatives of the capital accumulation process, with or without such autonomy, yield similar results in determining the political outcome of the state's actions, hence its class character.

Joachim Hirsh, in a manner similar to the analysis provided by Offe, derives his categories of discourse on the state directly from the accumulation process. Not particularly interested in Offe's preoccupation with the inner workings of the state apparatus, Hirsh focuses on what he views as the state's main task of countering the tendency of the falling rate of profit. As the class struggle against capital threatens the interests of the capitalist class and affects the rate of profit (thus affecting the survival of the state), the state is compelled to intervene to reverse this trend and promote further capital accumulation. Hirsh writes:

The bourgeois state, by reason of its essential character, cannot act as regulator of the social process of development, but must be understood in the determination of its concrete functions as a reaction to the fundamentally crisis-ridden course of the economic and social process of reproduction.... These can be condensed in terms of value theory in the law of the tendency of the rate of profit to fall, which also means that this law must be the conceptual point of departure for an analysis of state functions, to be developed out of the concrete course of capital accumulation and class conflicts.[58]

Although Hirsh characterizes the state as "the authority guaranteeing the rules of equal exchange and of commodity circulation, and autonomous from the social process of reproduction and the social classes,"[59] state intervention in the economy in favor of capital (and against labor) defines the class nature of the state (i.e., as a capitalist state). Contrary to the classical Marxist and recent instrumentalist formulations, Hirsh argues that "the bourgeois state does not originate historically as a result of the conscious activity of a society or class in pursuit of its 'general will' but rather as the result of often contradictory and short-sighted class struggles and conflicts."[60] Being autonomous from the production process and the dominant classes in society, yet operating within the parameters of a capitalist social order, the success of the state in securing its material base, Hirsh argues, depends on its success in the promotion of the continued and uninterrupted accumulation of capital. Thus, like Offe, Hirsh provides an analysis of the class nature of the state based on its economic role in mediating the accumulation of capital and its associated crises, which are rooted in the laws of motion of the capitalist mode of production and its logic of development.[61] The state's response to these crises and its interest in their resolution, prompted by its economic dependence on capital, then, by necessity bring the state to the aid of capital and, in this way, define its class role in society.

Therborn and Szymanski on the Contradictions of the Capitalist State

Focusing on the class contradictions and crises of the capitalist state, Goran Therborn and Albert Szymanski make an important contribution to the Marxist theory of the state by bringing back into the debate the analyses of the Marxist classics. After a brief pause during the early 1970s, when theorists associated with the Frankfurt School had a dominant influence in state theorizing, the efforts of Therborn, Szymanski, and others starting in the late 1970s set the stage for the resurgence of Marxist class analysis grounded in the historical-materialist conception of class, state, and society.

"This renaissance of Marxist political analysis in the 1980's," writes Therborn, "will appear unexpected,"[62] especially given the political climate of the period. But, he continues:

The irony is that while many former protagonists and adherents of various "schools" of neo-Marxism are now proclaiming a post-Marxist, beyond-class stance, a new, vigorous self-confident class theory of politics and the state is being launched, impeccably dressed in the best clothes of modern empirical social science, while making no secret of its inspiring commitment to the working-class movement....

There is, then, still a contingent of scholars arguing that states are a function of classes, rather than the other way round.[63]

To his credit, Therborn's contribution to this renaissance has led to a flood of studies in Marxist political economy and class theory of the state since the 1980s.

The origins of this new wave of Marxist theorizing on the state, however, go back to the 1970s, when Therborn and a number of other Marxist intellectuals set forth their class theory of the state,[64] setting the stage for the subsequent emergence of works bringing back into the debate questions of paramount importance originally formulated by Marx, Engels, and Lenin.

In his book *What Does the Ruling Class Do When It Rules?* Therborn argues in favor of an alternative historical-materialist conception of the state and politics. He writes:

In the present theoretical and political conjuncture, I think it appropriate to bend the stick in the other direction: to attempt to develop a formal, comparative analytical model of the class character of the state apparatus....

In my opinion, such a model should start not from the functionalist problematic of the role of the state in the reproduction of capital, but from the relations between antagonistic classes, as determined by the forces and relations of production.[65]

The aim of such a theoretical model, argues Therborn, "is to show that different types of class relations and of class power generate corresponding forms of state organization, and to elucidate the way in which the class character of the state apparatus is determined and revealed."[66]

According to the axioms of historical materialism, class and state condition each other: where there are no classes, there is no state. In class societies, moreover, social relations are first and foremost class relations. Thus, by definition, every state has a class character, and every class society has a ruling class (or bloc of ruling classes). In other words, Marxist discourse does not pertain at all to the subjectivist debate on whether there exists a ruling class. If it seeks to identify the ruling class and the class character of state power, it does so in order to discover the characteristic social structures and relations which are promoted and protected above all others by the material force of the state; and in order to determine the conditions under which they may be changed or abolished.[67]

Thus, Therborn reintroduces into the debate the "base-superstructure" problematic, interpreted in a new light. Basic to Therborn's analysis of the relationship of the economic base to the political superstructure is the role of the class struggle engendered by the dominant mode of production. "In very general terms," writes Therborn,

> the character of state power is defined by the two fundamental processes of determination of the superstructure by the base—processes which in reality are two aspects of the same determination. One of these is the systemic logic of social modes of production, that is to say, the tendencies and contradictions of the specific dynamic of each mode. The other is the struggle of classes, defined by their position in the mode of production. These two forms of determination by the base are logically interrelated in the basic theory of historical materialism, and serious distortions of an "economist" or "politicist" nature result from their dissociation. The former determination constitutes the structural fit of state and society; the second the manner in which it is actively experienced and fought out by the ruling and ruled classes.[68]

In this formulation, the state is no longer viewed simply as a passive recipient of directives from the dominant class but is actively involved in the reproduction of the dominant relations of production. "Invariably the state enters into the reproduction of the relations of production by providing the latter with a stabilizing legal framework backed by force."[69] Moreover, "Social relations of production are framed by legal rules which define relations" between dominant and subordinate classes, although "the range and modality of state intervention in the economy vary greatly according to the nature and stage of development of the mode of production."[70]

To sum up Therborn's position:

> The economic base determines the political superstructure by entering into the reproduction of state power and the state apparatus.... It shapes the character of state power by, among other things, providing the basic parameters of state action and structuring the population into classes.... By definition, the

ruling class exercises its ruling power over other classes and strata through the state—through holding state power. Consequently, two relationships must be ensured. The state, particularly its commanding personnel, must *represent*, that is to say, promote and defend, the ruling class and its mode of exploitation or supremacy. At the same time, the state must *mediate* the exploitation or domination of the ruling class over other classes and strata. In other words, it follows from the irreducible material specificity of the class state that it is simultaneously both an *expression* of class exploitation and domination, and *something more* than a simple expression—something other than the non-state ruling-class apparatuses necessary to support these relations.[71]

Viewing the class-state problematic in these terms, Therborn bridges the gap between structuralist and instrumentalist formulations of the state and provides a dialectical analysis of the relationship between base and superstructure, thus advancing the debate through a fresh look at historical materialism as the basis for a new, resurgent Marxist theory of the state.

Albert Szymanski, in his book *The Capitalist State and the Politics of Class*, makes a similar case in favor of the historical-materialist approach to the study of state and society.[72] Citing the works of Marx, Engels, and Lenin on the state, Szymanski argues that the state plays a central role in society and that "a Marxist political sociology must thus give careful and detailed consideration to the nature of the state."[73]

Examining the nature and role of the state in class-divided societies in general and capitalist society in particular, Szymanski writes:

> The state is an instrument by which the exploitation of the economically subordinate class is secured by the economically dominant class that controls the state.... The social relationships and the social order that the state guarantees are thus the social relationships of inequality and the order of property and exploitation. The historically specific manifestation of the state is always a product of the means and mode of production prevailing in society. Thus in capitalist society we speak of *the capitalist state. ...*
>
> The state in capitalist society is a capitalist state by virtue of its domination by the capitalist class *and* in that it functions most immediately in the interests of capital.[74]

Moreover, "The state must operate within an ideological, economic, military, and political environment structured by capitalist relations of production."[75] This means that the logic of capitalist economic relations, reinforced by capital's ideological hegemony, dictate the policies the state must follow, which are formulated within a very limited range of options allowed by the capitalist mode of production. Thus the state in capitalist society is controlled by the capitalist class through both direct and indirect mechanisms that foster the interests of this class.

Far from providing a simple instrumentalist view of the state, Szymanski reveals the full range and complexity of the state's actions in response to the ensuing class struggles in society: "Political outcomes are the result of the relative size, social location, consciousness, degree of organization, and strategies followed by classes and segments of classes in their ongoing struggles."[76] He goes on to point out:

> No one class or segment of a class is ever able totally to control all aspects of society. State policy is always influenced to some extent by the various classes, even while it is normally under the domination of the class that owns and controls the means of production, and even when other classes have no formal representation in the organs of government. The ruling class must take into account both the demands and likely responses of other classes when it makes state policy. If it does not it may suffer very serious consequences, including social revolution.[77]

This is especially true during an economic and social crisis, according to Szymanski, as the degree of relative autonomy of the state from direct control of the capitalist class determines the nature and effectiveness of policies adopted by the state to deal with the crisis.

> A state that is too directly dominated by the majority bloc of the capitalist class may be unable to handle such a crisis, because the narrow-minded self-interest of this bloc prevents the state it dominates from adopting the policies necessary to save and advance the system. Domination of the state by these groups also tends to discredit the state, which because of such control is obviously not alleviating an economic crisis. The legitimating function of the state thus comes into increasing conflict with direct capitalist-class control.[78]

Commenting on the question of "relative autonomy," David Gold, Clarence Y. H. Lo, and Erik Olin Wright make a similar argument when they point out that such autonomy "is not an invariant feature of the capitalist state. Particular capitalist states will be more or less autonomous depending upon the degree of internal divisiveness, the contradictions within the various classes and fractions which constitute the power bloc, and upon the intensity of class struggle between the working class and the capitalist class as a whole."[79]

Concluding Observations

Given the greater strength and militancy of the organized working-class movement in Europe versus the United States, and given capital's thorough penetration and control of the state in the United States and its relative weakness in Europe because of the effective opposition of independent workers' parties and organizations and their role in politics and the state, it is not surprising that an instrumentalist view of the state has so easily become the predominant mode of state theorizing among Marxists in the United States, while structuralism has been better able to explain the prevailing complex realities of politics and the state in Europe, where power has been distributed among a multitude of political parties and coalition governments within the framework of the structural imperatives of capital accumulation and the prevalence of the capitalist mode of production.

In Europe, for example, given the differential political development of some European formations (e.g., France, Italy, Spain, and Greece) where strong socialist and communist parties and movements have developed and flourished, it has been difficult for the capitalist class to maintain direct, exclusive control of the state apparatus and yield results always in line with its interests. In these formations, the state has been shaped not only by the various fractions of the capitalist class, but also by the representatives of rival opposition forces (labor), including the socialists and the communists, contending for state power. This situation has invariably been effected through the presence of these opposition forces within the very organs and institutions of the state. As the power and influence of these parties have increased disproportionately vis-à-vis that of the capitalists, a resurgence of the class struggle and struggles for state power have occurred—sometimes leading to the possession of political power by socialist and communist forces in key state institutions, such as the parliament or the presidency and cabinet posts within the executive branch, as in Spain during the latter phase of the Republic in the late 1930s and, more recently, in Spain, France, Italy, Greece, and Portugal, as well as elsewhere in Europe at various levels of government in local and national politics.

In the United States, in contrast, except possibly during crisis periods (such as the Great Depression of the 1930s) when there has been a resurgence of class politics, the state has been completely dominated and controlled by the capitalist class, now especially by its monopoly fraction.

Commenting on this variation in the nature of capitalist states across national boundaries, Szymanski concurs with the above analysis and explains:

In France, for example, it is often argued that the state bureaucracy is not directly controlled by capitalist interests because the capitalist class in France is rather fractionated; whereas in Great Britain, where the capitalist class has a tradition of unity, the state machinery is directly controlled by the upper class....

In the United States since World War II there has been no significant autonomy of the U.S. state. Throughout this period the capitalist class has maintained direct control of the state apparatus.[80]

Thus, the role of direct and indirect mechanisms of capitalist-class rule, as well as the degree of autonomy of the state, varies considerably among formations dominated by the capitalist mode of production and becomes even more pronounced in other, less-developed capitalist states. This, in turn, points to the need for a concrete analysis of states across national boundaries and over extended historical periods.

The next two chapters examine the origins and development of the state in general and the capitalist state in particular; subsequent chapters take up the task of analyzing its nature and transformation in different comparative and historical settings.

Notes

1. Friedrich Engels, *The Origin of the Family, Private Property and the State,* in Karl Marx and Friedrich Engels, *Selected Works* (New York: International Publishers, 1972), 587–588.

2. Karl Marx and Friedrich Engels, *Manifesto of the Communist Party,* in Marx and Engels, *Selected Works,* 53.

3. Friedrich Engels, *Ludwig Feuerbach and the End of Classical German Philosophy,* in Marx and Engels, *Selected Works,* 627.

4. Ibid.

5. V. I. Lenin, *The State,* in Karl Marx, Friedrich Engels, and V. I. Lenin, *On Historical Materialism* (New York: International Publishers, 1974), 641.

6. V. I. Lenin, *Selected Works,* Vol. 2 (Moscow: Progress Publishers, 1975), 374.

7. See Karl Marx and Friedrich Engels, *The German Ideology* (New York: International Publishers, 1969); Karl Marx, *The Poverty of Philosophy* (New York: International Publishers, 1963); Karl Marx, *Preface to a Contribution to a Critique of Political Economy,* in Marx and Engels, *Selected Works*; Karl Marx, *Capital,* Vol. 3 (New York: International Publishers, 1967); Friedrich Engels, *Anti-Duhring,* Part 2 (New York: International Publishers, 1976); and other writings of Marx and Engels, as well as their letters and correspondence.

8. Marx, Preface to *Critique of Political Economy,* 182.

9. Marx, *Capital,* Vol. 3.

10. Marx and Engels, *The German Ideology,* 59.

11. Marx and Engels, *Manifesto of the Communist Party,* 37.

12. Ibid., Part II.

13. Marx and Engels, *The German Ideology,* 39.

14. Marx is referring here to the uprising of the French workers in Paris in 1871.

15. Karl Marx, *The Civil War in France,* in Marx and Engels, *Selected Works,* 288.

16. Karl Marx, *Marx to L. Kugelmann in Hanover,* in Marx and Engels, *Selected Works,* 680 (emphasis in original).

17. V. I. Lenin, *The State and Revolution,* in *Selected Works* (New York: International Publishers, 1971), 268.

18. Ibid., 272.

19. By *hegemony,* Gramsci meant the ideological predominance of the dominant ruling class(es) over the subordinate. At the same time, and in response to this, he introduced the concept of counterhegemony, which occurs when the proletariat, with the aid of "organic" intellectuals, exerts hegemony and exercises its superiority over society through the establishment of a proletarian socialist state.

20. Antonio Gramsci, *Prison Notebooks* (New York: International Publishers, 1971), 244.

21. Carnoy, *The State and Political Theory,* 70.

22. Ibid., 66.

23. Ibid. (emphasis in original).

24. Giuseppe Fiori, *Antonio Gramsci, Life of a Revolutionary* (London: New Left Books, 1970), 238.

25. Martin Carnoy, *The State and Political Theory* (Princeton, NJ: Princeton University Press, 1984), 87.

26. Fiori, *Antonio Gramsci,* 238.

27. Ibid.

28. Lenin, *The State and Revolution,* 255 (emphasis in the original).

29. Karl Marx, *Critique of the Gotha Programme,* in Karl Marx and Friedrich Engels, *Selected Works,* 331 (emphasis in the original). For an extended discussion on the concept of the "dictatorship of the proletariat," see Etienne Balibar, *On the Dictatorship of the Proletariat* (London: NLB, 1977).

30. Lenin, *The State and Revolution,* 262 (emphasis in the original).

31. Ibid., 302 (emphasis in the original).

32. Engels, *Anti-Duhring,* 307.

33. Lenin, *The State and Revolution,* 302–303 (emphasis in the original).

34. See Louis Althusser, *For Marx* (London: Penguin, 1969) and Althusser, *Lenin and Philosophy and Other Essays* (New York: Monthly Review Press, 1971). Also see Louis Althusser and Etienne Balibar, *Reading Capital* (London: New Left Books, 1970).

35. Louis Althusser, *Lenin and Philosophy and Other Essays,* 135.

36. Ibid., 137.

37. The debate began with a review of Ralph Miliband's *The State in Capitalist Society* (London: Basic Books, 1969) by Nicos Poulantzas, "The Problem of the Capitalist State," *New Left Review,* no. 58 (1969), to which Miliband responded in the next issue of the same journal. See Ralph Miliband, "The Capitalist State-Reply to Nicos Poulantzas," *New Left Review,* no. 59 (1970). After some lapse of time, the debate continued with the publication in English of Poulantzas's book *Political Power and Social Classes* (London: New Left Books, 1973; originally

published in French in 1968), Miliband's subsequent article "Poulantzas and the Capitalist State," *New Left Review,* no. 82 (1973), and Poulantzas's response "The Capitalist State: A Reply to Miliband and Laclau," *New Left Review,* no. 95 (1976). Later works by Poulantzas include *Fascism and Dictatorship* (London: New Left Books, 1974; originally published in French in 1970); *Classes in Contemporary Capitalism* (London: New Left Books, 1975); *The Crisis of the Dictatorships* (London: New Left Books, 1976); *State, Power, Socialism* (London: New Left Books, 1978). Miliband's subsequent arguments can be found in his "Political Forms and Historical Materialism," in *Socialist Register, 1975,* eds. R. Miliband and J. Saville (London: Merlin Press, 1975); and his book *Marxism and Politics* (London: Oxford University Press, 1977).

38. See David Gold, Clarence Y. H. Lo, and Erik Olin Wright, "Some Recent Developments in Marxist Theories of the Capitalist State," Parts 1 and 2, *Monthly Review* (October and November 1975); Gosta Esping-Andersen, Roger Friedland, and Erik Olin Wright, "Modes of Class Struggle and the Capitalist State," *Kapitalistate* 4–5 (Summer 1976); Albert Szymanski, *The Capitalist State and the Politics of Class* (Cambridge, MA: Winthrop, 1978); Bob Jessop, *The Capitalist State* (New York: New York University Press, 1982); Carnoy, *The State and Political Theory.*

39. This line of reasoning, regarding the state's "relative autonomy," is also provided by Gold, Lo, and Wright, "Some Recent Developments in Marxist Theories of the Capitalist State," 38.

40. Miliband, *The State in Capitalist Society,* 23.

41. Gold, Lo, and Wright, "Some Recent Developments in Marxist Theories of the Capitalist State," 33.

42. Ibid., 32–33.

43. Poulantzas, "Problem of the Capitalist State," 73.

44. Ibid.

45. Poulantzas, *Political Power and Social Classes;* and Poulantzas, *State, Power, Socialism.*

46. Miliband, "Poulantzas and the Capitalist State," 85.

47. Miliband, *Marxism and Politics,* 83.

48. Ibid., 87.

49. Ibid., 91.

50. Nicos Poulantzas, "The Political Crisis and the Crisis of the State," in *Critical Sociology: European Perspectives,* ed. J. W. Freiberg (New York: Irvington, 1979), 374–381.

51. Ibid., 375.

52. Ibid., 357–393.

53. Gold, Lo, and Wright, "Some Recent Developments in Marxist Theories of the Capitalist State," 37–38.

54. Claus Offe, "Structural Problems of the Capitalist State," in *German Political Studies,* Vol. 1, ed. K. Von Beyme (London: Sage, 1974), 37–40, 46–54. Also see Claus Offe, "The Theory of the Capitalist State and the Problem of Policy Formation," in *Stress and Contradiction in Modern Capitalism,* eds. L. Lindberg, et al. (Lexington: Heath, 1975), 127; Claus Offe, "Crisis of Crisis Management: Elements of a Political Crisis Theory," *International Journal of Politics,* (Fall 1976): 91–97.

55. Offe, "Crisis of Crisis Management."

56. Gold, Lo, and Wright, "Some Recent Developments in Marxist Theories of the Capitalist State," 39.

57. This is all the more evident in Offe's more recent work. See Claus Offe, "The Separation of Form and Content in Liberal Democratic Politics," *Studies in Political Economy* 3 (Spring 1980); Claus Offe, "Some Contradictions of the Modern Welfare State," *International Praxis* 1, no. 3 (1981).

58. Joachim Hirsh, "The State Apparatus and Social Reproduction: Elements of a Theory of the Bourgeois State," in *State and Capital: A Marxist Debate*, eds. John Holloway and Sol Picciotto (Austin: University of Texas Press, 1979), 97.

59. Ibid., 65.

60. Ibid.

61. Ibid., 97. It should be pointed out that Hirsh's crisis theory of the state ultimately rests on the balance of class forces in the class struggle. And it is developments in this sphere that define the nature of the economic crisis.

62. Goran Therborn, "Neo-Marxist, Pluralist, Corporatist, Statist Theories and the Welfare State," in *The State in Global Perspective*, ed. A. Kazancigil (Aldershot, UK: Gower and UNESCO, 1986), 205–206.

63. Ibid.

64. See Goran Therborn, *Science, Class and Society* (London: New Left Books, 1976), esp. 317–429; Therborn, "The Role of Capital and the Rise of Democracy," *New Left Review*, no. 103 (1977); Therborn, *What Does the Ruling Class Do When It Rules?* (London: New Left Books, 1978); and Therborn, *The Ideology of Power and the Power of Ideology* (London: New Left Books, 1980).

65. Therborn, *What Does the Ruling Class Do When It Rules?*, 34.

66. Ibid., 35.

67. Ibid., 132.

68. Ibid., 162.

69. Ibid., 165.

70. Ibid.

71. Ibid., 169, 181.

72. Szymanski, *The Capitalist State and the Politics of Class*.

73. Ibid., 20–21.

74. Ibid., 21, 25.

75. Ibid., 24.

76. Ibid., 27.

77. Ibid.

78. Ibid., 273.

79. Gold, Lo, and Wright, "Some Recent Developments in Marxist Theories of the Capitalist State," 38. In their attempt to construct a general Marxist theory of the state, Gold, Lo, and Wright provide a number of general propositions that directly deal with this issue. The first, and central, proposition is as follows: "The capitalist state must be conceived both as a structure constrained by the logic of the society within which it functions and as an organization manipulated behind the scenes by the ruling class and its representatives. *The extent to which actual state policies can be explained through structural or instrumental processes is historically contingent.* There are periods in which the state can be reasonably understood as a self-reproducing structure which functions largely independently of any external manipulation, and other times when it is best viewed as a simple tool in the hands of the ruling class. Certain parts of the state apparatus may be highly manipulated by specific capitalist

interests while other parts may have much more structural autonomy. But in no situation can state activity be completely reduced to either structural or instrumental causation. The state is always *relatively* autonomous: it is neither completely autonomous (i.e., free from active control by the capitalist class) nor simply manipulated by members of the ruling class (i.e., free from any structural constraints)" (46) (emphasis in the original).

80. Szymanski, *The Capitalist State and the Politics of Class,* 272.

Chapter 3

The Origins and Development of the State

For THOUSANDS OF YEARS after the formation of human societies, no state existed; there was no bureaucratic institution of organized force and violence, and no political rule over an entire people. In fact, the first known states did not arise until about the fourth millennium BC. The institution of the state has thus been around for only six thousand years, a relatively short time considering the entire history of human societies. Moreover, most societies during this period were without states. The prevalence of the state among a large number of societies around the world became a fact only during the past several hundred years.

This chapter explores the origins and development of the state and examines its nature and role in various types of societies in history—including Oriental despotic, slaveowning, feudal, and capitalist societies. Providing a historically specific analysis of the state as it arose in societies with different modes of production, the chapter presents in detail the particular features of these states and their contradictions as they have evolved in world-historic context.

The Origins of the State

The emergence of the state coincided with the emergence of social classes and class struggles resulting from the transition from a primitive communal to more advanced modes of production when an economic surplus (i.e., a surplus beyond all that is necessary to feed and clothe a people at the subsistence level) was first generated. Ensuing struggles over control of this surplus led to the development of the state, and once captured by the dominant classes in society, it became an instrument of force to maintain the rule of wealth and privilege against the laboring masses, to maintain exploitation and domination by the few over the many. Without the development of such a powerful instrument of force, there could be no assurance of protection of the privileges of a ruling class, who clearly lived off the labor of the masses. Friedrich Engels points out:

> The newly wealthy needed a mechanism that would not only safeguard the newly-acquired property of private individuals against the communistic traditions of the gentile order, would not only sanctify private property, formerly held in such light esteem, and pronounce this sanctification the highest purpose of human society, but would also stamp the gradually developing new forms of acquiring property, and consequently, of constantly accelerating increase in wealth, with the seal of general public recognition; an institution that would perpetuate, not only the newly-rising class division of society, but also the right of the possessing class to exploit the non-possessing classes and the rule of the former over the latter.
>
> And this institution arrived. The *state* was invented.[1]

To trace the historical origins and development of the state, we must go back to the time when human social organization took the form of distinct societies. The first social organization was the commune. Under this mode of social relations, and it accounts for some 80 percent of human history, no state existed. In primitive hunting and gathering societies with communal social relations, political decisions were made on a collective basis; through tribal councils, all members took part in the decision-making process. Organized along kinship lines, primitive communal societies had no powerful chiefs or strong leaders. In the absence of an institution such as the state, no official authority structure could govern society through force. Instead, voluntary consent to assemblies of the whole tribe constituted the basis of social cooperation to maintain order and effect change. In the absence of class distinctions and private ownership of land, the wealth of society belonged to the whole tribe, and the protection of the tribe's possessions was considered the duty of all its members. In this sense, tribal property, held in common, assured the politics of the primitive commune without the need for a state.

Until about 10,000 years ago, all human societies were at the stage of primitive communism. In fact, until a few hundred years ago, most societies on earth were still of this type. Today, primitive hunting and gathering tribes are found only in a few remote areas of the world. But about 10,000 years ago, clan and tribal relations gradually began to change, largely as a result of the division of labor among communes and tribes. First, cattle-breeding communes and tribes split off; later, artisans followed suit. Labor productivity began to grow and gave rise to a surplus. The production of food and other necessities surpassed that required for subsistence, and the possibility of accumulation arose. With an increased and formalized division of labor came a rise in inequality and an inequitable distribution of the surplus among clan members. As a result, political power began to be expressed, not in the interests of all members of the clan, but to enrich the chiefs and elders. It also began to be more profitable to make slaves out of prisoners of war than to kill them because they could produce more than they consumed and thus add to the wealth of their owners. Thus, as Gennady Belov points out:

> In this way, a minority which amassed wealth was formed in the commune. Organs of self-government began to be changed into organs for the suppression of the majority by the minority. But custom, the moral authority enjoyed by chiefs and joint decision-making were not sufficient any more to turn these organs into regular organs of power. Special detachments (armies, first and foremost) were created to effect, by force of arms, or by the threat of using them, the will of the rich—those who owned the land, livestock and slaves. The appearance of organs of suppression and coercion ushered in the history of the state.[2]

Thus, the state developed as a social institution as a result of the growth of wealth and social classes:

> Former society, moving in class antagonisms, had need of the state, that is, an organization of the exploiting class at each period for the maintenance of its external conditions of production; that is, therefore, for the forcible holding down of the exploited class in the conditions of oppression (slavery, villeinage or serfdom, wage labor) determined by the existing mode of production. The state was the official representative of society as a whole, its embodiment in a visible corporation; but it was this only in so far as it was the state of that class which itself, in its epoch, represented society as a whole; in ancient times, the state of the slave-owning citizens; in the Middle Ages, of the feudal nobility; in our epoch, of the bourgeoisie.[3]

Table 3.1 illustrates the various kinds of states in relation to different modes of production in the historical process and provides a summary of their associated conditions, main contradictions, and social transformation.

Table 3.1 Modes of Production and Types of States in Historical Development

Modes of Production	Relations of Production	Superstructure
Primitive communist	No classes or division of labor, except by sex	No state; tribal council; primitive religion
Asiatic	Imperial court vs. communal villages	Centralized state; formalized religion; surplus for luxury
Ancient/slave	Master vs. slave	Centralized state and military organization; formalized religion
Feudal	Lords vs. serfs	Weak central state; formalized religion; manor based
Capitalist	Capitalists vs. wage laborers	Strong central state; formalized religion; individualistic ideology
Socialist*	Worker-worker; no antagonistic classes	Proletarian socialist ideology; strong central state
Communist	No division of labor; no class struggle	No state; communal consciousness; collective rule

Source: Adopted from Albert Szymanski, *The Capitalist State and the Politics of Class* (Cambridge, MA: Winthrop, 1978); and Szymanski, *Class Structure: A Critical Perspective* (New York: Praeger, 1983).

*Although Marx does not mention socialism as a mode of production, Marxists generally agree that between capitalism and communism, there exists a transitional phase called socialism, which Lenin called "the first phase of communist society." During this stage, the state is controlled by the

Associated Conditions	Contradictions	Transformations
Low population density; small-scale societies	Possibility of economic surplus and exchange	Commodity production; emergence of private property
High population density; need for irrigation and flood control	Court vs. village interests; external invasion	Stable system; resists change but can develop into any of the advanced modes
Centralized; city-based; division between town and country	Wars and expansion; constant increase in slaves	Undermining of social structure leads to breakdown of whole order
Low population density; division between town and country	Expanded demand for commodities; expanded trade; increased population	Bourgeois revolution against feudalism
Increasing population; city-based; division between town and country	Accumulation of capital; class polarization; increasing proletarian class consciousness	Proletarian socialist revolution against capitalism
Centralized; city-based; division between town and country	Factory system; division of labor; centralized state; division between town and country	Gradual withering away of these nonantagonistic contradictions
Decentralized; no division between town and country	None	None

working class, or what Marx calls "the dictatorship of the proletariat," through its political organ the communist party. The main characteristic of this period is the dismantling of the capitalist system and the building of communist society. A strong central state and factory-based industrial production exists; society is still city-based, although the division between city and country is being gradually reduced. Many nonantagonistic contradictions begin gradually to wither away, as does the state and other major institutions of society, as the society evolves toward full communism.

The Oriental Despotic State

The earliest form of the state emerging out of the primitive commune was Oriental despotism. With the disintegration of the tribal communal structure, the state emerged as the supreme political institution in society. It first developed in large river valleys, such as along the Nile, Tigris, Euphrates, Ganges, Yellow, and Yangtze rivers, where despotic empires were set up under the auspices of an imperial court. The consolidation of absolute power by the bureaucratic ruling class and the creation of the great empires of antiquity marked the beginning stage of the history of the state.[4] Over time, highly centralized states began to develop, with large numbers of full-time officials to collect taxes, keep official records, supervise the waterworks, and maintain the police and armies for enforcing the law.

> Side by side with the masses thus occupied with one and the same work, we find the "chief inhabitant," who is judge, police, and tax-gatherer in one; the bookkeeper, who keeps the accounts of the village and registers everything relating thereto; another official, who prosecutes criminals, protects strangers traveling through and escorts them to the next village; the boundary man, who guards the boundaries against neighboring communities; the water-overseer, who distributes the water from the common tanks for irrigation [etc.] ... This dozen of individuals is maintained at the expense of the whole community.[5]

Moreover, in these societies, the ruler or the emperor had absolute power. All the major institutions—economic, religious, military, and political—were merged into one, centered in an absolute ruler. As Marx put it:

> The despot here appears as the father of all numerous lesser communities, thus realizing the common unity of all. It, therefore, follows that the surplus product (which, incidentally, is legally determined in terms of [*infolge*] the real appropriation through labor) belongs to this highest unity. Oriental despotism therefore appears to lead to a legal absence of property. In fact, however, its foundation is tribal or common property, in most cases created through a combination of manufacture and agriculture within the small community which thus becomes entirely self-sustaining and contains within itself all conditions of production and surplus production.
>
> Part of its surplus labor belongs to the higher community, which ultimately appears as a *person*. This surplus labor is rendered both as tribute and as common labor for the glory of the unity, in part that of the despot, in part that of the imagined tribal entity of the god.[6]

The main contradictions in these early class societies, then, were between the masses of people who lived in village units and the ruling class, consisting of the ruler and the state bureaucracy.

An important characteristic of Oriental despotic societies was their strong resistance to change. The Egyptian, Aztec, Inca, Indian, Chinese, and Ottoman empires were highly stable, lasting several centuries. Because of their highly stable nature, change often had to come from external sources.

This was true, for example, in China and India. The despotic empires in these two regions were penetrated by British and, more generally, European capitalism during the later colonial phase of expansion, which broke down all internal barriers to development along the capitalist path. The contemporary capitalist (as well as the feudal) mode was "introduced" from outside the prevailing system of production. This was also true of the Aztec and Inca empires, which underwent a similar process of change with the impact of European mercantile expansion to the Americas and the subsequent penetration of commercial and feudal interests in transforming local economic and sociopolitical structures.

With Ottoman despotism, a combination of external *and* internal developments brought change to this centuries-old social formation. Although the expansion of European mercantile capital to the East undermined the Ottoman monopoly on trade in the Mediterranean, an equally important internal process was at work. This was the allocation of parcels of land in rural areas to warriors engaged in the despotic bureaucracy's militaristic adventures in Europe, the Middle East, North Africa, and elsewhere. This system of land allocation (*timar*) and the subsequent introduction of tax farming (*iltizam*) brought about a major transformation of the Ottoman agrarian structure.[7] The accumulation of large tracts of land, initially by these warriors and later by an emerging landed gentry (*ayan*), led to the development of a landowning class that came to subordinate local communal villagers to its dictates. Through this process, the majority of the local population was turned into an unpaid laboring class tied to local landed interests and in a position not unlike the serfs under European feudalism. At the same time, interaction with Europe facilitated the expansion of European commercial capital into the empire and led to the transformation of the local merchant class into an intermediary of European capital. In this way, the state came to represent the interests of the landed gentry, local merchants, and European capital, as well as the political bureaucracy on which it was based.[8]

In other despotic societies, an alternative path of development led to the emergence of slavery and feudalism as dominant modes of production. The transition from Oriental despotic state under the Asiatic mode of production to its varied forms under slavery and feudal landlordism was a slow process that took hundreds of years. But, in time, the development of new modes of production resulted in the transformation of the superstructure as well, in a way that directly corresponded to the prevailing relations of production and the ensuing class struggles. Thus, the evolution of changing property relations in society ushered in a new form of the state—a state that served the interests of new ruling classes (of slaveowners, landlords, and subsequently, capitalists) for purposes of control, domination, and exploitation of the laboring masses.

The Ancient Slaveowning State

In some societies, the state possessed immense power and served to advance the interests of masters against slaves. Societies based on the slave mode of production, such as Athens, were located along major trade routes and at the mouths of important rivers. They became major trading centers with strong military power. "In the ancient world," writes Marx, "commerce and the development of commercial capital ... resulted in a slave economy, or sometimes, depending on the point of departure, it resulted simply in the transformation of a patriarchal slave system devoted to the production of direct means of subsistence into a similar system devoted to the production of surplus value."[9] Ancient society, then, was based on slavery as the dominant mode of production and exchange. Surplus value was extracted from slaves and appropriated, in turn, by the citizen ruling class, or masters.

Slaveowning societies, such as Athens, conquered large numbers of people and made them slaves. This practice enabled Athens to maintain a democracy for Athenian citizens while enslaving virtually all the people in the surrounding environs: "In Athens," writes V. Gordon Childe, "democracy was made completely effective.... Every citizen was expected to attend assemblies and to sit on juries.... In the latter part of the fifth century, countrymen did in fact attend the assembly and vote on questions of general policy."[10] Childe goes on to add:

> Fifth-century Athens thus provides the first adequately documented example of a through-going popular government. Its popular character must not be exaggerated. In the first place women had no place in public life.... Secondly, citizenship was now a hereditary privilege from which resident aliens were rigorously excluded.... Finally, industry was based on slavery; even the small farmer generally owned a slave or two, and the majority of the employees in mines and factories ... were slaves.... Aliens had no share in the government and slaves had no rights whatever.[11]

The primary contradiction in the productive scheme of ancient societies such as Athens and early Rome was between slaves and masters. While the surplus product created by forced (slave) labor was converted into unproductive expenditure—on public works, religious monuments, and works of art, as well as the extravagant, aristocratic way of life of the citizen ruling class—the condition of the slave masses deteriorated, and their position of subsistence became more precarious as their impoverishment grew.[12]

The decay of ancient social organization was the result of a decline in trade, the money economy, and cities, all of which—accompanied by war, expansion, and a constant increase in slavery and, with it, widespread slave rebellions[13]—made slavery no longer profitable and undermined the entire community structure. These developments led to the slaves' conversion into proto-serfs, that is, neither citizens nor slaves. Although this meant a certain level of improvement in their position compared to earlier periods, the slaves nonetheless remained tied to the land and were bought and sold with it. Herein lay the preconditions for the transition to feudalism.

The Feudal State

The origins of classical European feudalism go back to the Germanic invasions of the Roman Empire and the fusion of the essentially household-based Germanic mode with Roman proto-feudalism, which occurred after the collapse of the slave system of ancient Rome. The forced unity of the two societies, originally at different stages of development, led to the eventual dissolution of the old forms and gave rise to the development of a yet new (feudal) mode of production. "The last centuries of the declining Roman Empire and its conquest by the barbarians," writes Marx,

> destroyed a number of productive forces; agriculture had declined, industry had decayed for lack of markets, trade had died out or had been violently interrupted, and the rural and urban population had diminished. These conditions and the mode of organization of the conquest determined by them gave rise, under the influence of the Teutonic military constitution, to feudal property.[14]

The essential social relation of production in feudal societies was between lord and serf. There was very little division of labor, minimal trade or commerce (as all goods were produced in self-sufficient communities), and constant warfare among feudal lords to expand land. The village was the basic unit of the agrarian feudal economy and consisted of a population ranging from about a dozen to several hundred peasant families living in a cluster. The manor, in contrast, was a unit of political jurisdiction and economic exploitation controlled by a single lord; it was often geographically identical with the village, although some manors embraced two or more villages. "The village community," writes Hollister, was

> a closed system, economically self-sufficient, capable of sustaining the material and spiritual needs of the villages without much contact with the outside world.... The economy of the Early Middle Ages, lacking a vigorous commercial life and a significant urban population, failed to provide villages with much incentive to produce beyond their immediate needs. There was only the most limited market for surplus grain. Accordingly, village life tended to be uneventful, tradition-bound, and circumscribed by the narrowest of horizons....
>
> Superimposed on the economic structure of the village was the political-juridical structure of the manor. The average peasant was bound to a manorial lord.... They owed various dues to their manorial lord, chiefly in kind, and were normally expected to labor for a certain number of days per week—often three—on the lord's fields.[15]

The obligations placed on the peasants were immense, and their function within the manorial system was one of productive subordination to the lord. In addition to their obligation to work on the lord's fields, the peasants paid their lord a percentage of the produce of their fields, as well as paying various fees and taxes. The following key excerpt from Engels's *The Peasant War in Germany* captures the condition of life of the peasant in feudal Germany:

> At the bottom of all the classes, save the last one, was the huge exploited mass of the nation, the peasants. It was the peasant who carried the burden of all the other strata of society: princes, officialdom, nobility, clergy, patricians and middle-class. Whether the peasant was the subject of a prince, an imperial baron, a bishop, a monastery, or a city, he was everywhere treated as a beast of burden and worse. If he was a serf, he was entirely at the mercy of his master. If he was a bondsman, the legal deliveries stipulated by agreement were sufficient to crush him; even they were being daily increased. Most of his time, he had to work on his master's estate. Out of that which he earned in his few free hours, he had to pay tithes, dues, ground rents, war taxes, land taxes, imperial taxes and other payments. He could neither marry nor

die without paying the master. Aside from his regular work for the master, he had to gather litter, pick strawberries, pick bilberries, collect snail shells, drive the game for the hunting, chop wood, and so on. Fishing and hunting belonged to the master. The peasant saw his crop destroyed by wild game. The community meadows and woods of the peasants had almost everywhere been forcibly taken away by the masters.[16]

Engels points out that the domination of the lord or master over the peasant extended not only over the peasants' property but also over his person:

And in the same manner as the master reigned over the peasant's property, he extended his willfulness over his person, his wife and daughters. He possessed the right of the first night. Whenever he pleased, he threw the peasant into the tower, where the rack waited for him just as surely as the investigating attorney waits for the criminal in our times. Whenever he pleased, he killed him or ordered him beheaded. None of the instructive chapters of the Carolina[17] which speaks of "cutting of ears," "cutting of noses," "blinding," "chopping of fingers," "beheading," "breaking on the wheel," "burning," "pinching with burned tongs," "quartering," etc., was left unpracticed by the gracious lord and master at his pleasure. Who could defend the peasant? The courts were manned by barons, clergymen, patricians, or jurists, who knew very well for what they were being paid. Not in vain did all the official estates of the empire lie on the exploitation of the peasants.[18]

Although state rule was highly decentralized, and there was little in the way of a state bureaucracy, the power of the feudal lords rested on their military strength: "The hierarchical system of landownership, and the armed bodies of retainers associated with it gave the nobility power over the serfs. This feudal structure was, just as much as the communal property of antiquity, an association against a subject producing class, but the form of association and the relation to the direct producers were different because of the different conditions of production."[19]

The Transition from Feudalism to Capitalism

Historically, the feudal mode of production in Western Europe began to give way to mercantilism in the sixteenth century and later to capitalism in the eighteenth century. The growth of trade and the rise of the merchant class strengthened the rule of the state, which obtained complete control over trade and the economy in general during the mercantile era and set the groundwork for the subsequent emergence of capitalism and the capitalist state.[20]

The transition from feudalism to capitalism was marked by a transformation of the state from a coordinating institution of dispersed landed interests over a large agrarian territory to a centralized power representing the new merchant class and later the emerging industrial capitalists concentrated in urban trading centers and port cities and subsequently manufacturing. The shift in the center of political rule thus resulted from a shift in production relations, and relations of exploitation in general, in favor of the merchant class in league with the early capitalists in transition from crafts production to large-scale manufacturing and industry. The protection provided to the merchants by the mercantile and later capitalist state in the transitional period resulted from the increasing power and influence of the merchants and capitalists in economic life and consequently in politics. In time, the merchants and the capitalists constituted the new ruling class in Europe (and elsewhere).[21]

The reappearance of a strong central state coincided with the dissolution of the feudal mode of production and the rise to prominence of the commercial and industrial capitalist class. Through the powers of the state, the merchants and the traders ushered in a period of mercantilism and later capitalism. At the height of this period, and with a greatly expanded overseas trade during the sixteenth to eighteenth centuries in Europe, we begin to see the emergence of the original accumulation of capital that subsequently gave rise to capitalism in Western Europe. Thus, overseas trade, the basis of the original accumulation of capital, played a crucial role in weakening the position of the landlords, in laying the foundations of capitalism and thereby facilitating the process of transition.[22] As Marx and Engels observed:

> The discovery of America, the rounding of the Cape, opened up fresh ground for the rising bourgeoisie. The East-Indian and Chinese markets, the colonization of America, trade with the colonies, the increase in the means of exchange and in commodities generally, gave to commerce, to navigation, to industry, an impulse never before known, and thereby, to the revolutionary element in the tottering feudal society, a rapid development.[23]

As trade and merchants' capital set the stage for the shift toward manufacturing and industrial production for further accumulation, the balance of forces in the economy began to swing in favor of the rising bourgeoisie, whose growing wealth and economic strength brought changes in the nature and role of the state as well—in favor of the bourgeoisie.

> At the same pace at which the progress of modern industry developed, widened, intensified the class antagonism between capital and labor, the State power assumed more and more the character of the national power of capital over labor, of a public force organized for social enslavement, of an engine of class despotism.[24]

The absolutist monarchies that ruled much of Europe in an earlier period and were strengthened during the mercantilist era through strong state intervention in the economy worked to the benefit of the bourgeoisie as its expanded economic position vis-à-vis the landlords and the merchants, and the subsequent political pressure it exerted upon the state, resulted in the state's increasing isolation from the control and influence of the former ruling classes in both the economy and the polity. In time, the bourgeoisie forced the dissolution of the absolutist state and established republics (in France and Switzerland) or constitutional monarchies (in England and Holland). Eventually, the bourgeoisie set up its own states throughout much of Europe and ushered in a new era of capitalist expansion promoted and safeguarded by the new capitalist state.

It is to the analysis of the capitalist state that we turn in the next chapter.

Notes

1. Friedrich Engels, *The Origins of the Family, Private Property, and the State* (New York: International Publishers, 1972), 263.

2. Gennady Belov, *What Is the State?* (Moscow: Progress Publishers, 1986), 21.

3. Friedrich Engels, *Anti-Duhring* (New York: International Publishers, 1976), 306.

4. For a discussion of the Oriental despotic state and the Asiatic mode of production, see Perry Anderson, *Lineages of the Absolutist State* (London: New Left Books, 1974), 462–549; Hal Draper, *Karl Marx's Theory of Revolution* (New York: Monthly Review Press, 1977), 515–571; D. R. Gandy, *Marx and History* (Austin: University of Texas Press, 1979), 18–25; and Lawrence Krader, *The Asiatic Mode of Production* (Assem: Van Gorcum, 1975).

5. Karl Marx, *Capital* (New York: International Publishers, 1967), 1: 357–358.

6. Karl Marx, *Pre-Capitalist Economic Formations* (New York: International Publishers, 1965), 69–70.

7. Halil Inalcik, *The Ottoman Empire* (New York: Praeger, 1973); H. Islamoğlu and S. Faroqhi, "Crop Patterns and Agricultural Production Trends in Sixteenth Century Anatolia," *Review* 2, no. 3 (Winter 1979): 401–436. For a detailed discussion of the land-tenure system and the emergence of a landed gentry in the Ottoman Empire, see "The State in the Middle East" in Chapter 6 of this book.

8. For further discussion on the nature of the Ottoman Empire and the controversy surrounding the applicability of the Asiatic mode of production to the Ottoman social formation, see Sencer Divitçioğlu, *Asya Üretim Tarzı ve Osmanlı Toplumu* (The Asiatic Mode of Production and Ottoman Society) (Istanbul: Koz Yayınevi, 1971).

9. Karl Marx, *Selected Writings in Sociology and Social Philosophy* (New York: McGraw-Hill, 1964), 113.

10. V. Gordon Childe, *What Happened in History* (Baltimore: Penguin, 1971), 215.

11. Ibid., 216.

12. Engels, *Origins,* 217–37.

13. As Childe points out, "Slave revolts ... assumed serious proportions for the first time in history after 134 B.C. Attica, Macedonia, Delos, Sicily, Italy, and Pergamon. The rebels were often joined by small peasants and tenants and even by 'free' proletarians." Childe, *What Happened in History,* 267.

14. Marx, *Selected Writings in Sociology,* 117–118.

15. C. Warren Hollister, *Medieval Europe,* 3rd ed. (New York: Wiley, 1974), 131–132.

16. Friedrich Engels, *The Peasant War in Germany* (New York: International Publishers, 1973), 47.

17. Carolina, a criminal code of the sixteenth century, published in 1532 under Emperor Charles V.

18. Engels, *The Peasant War in Germany,* 47–48.

19. Marx, *Selected Writings in Sociology,* 118.

20. See Immanuel Wallerstein, *The Modern World System* (New York: Academic Press, 1974); Wallerstein, *The Capitalist World Economy* (Cambridge: Cambridge University Press, 1979); and Wallerstein, *The Politics of the World Economy* (Cambridge: Cambridge University Press, 1984).

21. Berch Berberoglu, "The Transition From Feudalism to Capitalism: The Sweezy-Dobb Debate," *Revista Mexicana de Sociologia* (December 1977).

22. For an analysis of the debate on the transition from feudalism to capitalism in Western Europe, see Berberoglu, "The Transition From Feudalism to Capitalism." The original debate between Sweezy and Dobb, which took place in the pages of the journal *Science and Society* in the early 1950s, is compiled, with additional commentaries and discussion, in Rodney Hilton, ed., *The Transition From Feudalism to Capitalism* (London: New Left Books, 1976).

23. Karl Marx and Friedrich Engels, *Manifesto of the Communist Party,* in Karl Marx and Friedrich Engels, *Selected Works* (New York: International Publishers, 1972), 36.

24. Karl Marx, "The Civil War in France," in Marx and Engels, *Selected Works,* 289.

Chapter 4

The Development of the Capitalist State

THE DECLINE OF FEUDALISM AND THE RISE of capitalism in Europe marked the beginning of a new chapter in world history. The transition from feudalism to capitalism was accompanied by a number of preconditions that gave rise to capitalism and the capitalist state that came to dominate the social formations of Western Europe by the early eighteenth century.

This chapter examines the origins of the capitalist state in Europe and the United States, providing an analysis of its nature, dynamics, and contradictions through its development over the centuries. It also provides a comparative analysis of variations in its development in the two settings, highlighting its emergence under feudalism and plantation slavery and its maturity under conditions of advanced capitalist society.

The Origins of the Capitalist State in Europe

In examining the decline of feudalism and the rise of capitalism in Western Europe, Marx conceived of two possible paths of development that could lead to the emergence of capitalism in formations previously dominated by the feudal mode of production: one, merchant to capitalist, and two, craftsman to capitalist. Of the two, Marx characterized the second as the "really revolutionary way," pointing to the centrality of the internal contradictions lodged in the productive process under feudalism, which contained the seeds of the emergent capitalist mode in the form of petty commodity production based on crafts.[1]

This was clearly true in Britain and France, where the new forces of production came into the hands of small craftsmen, who set up workshops and factories employing wage labor, thus transforming themselves into capitalists. In Prussia and most of Eastern Europe, however, the big merchants and landlords became the owners of industry. In the absence of a strong, independent capitalist class, and with power in the hands of the merchants and landlords, capitalism in this region developed gradually and over an extended time; monarchist and feudal forms of the state continued to dominate society well into the twentieth century.[2]

Marx's careful examination of the European experience convinced him that, on balance, a combination of the two paths, dominated more by the first, actually led to the emergence of capitalism and capitalist relations in much of Europe. This prompted him to emphasize the importance of trade (especially colonial trade) as a major contributing factor in the dissolution of feudalism and the original accumulation of capital. This was the case in addition to the fundamental internal contradictions of the feudal mode, where trade provided the added impetus in bringing about the collapse of feudalism:

> Trade with the colonies, the increase in the means of exchange and in commodities generally, gave to commerce, to navigation, to industry, an impulse never before known, and thereby, to the revolutionary element in the tottering feudal society, a rapid development....
>
> In proportion as industry, commerce, navigation, railways extended, in the same proportion the bourgeoisie developed, increased its capital, and pushed into the background every class handed down from the Middle Ages.[3]

Historically, a number of conditions set the stage and led to the emergence of capitalism and the capitalist state in Western Europe and elsewhere. These included the availability of free laborers, the generation of moneyed wealth, a sufficient level of skills and technology, markets, and the protection provided by the state. In general, these conditions were the foundations on which a precapitalist society transformed itself into a capitalist one until capitalism developed through its own dynamics.[4] Once capitalism was established, it began to produce and reproduce the conditions for expanded commodity production and capital accumulation. From this point on, capitalism developed in accordance with its inherent contradictions.

During the development of capitalism since the late eighteenth century, the commercial and industrial interests that merged into a single unified class forming the rising bourgeoisie increasingly viewed their interests as tied-up with the nation in which they amassed their growing wealth and came to require the protection of the state to safeguard their increasingly privileged position in society. This led to the control of state power during the transition from feudalism to capitalism in order to advance the interests of capital as distinct from the interests of the overthrown landed aristocracy on the one hand and the emerging working class on the other. The early capitalists thus came to articulate, through the instrumentality of the state, not only their own particular class interests, but *appeared* to represent the interests of the nation as a whole, hence promoting the illusion that the state is the expression of the national will and that its role is to protect and advance the rights of all citizens. "At first glance, it may seem that the exploiter state really does express the interests of society as a whole, uniting all of its members within a structure," writes G. Belov:

> But no state has ever existed which served the interests of the exploiters and the exploited in equal measure. In those countries where the minority gathers to itself the bulk of the national wealth, the state primarily acts out as an oppressor of the majority rather than as the promoter of the interests of all citizens. This is the basic postulate one must bear in mind in order to fathom the essence, or the class nature of the state; only then can the true meaning of the state's activities be understood.[5]

With the principal relations of production being that between wage labor and the owners of the means of production, capitalism established itself as a mode of production based on the exploitation of wage labor by capitalists, whose power and authority in society derived from their ownership and control of the means of production. Lacking ownership of the means necessary to gain a living, producers were forced to sell their labor power to capitalists in order to survive. As a result, the surplus value produced by labor was appropriated by the capitalists in the form of profit. Thus, private profit, generated through the exploitation of labor, became the motive force of capitalism.

The contradictions imbedded in such antagonistic social relations in time led to the radicalization of workers and the formation of trade unions and other labor organizations that were to play important roles in the struggles between labor and capital. The history of the labor movement in Europe, the United States, and elsewhere in the world is replete with bloody confrontations between labor and capital and the latter's repressive arm, the capitalist state. From the early battles of workers in Britain and on the Continent in the late eighteenth and early nineteenth century, to the decisive role played by French workers in the uprising of 1848 to 1851, to the Paris Commune in 1871 and beyond, the working class put up a determined struggle in its fight against capital—a struggle spanning over two centuries.

Established to protect and advance the interests of the capitalist class, the early capitalist state assumed a pivotal role that assured the class rule of capitalists over society and thus became an institution of legitimization and brute force to maintain law and order in favor of capitalism. Sanctioning and enforcing laws to protect the rights of the new property owners and disciplining labor to maintain a wage system that generated profits for the wealthy few, the capitalist state became the instrument of capital and its political rule over society.

Among the major functions of the early capitalist state were guaranteeing private property at home and abroad; collecting taxes; recording births, deaths, and income for purposes of taxation and raising armies; guaranteeing contracts; providing the infrastructure (railroads, canals, communication) for the new industries; facilitating the growth of private industry; mediating among various wealthy interests; securing a cheap and disciplined labor force for private enterprise; and preserving law and order to keep the masses under control. Corresponding to conditions under early industrial capitalism, the state had only a small bureaucracy, spent little on social programs, and had a relatively small standing army; taxes were greatly reduced and were collected largely through tariffs on imports in order to protect home industry.[6]

The central task of the early capitalist state in Europe was that of disciplining the labor force. Union activity, strikes, or collective actions of any kind by workers against businesses were prohibited; demonstrations, agitation, and propaganda initiated by workers against the employers and the system were systematically repressed. Thus, while state intervention in the economy was kept to a minimum to permit the capitalists to enrich themselves without regulation, the capitalist-controlled state became heavily involved in the conflict between labor and capital on behalf of the capitalist class, bringing to bear its repressive apparatus on labor and its allies who threatened the capitalist order. Law and order enforced by the state in early capitalism (and right up to the present) served to protect and preserve the capitalist system and prevent its transformation. In this sense, the state came to see itself as a legitimizing agency of the new social order and identified its survival directly with the capitalists who controlled it. This mutual relationship between state and capital in time set the conditions for the structural environment in which the state functioned to promote capitalist interests, now without the necessity of direct control by individual capitalists through specific state agencies. Within this process of the state's development from early to mature capitalism, the structural imperatives of capital accumulation placed the state in the service of capital, thus transforming it into a capitalist state.

With the growth and development of capitalism and its contradictions, and, in response to this, the growth of the working class and the trade union movement, the state began to take a more active role in the economy in order to regulate business activity and cyclical crises (e.g., the business cycle, finance, trade, the stock market). At the same time, to control the demands of labor and secure the long-term stability of the capitalist system, it granted certain concessions to the masses. The limited social programs enacted by the state, and the extension of the franchise to the masses, came to serve a legitimizing role and rationalized the actions of the state as "representing the interests of the entire society" (i.e., that it was a "democratic state"). "But this democracy," we are reminded,

> is always bound by the narrow framework of capitalist exploitation, and consequently always remains, in effect, a democracy for the minority, only for the propertied classes, only for the rich. Freedom in capitalist society always remains about the same as it was in the ancient Greek republics; freedom for the slave-owners. Owing to the conditions of capitalist exploitation, the modern wage slaves are so crushed by want and poverty that "they cannot be bothered with democracy," "cannot be bothered with politics"; in the ordinary, peaceful course of events, the majority of the population is debarred from participation in public and political life....
>
> Democracy for an insignificant minority, democracy for the rich—that is the democracy of capitalist society....
>
> Marx grasped this essence of capitalist democracy splendidly when, in analyzing the experience of the Commune, he said that the oppressed are allowed once every few years to decide which particular representatives of the oppressing class shall represent and repress them in parliament![7]

The increasing involvement of the state in social life in order to promote the capitalist system accomplished its desired ends: The masses were in general unable clearly to distinguish the state's democratic-appearing concessions from its real class agenda, as an instrument of capitalist rule. What's more, class-conscious workers and labor organizations that were aware of this fact and tried to expose it through mass political action were severely repressed.

The Development of the Capitalist State in the United States

The transformation of the state in the United States from a colonial appendage of the British Empire to an independent capitalist state with jurisdiction over the entire national territory did not occur until the late nineteenth century. The War of Independence did, to be sure, change the political relations between Britain and its former American colony, but this change was not accompanied by a social transformation transferring power from one class to another. In this sense, the American Revolution was not a social revolution; rather, it constituted the transfer of power from Britain to its ex-colony, similar to that achieved by wars of national liberation, without effecting a change in internal class power and class relations. From 1776 to the end of the Civil War in 1865, the United States developed within the framework of a "neocolonial" relationship with Britain, when the state represented the interests of both the emerging capitalist class in the North and the dependent slaveowning class in the South, which was tied to the British-dominated world economy. Specializing in agroindustrial raw material production (e.g., cotton) geared to the needs of the textile industry in England, the slaveowning planter class in the South came to articulate the interests of its ex–colonial master poised against northern capital, from which it carved out for itself a portion of the profits guaranteed by the imperial crown. The contradictory class relationship between the two rival ruling classes in postcolonial America continued to evolve and develop within the framework of a truce that permitted the coexistence of two distinct modes of production through the sharing of state power, at least for a time.

The balance of class forces in the state apparatus from the postindependence period to the Civil War was maintained by the Constitution drawn up by the two rival propertied classes in 1787. Intent on replacing the Articles of Confederation (the law of the land at the time) with a Constitution that would give power to a central state, the delegates to the Constitutional Convention in Philadelphia pushed through a document designed to protect their class interests and prevent popular democratic control of the U.S. state. Fifty-three of the fifty-five delegates to the Convention were or represented the economic interests of the propertied classes of slaveowners, merchants, creditors, and manufacturers.[8] Forty of the delegates held the paper money issued by the Continental Congress to finance the Revolutionary War, fourteen held vast tracts of land, twenty-four were creditors and mortgage holders, eleven were merchants or manufacturers, and fifteen were slaveowners.[9] They included James Madison, plantation owner and lawyer; Edmund Randolph of Virginia, owner of five thousand acres and two hundred slaves; Robert Morris, the Philadelphia banker; and Gouverneur Morris, land speculator of New York and Philadelphia.[10] Moreover, "according to James McHenry, a delegate from Maryland, at least twenty-one of the fifty-five delegates favored some form of monarchy. Yet few dared venture in that direction out of fear of popular opposition."[11] Aware of widespread opposition among the people to the new Constitution, the delegates passed a resolution at the beginning of the convention to keep what they were doing completely secret; they even passed a subsequent resolution that no one was to take notes.[12] This was done to prevent the public from finding out the true nature of the document being written and the motives of those responsible for it. Despite the fact that the delegates were instructed both by the Congress and their own states to consider only a revision of the Articles of Confederation, and to submit their recommendations to the Congress and the states for approval,[13] they ignored these instructions and came up with a new document to replace the Articles:

> They did not amend the Articles of Confederation; they cast that instrument aside and drafted a fresh plan of government. Nor did they merely send the new document to Congress and then to the state legislatures for approval; on the contrary they appealed over the heads of these authorities to the voters of the states for a ratification of their revolutionary work. Finally, declining to obey the clause of the Articles which required unanimous approval for every amendment, they frankly proposed that the new system of government should go into effect when sanctioned by nine of the thirteen states, leaving the others out in the cold under the wreck of the existing legal order, in case they refused to ratify.[14]

Despite these maneuvers, the convention was unable to meet even its own requirements and secure the nine states necessary for ratification: the people of New York, New Hampshire, Massachusetts, Rhode Island, and North Carolina voted against ratification. Keenly aware of the need to reverse the situation by securing the votes, the pro-Constitution forces persuaded some of the delegates to the state conventions who had been elected to vote against the Constitution to vote for it instead. This maneuver reversed the results in three crucial states—New York, New Hampshire, and Massachusetts:

> In New Hampshire, New York, and Massachusetts, where the election returned avowed majorities opposed to the Constitution, a great deal of clever engineering induced several delegates to depart from their apparent instructions and cast their ballots for ratification. But to the very end, two states, North Carolina and Rhode Island, refused to give their consent.... From the fragmentary figures that are available, it appears that no more than one-fourth of the adult white males in the country voted one way or the other in the elections at which delegates to the state ratifying conventions were chosen. According to a cautious reckoning, probably one-sixth of them—namely, one hundred thousand—favored the ratification of the new form of government.[15]

After the Constitution was finally ratified and became the basis of government, both the intent of the framers and the content of the document became increasingly clear to people, especially small farmers, who constituted the majority of the population:

> The people as a whole were opposed to the document. Particularly hostile were the small farmers of the country.... They were quick to point out the essentially undemocratic character of the new frame of government.... They resented the fact that the proposed instrument was more concerned with the protection of property rights than in the maintenance of human rights. They did not fail to note that what the constitution was trying to do was to establish the same centralized system of political, judicial, and economic controls that the British ruling classes had attempted to foist upon them in the days of Grenville, Townshend, and North.[16]

Under pressure from the small farmers and other democratic forces in society, the newly emerging U.S. state, controlled by the wealthy, had no choice but to come forward with a Bill of Rights—the first ten amendments to the Constitution, which were added to the document in 1791.[17]

That the framers of the Constitution wanted to establish a state guided by laws and principles reflecting the interests of the propertied classes is no secret even to a casual observer of the events of the time. Their antidemocratic pronouncements were in line with their class interests and against those of the slaves, the workers, the artisans, and the farmers, as well as the Native American people—in effect, the vast majority of the population.[18] The critical linkage between class and state in postcolonial America, then, was established precisely by the class nature and role of the U.S. Constitution, which provided the basis of the rule of property over labor and gave the state its subsequent class character.[19] For this reason, the Constitution can be seen both as a product and an instrument of the class forces that came to dominate the U.S. state until the Civil War.

Nevertheless, it soon became clear that the state apparatus that came under the control of the ruling classes could not function properly unless some mechanisms of mediation of conflict were instituted to resolve differences between rival forces within the ruling-class coalition. Thus: "In order to regulate the conflict of interests between capitalists and landowners, a series of checks and balances between judiciary, congressional, and executive powers were introduced, as well as different methods of representation for the Senate and the House of Representatives."[20] This was also recognized and articulated in no uncertain terms by the framers of the Constitution who established the foundations of the modern U.S. state, as the following passage from James Madison's *Federalist Papers* indicates:

But the most common and durable source of factions has been the various and unequal distribution of property. Those who hold and those who are without property have ever formed distinct interests in society.... A landed interest, a manufacturing interest, a mercantile interest, a moneyed interest, with many lesser interests, grow up of necessity in civilized nations, and divide them into different classes, actuated by different sentiments and views. The regulation of these various and interfering interests forms the principal task of modern legislation, and involves the spirit of party and faction in the necessary and ordinary operations of the government.[21]

During the first half of the nineteenth century, slaveowners were the dominant force within the ruling-class alliance. This is evidenced by the fact that key positions within the federal machinery were controlled by slaveowners, assisted by their financial and mercantile allies in the North. The executive and legislative branches of the state were pro-slaveowner, and seven of the nine Supreme Court justices were either slaveowners or supported slavery.

By the middle of the nineteenth century, capitalist development had reached new heights throughout the North, requiring new markets, access to raw materials, cheap and abundant labor, and further capital accumulation. The slaveowning class in the South held on to its source of wealth through the exploitation of slave labor and safeguarded its neocolonial role in the world economy. The contradictions that had been developing between the two systems since the formation of the Union could no longer be contained within the existing state. Thus the two exploiting classes finally clashed, to solve, once and for all, the question of state power.

The level of development reached by the different modes of production at the time of independence was such that it took nearly a century for these contradictions to burst open and culminate in a civil war that would finally decide the answer to the decisive question: Which class alone shall rule the state? The Northern, capitalist victory against the slaveowning South resulted in the transfer of state power to the capitalist class and thereby ushered in the rule of the capitalist state. In this sense, the Northern victory in the Civil War marked a turning point in the social transformation of postcolonial America, when capitalism became the dominant mode of production and the capitalist state the dominant political authority in the land.

As capitalism came to dominate the national economy and the state following the Civil War, the primary struggle became that between industrial capital (and its associated moneyed interests) and the small farmers and a growing class of industrial workers. During this period of "reconstruction" (i.e., the period of transition to and establishment of capitalist dominance),

> The capitalist class turned the state completely into its instrument. The state heavily subsidized the building of the railways and internal improvements. High protective tariffs were established. Immigration of laborers was encouraged. Free land was given to the farmers and the railroads. The working class was kept in line and prevented from organizing. In every way the state facilitated the rapid and unimpeded advance of industrial capital.[22]

As a result, a tremendous expansion of capital took place, leading to the concentration and centralization of wealth in the hands of the capitalists, whose base of exploitation expanded through the accumulation of surplus value from both local and immigrant labor. As industry grew, production expanded, and capitalism spread throughout the nation, the ex-slaves (now paid labor), together with the established industrial proletariat of the Northern cities, generated ever-higher rates of surplus value for the capitalists, yielding huge profits and fueling the fortunes of the super-rich, who set up immense financial empires that generated the first capitalist monopolies, cartels, and trusts. Through this process of expansion, capital, now in its monopoly stage, came to dominate the U.S. economy and the state by the late nineteenth and early twentieth century. As a result, the state's role in regulating the economy on behalf of capital began to increase, as did its role in repressing an increasingly militant working class.

> The fierce conflicts of Chicago and Colorado, the strikes of steel workers, metal miners, and railroad men, the jailing of literally thousands of labor's rank and file ... were cruel and bloody years that stretched between 1890 and 1900....
>
> It was the time in which American finance underwent a qualitative change, beginning to export its money and Marines into the Caribbean and the Pacific, grabbing Puerto Rico and the Philippines by force of arms, controlling Cuba as a protectorate, and annexing Hawaii outright.
>
> And it was the decade which saw one more gallant effort by the common people, the workers and farmers, to wrest the country from the control of Wall Street through independent political action. It was the time of labor's tall Gene Debs and the miners' Big Bill Haywood, of Sockless Jerry Simpson and Mary Elizabeth Lease, who advised the nation's farmers to "raise less corn and more hell." It was a decade in which monopoly, steadily growing since the Civil War, pyramided into new heights of power ... [while] the Knights of Labor ... called for the abolition of the wage system and the establishment of an order whose

factories, mines, mills, railroads, and utilities were owned and operated by the people....

Despite these political struggles, monopoly steadily grew ... ever increasing their grip on every aspect of American life.... And the great age of financial concentration, of the narrowing control of the few who reaped fabulous profits from the work of the many, had just begun.[23]

Beginning in the first two decades of this century and continuing throughout the Great Depression and World War II, the state played a key role in safeguarding and promoting the capitalist economy. With the U.S. entry into World War II, the United States embarked on the road to full recovery and thereby became a powerful force on the world scene, its economy rivaling that of Britain, France, Germany, and other mature capitalist states. In fact, with the devastation of Europe during World War II and the de facto defeat of the major European states at the conclusion of the war, the United States emerged as the leading imperial state among the rival powers dominating the world economy. The growth and expansion of U.S. transnational corporations in the postwar period thus corresponds to the rise to power and prominence of the United States in the postwar period.

The Postwar Expansion of the U.S. State

The transfer of political and economic control from Britain to the United States in the British spheres of influence (Latin America, Asia, Africa, and the Middle East) in the aftermath of World War II gave the United States access to oil and other raw materials and investment outlets in manufacturing to tap sources of cheap and abundant labor. With the postwar expansion of U.S. capital on a global scale came the political expansion of the U.S. state; together they came to articulate the interests of U.S. capitalism throughout the world.

The turning point for the rise to world prominence of the United States is the end of World War II. While Europe was devastated and in ruins, the United States emerged as the leading center of the capitalist world, practically unaffected by the war. In fact, the collapse of the infrastructure of the major European economies by war's end worked to the advantage of U.S. capital and permitted its penetration into Western Europe through the Marshall Plan.

From 1945 to the early 1970s, U.S. capital maintained its dominance of the global economy, supported by the political and military might of the U.S. state. The expanded role of the state in overseas political or military ventures during this period led both to the projection of U.S. power on a global scale and a tremendous expansion of overseas investments by large U.S. corporations throughout the world.

The ascendancy of the United States in the global economy thus dates mainly from the end of World War II, when weakened European economies coincided with a tremendous growth and expansion of U.S. corporations on the world scene. The globalization of production began to take root on a world scale under the auspices of U.S. transnational corporations. From this point on, therefore, we begin to see a rapid increase in the volume of U.S. direct investment around the world.

In the early part of the twentieth century, U.S. foreign direct investment amounted to less than $1 billion, reaching a mere $1.6 billion in 1908.[24] Even by 1920, the total came to less than $4 billion. But by 1950, it had climbed to $11.8 billion, by 1970 to $76 billion, by 1990 to $431 billion, by 2000 to $1.5 trillion, and by 2009 to a record $4.1 trillion.[25] Together with all other forms of investments in 2009, the market value of total U.S. private assets abroad reached $14.4 trillion![26]

The massive nature of U.S. transnational corporate expansion abroad and the hundreds of billions of investment dollars tied up in distant lands during the past several decades have led the U.S. state to take a more aggressive role in foreign policy in order to protect U.S. transnational interests abroad. This has become an enormous burden on the U.S. state, greatly affecting both the U.S. economy and the working people of the United States who have come to shoulder through increasing taxation the colossal cost of maintaining a global empire whose vast military machine now encompasses the world.[27]

Parallel to this expansion, the state's growing role in domestic spending, especially military spending, has served to protect and advance the interests of U.S. corporations through the public purse. Total U.S. government spending increased from $92 billion in 1960 to $591 billion in 1980 to $1.8 trillion in 2000 to $3.5 trillion in 2010.[28] Much of this spending was on the military, as military contracts to private capital became the decisive factor in the postwar expansion of the U.S. economy. Military spending, as a percentage of all governmental expenditures, rose from 6 percent in the 1930s to around 30 percent during the 1950s and 1960s, increasing from about 1 percent of the GNP to about 10 percent during this period.[29] In 2010, military spending (at $694 billion) accounted for 20 percent of total federal expenditures of $3.5 trillion.[30]

Together with increased government intervention in the economy, the state played a key role in facilitating political stability of the system through the regulation of national politics via the two-party monopoly. The electoral arena thus became the centerpiece of party politics and the mechanism of control and domination of the state by capital in the postwar period. However, continued state expenditures in favor of capital led, starting in the early 1970s, to the state's budgetary crisis and exacerbated related economic problems confronting the state, such as rising public debt; together with other factors (discussed in the next chapter), this has contributed to the crisis of the U.S. state.

Notes

1. Karl Marx, *Capital,* vol. 1 (New York: International Publishers, 1967).

2. See Perry Anderson, *Passages from Antiquity to Feudalism* (London: New Left Books, 1974).

3. Karl Marx and Friedrich Engels, *Manifesto of the Communist Party,* in *Selected Works* (New York: International Publishers, 1972), 36–37.

4. Karl Marx, *Pre-Capitalist Economic Formations* (New York: International Publishers, 1965).

5. G. Belov, *What Is the State?* (Moscow: Progress Publishers, 1986), 22–23.

6. In other parts of the world (e.g., Germany and Japan), the state took a more active role in production and industrial expansion as it came to manage major sectors of the economy directly. See Barrington Moore Jr., *The Social Origins of Democracy and Dictatorship* (London: Penguin, 1968); and John Clapham, *The Economic Development of France and Germany* (Cambridge: Cambridge University Press, 1948).

7. V. I. Lenin, *The State and Revolution,* in *Selected Works in One Volume* (New York: International Publishers, 1971), 326–327.

8. The only exceptions were Benjamin Franklin (Pennsylvania) and Luther Martin (Maryland). Martin refused to sign the Constitution, and both Martin and Franklin campaigned against the ratification of the Constitution in their respective states.

9. Charles Beard, *An Economic Interpretation of the Constitution of the United States* (New York: Macmillan, 1962).

10. Kenneth Neill Cameron, *Humanity and Society: A World History* (New York: Monthly Review Press, 1977), 421.

11. Michael Parenti, *Democracy for the Few,* 9th ed. (Boston: Wadsworth, 2011), 50.

12. One of the delegates, James Madison, did not abide by the group's decision, and his notes were later published, which contain revealing statements by some of the delegates during the convention. See also the essays by James Madison and others in *The Federalist Papers,* especially No. 10.

13. Herbert M. Morais, *The Struggle for American Freedom* (New York: International Publishers, 1944), 248–249.

14. Charles Beard and Mary Beard, *The Rise of American Civilization* (New York: Macmillan, 1930), 313–314.

15. Ibid., 332. Of course, women, who constituted half the adult population; slaves, who made up one-fourth of the population; Native Americans; and poor, propertyless whites were not allowed to vote. This, many have argued, is another testimony to the racist, sexist, elitist, and class-biased nature of the early U.S. state and the Constitution, both of which reflected the class interests of the forces that came to dominate the state after independence.

16. Morais, *The Struggle for American Freedom,* 253–254.

17. Colonel Mason recommended at the Constitutional Convention that a committee be formed to draft "a Bill of Rights," but his motion was voted down unanimously.

18. Herbert Aptheker, *The American Revolution, 1763–1783* (New York: International Publishers, 1976).

19. Ibid.

20. Cameron, *Humanity and Society,* 421.

21. Madison, *The Federalist Papers,* No. 10.

22. Albert Szymanski, *The Capitalist State and the Politics of Class* (Cambridge, MA: Winthrop, 1978), 160.

23. Richard O. Boyer and Herbert M. Morais, *Labor's Untold Story,* 3rd ed. (New York: United Electrical, Radio and Machine Workers of America, 1980), 1057.

24. Cleona Lewis, *America's Stake in International Investments* (Washington, DC: Brookings Institution, 1938), 605–606.

25. U.S. Department of Commerce, *Selected Data on U.S. Direct Investment Abroad;* U.S. Department of Commerce, *Statistical Abstract of the United States, 1999,* 797 and *1981,* 833; U.S. Council of Economic Advisers, *Economic Report of the President, 2007,* 353 and *2011,* 313.

26. U.S. Department of Commerce, *Survey of Current Business* (July 1999); U.S. Department of Commerce, *Statistical Abstract of the United States, 1999,* 793; U.S. Council of Economic Advisers, *Economic Report of the President, 2000,* 427 and *2011,* 313.

27. For an extended discussion and data on the cost of maintaining the U.S. empire and its impact on the U.S. working class, see Berch Berberoglu, *The Legacy of Empire: Economic Decline and Class Polarization in the United States* (New York: Praeger Publishers, 1992), Chap. 4–6; and Berberoglu, *Globalization and Change: The Transformation of Global Capitalism* (Lanham, MD: Lexington Books, 2005), Chap. 5.

28. U.S. Department of Commerce, Table 469, *Statistical Abstract of the United States, 2012,* 310.

29. U.S. Department of Commerce, *Statistical Abstract of the United States* (various issues). For detailed discussion and data on the role of military spending in the postwar expansion of the U.S. economy, see Paul Baran and Paul M. Sweezy, *Monopoly Capital* (New York: Monthly Review Press, 1966). See also Szymanski, *The Capitalist State and the Politics of Class,* Chap. 9.

30. U.S. Department of Commerce, Table 473, *Statistical Abstract of the United States, 2012,* 312.

Chapter 5

The Crisis of the Advanced Capitalist State

WHILE THE CHANGES AT WORK in the U.S. economy and society have their roots in earlier decades when the consolidation of U.S. political and economic power began to take hold on a world scale, the increased globalization of U.S. capital under the auspices of U.S. transnational corporations in recent decades has affected various classes and segments of U.S. society unevenly. The diverse impact of economic changes during this period on different classes and fractions of classes are precipitating causes of the unfolding political crisis of the capitalist state in the United States. In this context, the intensified globalization of U.S. capital and the decline of the U.S. domestic economy since the early 1970s constitute the material basis of the crisis of the advanced capitalist state in the United States during the past four decades.

This chapter examines the crisis of the advanced capitalist state in the United States, focusing on the various levels of its internal contradictions in the postwar period, especially in the late twentieth and early twenty-first centuries. The chapter then turns to an analysis of the crisis of the U.S. economy in relation to the crisis of the U.S. state. Finally, the impact of the twin crises of the U.S. economy and the state are assessed in terms of the emergence and development of class struggle in the United States in the period ahead.

The Crisis of the U.S. State

The period from 1945 to the present saw an unparalleled growth of U.S. transnational capital throughout the world, but the postwar boom that reached its peak during the Vietnam war came to an abrupt end when the U.S. defeat in Southeast

Asia (which brought to a halt major war contracts to U.S. corporations) plunged the economy into a severe recession by the mid 1970s. So powerful was the impact of the defeat in Vietnam that the United States has been unable to alter the situation ever since. As a result, the decline of U.S. hegemony on the world scene has become irreversible.

A major problem endemic to the present U.S. political economy is the budget deficit. As an extension of postwar Keynesian "remedies" to recessions and depressions brought about by the capitalist business cycle, as well as military intervention, from Vietnam in earlier periods to Iraq and Afghanistan in the more recent period, government spending has led to an enormous growth in the national debt over the past several decades. The situation worsened from the 1980s through the 2000s when a huge increase in military spending combined with large tax cuts for business resulted in record annual budget deficits, vastly increasing the total government debt and the interest paid on the debt. As military spending has more than doubled since 1990 and more than quadrupled since the early 1980s (reaching nearly $700 billion in 2010), the gross federal debt has increased immensely, from $909 billion in 1980 to $3.2 trillion in 1990 to $5.6 trillion in 2000 to $13.5 trillion in 2010, while the net interest paid on the debt rose from $52 billion in 1980 to $184 billion in 1990 to $223 billion in 2000, dropping to $196 billion in 2010 (see Table 5.1).[1]

Table 5.1 Military Spending, Federal Deficit, and Interest Paid on Debt, 1970–2010 (in billions of current $)

Year	Military Spending	Gross Federal Debt	Annual Budget Deficits	Net Interest Paid
1970	81.7	380.9	−2.8	14.4
1975	86.5	541.9	−53.2	23.2
1980	134.0	909.0	−73.8	52.5
1985	252.7	1,817.4	−212.3	129.5
1990	299.3	3,206.3	−221.0	184.3
1995	272.1	4,920.6	−164.0	232.1
2000	294.4	5,628.7	236.2	222.9
2005	495.3	7,905.3	−318.3	184.0
2010	693.6	13,528.8	−1,293.5	196.2

Source: Council of Economic Advisers, *Economic Report of the President, 2011,* Table B-78, p. 283, and Table B-80, p. 285.

This vast amount of government spending, especially on the military and the interest paid on the debt, together with an expanded consumer credit system in the trillions, has thus far averted the total collapse of the U.S. economy. The widening gap between the accumulated wealth of the capitalist class and the declining incomes of workers and the self-employed (within a deteriorating national economy and the state's budgetary crisis) has led to the ensuing political crisis within the state.

The crisis of the advanced capitalist state in the United States manifests itself at different levels, ranging from international conflicts (inter-imperialist rivalry, disintegration of regional political and military alliances, inability to suppress national liberation struggles and revolution around the world) to domestic economic problems (trade and budget deficits, monetary and fiscal crisis, inflation, unemployment, recession, etc.) to national political crisis (factional struggles within the capitalist class, problems of legitimacy, repression of the working class and mass movements, militarization of the polity and society, and so on).[2]

The most critical problem facing the advanced capitalist state, however, is the crisis emanating from the restructuring of the international division of labor involving plant closings in the center states and the transfer of the production process to overseas territories, in line with the globalization of capital.[3] Given the logic of capital accumulation on a global scale in advanced capitalist society, it is no accident that the decline of the U.S. domestic economy since the early 1970s corresponds to the accelerated export of U.S. capital abroad in search of cheap labor, access to raw materials, new markets, and higher rates of profit. The resulting deindustrialization of the U.S. economy has had a serious impact on workers and other affected segments of the laboring population and has brought about a major dislocation of the domestic economy. The deindustrialization of advanced capitalist centers, especially the United States,[4] has led to higher unemployment and underemployment, pressing down wages to minimum levels, while imperial-installed puppet regimes have intensified the repression of workers and peasants abroad and forced on them starvation wages in order to generate superprofits for the U.S. transnational corporations.

The contradictions of this process of global expansion and accumulation have brought to the fore new realities of capitalist economics, now character-ized by industrial decline and decay in the center states, which has necessitated further state intervention on behalf of the corporations and has heightened the contradictions that led to the crisis of the U.S. state, resulting in renewed repression at home and abroad to control an increasingly frustrated and angry working class.

The Crisis of the U.S. Economy

A number of factors have brought about the crisis of the advanced capitalist state in the United States, all of which are based on crises afflicting the U.S. economy during the past four decades—the ending of the war in Vietnam, the oil crisis, the rise to world prominence of European and Chinese economies, the effects of the globalization of U.S. capital on the U.S. economy, and problems associated with the capitalist business cycle. The structural transformation of the U.S. economy in line with its role in the new international division of labor during the three decades following World War II, brought forth in 1974 and 1975 the most severe recession since the 1930s.[5] The gravity of the situation in the mid 1970s was such that the post-1975 recovery could not sustain itself for more than a few years, then sank the economy into another recession from 1979 to 1980, and a much deeper one in 1982.[6] While short-term government policies since 1983 have managed to regulate symptoms of the underlying structural defects in the economy and postponed a major crisis of depressionary proportions, the latest crash in 2008 and 2009 has proven to be much worse than any crash previously, for the cumulative impact of the crisis has been such that it has brought the global economy to a head, especially in its nucleus, the United States.[7]

The highly speculative nature of the stock market in the 1990s (a situation similar to that of the 1920s) has led to such an outcome in the early years of the twenty-first century. Decline in capacity utilization in manufacturing industry, record trade deficits, growing unemployment, decline in real wages and purchasing power, small business bankruptcies and farm and home foreclosures, collapse of the real estate market, bank failures, a shaky global financial system, record government deficits, as well as a highly speculative stock market, have all led to decline of the national economy following a decade-long bull market, record corporate profits, megamergers, and wholesale acquisitions and takeovers favorably affecting the biggest U.S. corporations.[8]

In examining the data for the period from the mid 1960s to the early 1980s, we see that capacity utilization in manufacturing fell from 89.5 percent in 1965 to 77 percent in 1971, to 72 percent in 1975, to 70 percent in 1982—during the three consecutive recessions. The decline in durable goods production was even more pronounced as it fell from 87 percent in 1967 to 73 percent in 1971 to 70 percent in 1975 to 67 percent in 1982.[9] Similarly, there was a sharp decline in net private domestic investment during the 1975 and 1982 recessions, falling from $257 billion in 1973 to $96 billion in 1975, and from $253 billion in 1978 to $64 billion in 1982.[10] The ups and downs of the business cycle over this period show that the general trend in business activity is in a downward direction, with each peak lower than the one that preceded it and each trough deeper and worse than what came before.

This is also indicated by the data on unemployment rates: The rate was 6 percent at the height of the 1971 recession, 8.3 percent during the 1975 recession, and 9.5 percent during the 1982 recession; similarly, the rate was higher at the peak of each of the three succeeding recoveries: 4.8 percent in 1973; 5.8 percent in 1979; and 6.9 percent in 1986.[11] Although the overall unemployment rate fell to as low as 4.5 percent in 1998 and was at around this rate before the start of the great recession of 2008 and 2009, it rapidly climbed from 4.6 percent in 2007 to 5.8 percent in 2008 to 9.3 percent in 2009 to 9.6 percent in 2010.[12] By early 2012, more than two years after the recession had officially "ended" in September 2009, the unemployment rate continued to remain high at around 9 percent.[13]

Turning to wages, with increasing unemployment and spiraling inflation during the 1970s and early 1980s,[14] real wages of workers declined during the two previous recessions, registering a drop of 7.2 percent from 1974 to 1975 and nearly 12 percent from 1979 to 1982. Thus, during the two decades from 1974 to 1995, U.S. workers showed a net loss of 20 percent in their real income. Although the situation improved a bit during the second half of the 1990s, when workers were able to gain some in real wages, the trend reversed again during the 2000s, when real wages stagnated or fell (see Table 5.2). The general decline in real wages since the mid 1970s, has led to a decline in purchasing power and living standard for U.S. workers, such that in 2010, the purchasing power of the dollar, as measured by consumer prices in 1982–1984 dollars, declined to its lowest level in forty years (forty-six cents!).[15]

A key factor in the decline in purchasing power and living standard for workers in the United States has been a rise in the rate of exploitation (surplus value) and a consequent drop in labor's share over the years. Thus, the rate of exploitation in U.S. manufacturing industry doubled in the period from 1950 to 1984, from 150 percent in 1950 to 302 percent in 1984. By 2006, the rate of exploitation again had nearly doubled in little over two decades to 539 percent.[16] At the same time, labor's share drastically fell during this period, from 40 percent in 1950 to 25 percent in 1984. By 2006, labor's share had further dropped to 15.6 percent.[17] This, together with favorable government policies toward big business (e.g., capital gains tax cuts), resulted in record corporate profits. Thus, we find that total net corporate profits increased enormously in the period from 1970 to 2010, from $74 billion in 1970 to $211 billion in 1980, $399 billion in 1990, $756 billion in 2000, and $1.8 trillion in 2010 (see Table 5.3). Paralleling this, profits of domestic industries likewise increased several-fold during this period, mostly accounted for by nonfinancial industries. Even taking inflation into account, net corporate profits surged during this period.[18]

Table 5.2 Inflation and Wages: Consumer Price Index and Average Weekly Earnings for Private Nonagricultural Workers, 1970–2010

| | CPI | | Average Weekly Earnings | | |
| | | | Money Wages | Real Wages | |
Year	(1982–84 = 100)	(% incr.)	(current dollars)	(1982–84 dollars)	(% chg. /year)
1970	38.8	5.7	126	323	−1.4
1975	53.8	9.1	170	315	−3.2
1980	82.4	13.5	241	291	−5.8
1985	107.6	3.6	305	285	−1.1
1990	130.7	5.4	350	271	−1.7
1995	152.4	2.8	400	267	−0.6
2000	172.2	3.4	481	285	0.4
2005	195.3	3.4	544	285	−0.6
2010	218.1	1.7	636	297	1.0

Note: Percent increase in CPI for 2000–2010 calculated by the author from data provided in the *Economic Report of the President, 2011,* Table B-60, p. 259.

Source: Council of Economic Advisers, *Economic Report of the President, 2000,* Table B-62, p. 378; *2011,* Table B-47, p. 246, and Table B-60, p. 259.

Table 5.3 Corporate Profits: Financial and Nonfinancial Industries, 1970–2010 (in billions of current $)

| Year | Total Corporate Profits[2] | Domestic Industries[1] | | |
		Total	Financial	Nonfinancial
1970	74.4	67.3	15.4	52.0
1975	135.0	120.4	20.2	100.2
1980	211.4	175.9	34.0	142.0
1985	257.5	219.4	45.9	172.5
1990	398.8	322.7	92.3	230.4
1995	666.0	573.1	160.1	413.0
2000	755.7	610.0	194.4	415.7
2005	1,609.5	1,370.0	443.6	926.4
2010[3]	1,776.8	1,389.5	371.9	1,017.5

Notes: [1]Domestic profits, with inventory valuation adjustment and without capital consumption adjustment. [2]Includes domestic and foreign profits, with inventory valuation adjustment and without capital consumption adjustment. [3]Estimates based on data for the first three quarters of 2010.

Source: Council of Economic Advisers, *Economic Report of the President, 2011,* Table B-91, p. 296.

The enormous profits made by U.S. corporations over the years have translated into great riches for their owners, such that it has created vast disparities in the distribution of wealth in the United States. Looking at the latest data available for 2007, we find that the top 1 percent of households owned 49.7 percent of the total wealth, the top 10 percent of households owned 87.8 percent of the total wealth and the bottom 90 percent of households owned a mere 12.2 percent of the total wealth (see Table 5.4). Moreover, the top 1 percent owned more than 60 percent of financial securities and business equity, while the top 10 percent owned 89.4 percent of stocks and mutual funds, 93.3 percent of business equity, and 98.5 percent of financial securities (Table 5.4).

Turning to the economy in general, we observe that while record bankruptcies among small businesses, especially family farms, led to further centralization of the U.S. economy during the recessions of the 1970s and early 1980s, the intensi- fied overseas expansion of U.S. transnational corporations had a serious impact on the U.S. export-import structure, resulting in large trade deficits. This came about as a result of a relative drop in U.S. exports due to plant closings, and a sharp increase in imports from overseas subsidiaries of U.S. transnational corporations during the past four decades.[19] Data on U.S. imports and exports show that the U.S. trade deficit has greatly increased since the mid 1970s, reaching $25 billion in 1980, $111 billion in 1990, $446 billion in 2000, and $663 billion in 2010. While U.S. transnational expansion abroad took off with exceptional speed during the 1970s, it took on a new significance by the early 1980s, as imports into the United States of manufactured goods produced by U.S. transnational subsidiaries over- seas began to affect the U.S. trade balance in a significantly negative direction beginning in 1982. Thus, as imports of manufactured goods increased from $170 billion in 1980 to $436 billion in 1990 to $1.1 trillion in 2000 to $1.2 trillion in

Table 5.4 Distribution of Wealth in the United States, 2007,
by Type of Asset (in percentages)

Investment Assets	Top 1%	Top 10%	Bottom 90%
Stocks and mutual funds	49.3	89.4	10.6
Financial securities	60.6	98.5	1.5
Trusts	38.9	79.4	20.6
Business equity	62.4	93.3	6.7
Non-home real estate	28.3	76.9	23.1
Total for group	**49.7**	**87.8**	**12.2**

Source: Edward N. Wolff, "Recent Trends in Household Wealth in the United States: Rising Debt and the Middle Class Squeeze," Working Paper No. 589 (March 2010), p. 51.

2010, the trade deficit for manufactured goods increased from $89 billion in 1990 to $373 billion in 2000 to $585 billion in 2005, dropping to $309 billion in 2010, due to the great recession in 2008 and 2009.[20] Although foreign imports are partly responsible for the shift in the balance of U.S. merchandise trade in manufactured goods, subcontracting with foreign firms, especially in China, and increasing penetration of the Japanese and European economies by U.S. transnationals has led to the acquisition of a growing percentage of the stocks of foreign competitors in their home territories. This development, coupled with the transfer of productive facilities of U.S.-based transnational corporations to cheap labor areas overseas and subcontracting (not "unfair competition" by foreign companies, or imports from China of goods purchased from Chinese companies) explains in large part the record U.S. trade deficit in recent years.[21] The trade deficit is thus mainly the result of U.S. corporations having their products made in low-wage sweatshops overseas for sale in the United States to increase profits, and this has resulted in a consequent decline in production and an increase in unemployment in the United States—a situation that will be leading to increased class conflict and struggle in the United States in the coming years.

The Emergence of Class Struggle in the United States

The persistent crisis of the U.S. economy since the early 1970s has had a contradictory effect on state and class politics in the United States. On the one hand, there has been a sharp turn to the right during the Reagan Administration in the 1980s, and through the rise of the New Right and right-wing religious fundamentalism during the 1990s and 2000s, culminating in the right-wing Tea Party movement in the late 2000s, leading to an all out assault on labor, reversals of civil rights gains, attacks on women's rights, a repressive immigration policy, renewed militarization, an increase in FBI domestic surveillance, and covert CIA operations to accompany an interventionist policy in Central Asia and the Middle East. On the other hand, there has been a rise in the militancy of workers and other progressive forces in the United States in response to this assault, through mass strikes and demonstrations against the capitalist offensive, the wars in Iraq and Afghanistan, and the corporations and banks that profited from the government bailout of failed financial institutions and corporations during the great recession of 2008 and 2009, which led to the emergence of the Occupy Wall Street movement in 2011, targeting the banks, the corporations and the super rich (the top 1 percent) whose fortunes have multiplied many-fold while working people have suffered from unemployment, home foreclosures, poor health, and a decline in their standard of living.

As the crisis of the capitalist economy has brought the advanced capitalist state to the center stage of economic life and revealed its direct ties to the corporations and the banks (i.e., Wall Street),[22] thus exacerbating the state's legitimation crisis, the struggles of the working class and the masses in general have become more political than ever and are directed not merely against capital, but against the state itself, as revealed in a highly publicized slogan of the Occupy Wall Street movement: "Wall Street occupies our government, Occupy Wall Street!" Later, to highlight the importance of state power, the Occupy Wall Street movement shifted tactics and began targeting politicians in Washington as puppets of Wall Street and the wealthy, and waged a campaign for Americans to take back their government from the capitalists. This shift in the mass struggle from the economic to the political sphere focusing on the state as the political tool of powerful economic interests will set the stage for protracted class struggles that will become more and more political in the years ahead.

While capital's answer to the growing ills of the U.S. economy has been further repression of the working class and people's movements, the mass struggle against capital and the state by strikes, protests, demonstrations, and other forms of defiance is bound to continue and become stronger. These actions are clear examples of a growing class consciousness within the U.S. working class and the oppressed in general; they are taking place in the context of an intensifying world-wide capitalist crisis and in the midst of a much more politicized global labor movement, from the Philippines and South Korea to Central and South America, North Africa, the Middle East, Western Europe, and the United States.

The globalization of U.S. capital is bound to accelerate the politicization of the U.S. working class and lead to the building of a solid foundation for international solidarity of workers on a global scale, directed against transnational capital and the advanced capitalist state in labor's long-term struggle for state power.

Notes

1. Council of Economic Advisers, Table B-78 and Table B-80, *Economic Report of the President, 2011*, 283, 285.

2. For a discussion of various aspects of the capitalist crises of the 1970s and 1980s, see James O'Connor, *The Fiscal Crisis of the State* (New York: St. Martin's, 1973) and O'Connor, *Accumulation Crisis* (New York: Basil Blackwell, 1984); Ernest Mandel, *Late Capitalism* (London: New Left Books, 1975) and Mandel, *The Second Slump* (London: Verso, 1980); Albert Szymanski, *The Capitalist State and the Politics of Class* (Cambridge, MA: Winthrop, 1978); Victor Perlo, *Super Profits and Crises: Modern U.S. Capitalism* (New York: International Publishers, 1984); and Howard Sherman, *The Business Cycle: Growth and Crisis Under Capitalism* (Princeton, NJ: Princeton University Press, 1991). For subsequent crises in the 1990s

and 2000s, especially the most recent 2008–2009 great recession, see Gerald Friedman, Fred Moseley, and Chris Sturr, eds., *The Economic Crisis Reader* (Boston: Economic Affairs Bureau, Inc., 2009); Henry Veltmeyer, ed., *Imperialism, Crisis, and Class Struggle* (Leiden: E. J. Brill, 2010); Howard Sherman, *The Roller Coaster Economy: Financial Crisis, Great Recession, and the Public Option* (Armonk, NY: M. E. Sharpe, 2010); Josh Bivens, *Failure by Design: The Story Behind America's Broken Economy* (Ithaca: ILR Press, 2011).

3. See Berch Berberoglu, *The Internationalization of Capital* (New York: Praeger, 1987) and Berberoglu, *Globalization of Capital and the Nation-State* (Lanham, MD: Rowman & Littlefield, 2003).

4. Barry Bluestone and Bennett Harrison, *The Deindustrialization of America* (New York: Basic Books, 1982); and Bluestone and Harrison, *The Great U-Turn: Corporate Restructuring and the Polarizing of America* (New York: Basic Books, 1988).

5. See Mandel, *The Second Slump*; Howard Sherman, *Stagflation* (New York: Harper & Row, 1976).

6. See Jim Devine, "The Structural Crisis of U.S. Capitalism," *Southwest Economy and Society* 6, no. 1 (Fall 1982).

7. While the massive 508-point drop in the stock market on "Black Monday" in October 1987 was a reflection of long-term structural defects in the financial system and the economy in general, it was actually the precursor of a much worse decline during the 2008–2009 recession when the stock market lost 50 percent of its value over the course of a year, the Dow declining from 14,000 at the end of 2007 to 6,500 in early 2009.

8. Harry Magdoff and Paul Sweezy, *Stagnation and the Financial Explosion* (New York: Monthly Review Press, 1987). See also Berch Berberoglu, *The Legacy of Empire: Economic Decline and Class Polarization in the United States* (New York: Praeger Publishers, 1992).

9. Council of Economic Advisers, *Economic Report of the President, 1989*, 365.

10. Ibid., 327.

11. U.S. Department of Commerce, *Statistical Abstract of the United States, 1988*, 382; Council of Economic Advisers, *Economic Report of the President, 1989*, 352.

12. U.S. Department of Commerce, *Statistical Abstract of the United States, 2011*, 401.

13. The unemployment rate dropped to 8.8 percent at the end of 2011 and continued at this level close to 9 percent in early 2012.

14. During the first half of the 1970s, the rate of inflation averaged 7 percent per year; during the second half of the 1970s, it averaged 9 percent per year, reaching a high of 13.5 percent in 1980. In comparison, it was about 1 percent per year in the early 1960s and 3 percent per year in the late 1960s. U.S. Department of Commerce, *Statistical Abstract of the United States, 1987*, 455.

15. U.S. Department of Commerce, Table 724, *Statistical Abstract of the United States, 2012*, 473.

16. Victor Perlo, *Super Profits and Crises: Modern U.S. Capitalism* (New York: International Publishers, 1988), 512; U.S. Census Bureau, *2006 Annual Survey of Manufactures* (November 18, 2008).

17. Ibid.

18. Except for 1981, when the inflation rate was 10.3 percent, and 1982, when it was 6.2 percent, annual increases in the inflation rate have averaged between 3 to 5 percent during the rest of the 1980s and between 2 to 3 percent during much of the 1990s and 2000s (see Table 5.2).

19. It is now estimated that nearly 50 percent of all imports entering the United States are goods produced by overseas subsidiaries of U.S. transnational corporations. In addition, a substantial part of the remainder are produced through subcontracting arrangements between U.S. transnationals and local firms—goods produced in accordance with U.S. corporate specifications for sale at major U.S. retail outlets, such as Walmart, Sears, and J. C. Penney.

20. Council of Economic Advisers, Table B-104, *Economic Report of the President, 2011,* 310.

21. Imports from China consist of goods produced primarily through subcontracting arrangements or by joint ventures with U.S., European, and Japanese corporations that keep much of the profits themselves.

22. For a detailed discussion on the relationship of the state to capital and the mechanisms of direct and indirect domination of the state by capital, see Szymanski, *The Capitalist State and the Politics of Class,* 163–273. See also Michael Parenti, *Democracy for the Few,* 9th ed. (Boston: Wadsworth, 2011) and G. William Domhoff, *Who Rules America? Challenges to Corporate and Class Dominance,* 6th ed. (New York: McGraw-Hill, 2010).

Chapter 6

The State in the Less-Developed Countries

As a central political institution ruling over society, the state has played an especially pivotal role in the less-developed countries throughout the world. From earlier empires in the Americas to the various dynasties in China, from the distant colonial administrations of the Spanish, the Portuguese, the French, and the British to the postcolonial states in Africa, Asia, and the Middle East, the state—especially its military and bureaucratic apparatus—has been a key, defining institution of societies throughout the less-developed world for decades and often centuries.

This chapter explores the nature and dynamics of the state in the less-developed countries across the globe, historically and today—from the despotic rule of succeeding dynasties of the past to the despotic authoritarian rulers of today who have been challenged by the Arab Spring—the uprising of an entire people shaking the institutional foundations of societies across North Africa and the Middle East through political action leading to rebellion and revolution. We will address these issues and examine the origins and development of the state in Latin America, Asia, Africa, and the Middle East by exploring the historical roots of contemporary postcolonial states that dominate the social formations of these regions across the globe.[1]

Historically, the state has served as a powerful superstructural institution to maintain the prevailing social order ever since its original formation in the transition from communal to despotic societies going back several thousands of years. With the collapse of primitive communal society and the emergence of social classes and class conflict that led to the formation of the state to protect dominant class interests (first despots and a bureaucratic stratum, later slaveowners, landlords, and capitalists), the rise of the state as the political instrument of the

97

wealthy established the framework for the state's role as protector of prevailing social order sanctioned by law. Thus the state became the arena of conflict between those in control of this institution and those controlled and oppressed by its actions to maintain order. It is for this reason that the state has become a battleground of the class struggle since its inception.

Today, the class forces that have been in control of the state in the less-developed countries are the local capitalists (consisting of national and comprador segments), the large landowners, and the transnational corporations and their imperial states. The bureaucratic political-military apparatuses of the peripheral capitalist states have always operated within the framework of control of the state by one or a combination of these class forces, whose class interests are served by the state's juridical and repressive bureaucratic machine.

In societies dominated by large landowners and commercial capitalists dependent on imperialism, a variant of the capitalist state has taken on a neocolonial character as its survival is based on its role as an appendage of the transnational corporations and the imperial state. In these societies, the state has become increasingly repressive and authoritarian in order to crush any popular opposition to its role in promoting the interests of local and transnational ruling classes.[2] As the states in these settings have found it necessary to legitimize their increasingly unpopular rule to maintain law and order, protect private property, and prevent a revolution against the prevailing social order, they have attempted to convey a "technocratic" image with a focus on capital accumulation and economic growth, combined with severe repression of labor and marginalized sectors of society. Characterized by some as "corporatist" and by others as "bureaucratic authoritarian," or even "neofascist," these states have played a key role in the globalization of capital and its predominance in much of the less-developed world, promoting further penetration of their economies and societies by the transnational corporations.[3] This process of integration of neocolonial states into the global economy, seeking the protection of the imperial state, has been to a large degree a reaction to a perceived threat to the survival of capitalism around the globe—one that is becoming a serious concern for both imperialism and the local bureaucratic authoritarian states.

In societies where popular uprisings, based on different alliances of class forces struggling against imperialism and the local authoritarian state, have succeeded in taking state power, they have followed a path in the direction of state-capitalism or socialism. Class forces mobilized by the petty bourgeoisie and other intermediate sectors of society in state-capitalist formations have seized power by rallying the people around a nationalist ideology directed against imperialism and its internal reactionary class allies, the landlords and compradors.[4] Contrary to the role of its bureaucratic authoritarian counterpart, the state in state-capitalist formations has attempted to promote the interests of the national and petty bourgeoisies against imperialism and the transnationals. Nevertheless, the class agenda of these anti-imperialist states yields similar results with regard to the exploitation and repression of labor. Capital accumulation, however nationalistically defined, accrues profits and wealth to (local) capitalists and the state while subjecting the working class to the dictates of state-directed capitalism, the central priority of which is the extraction of surplus value from wage labor, as in any other form of capitalism.

Going beyond the state-capitalist alternative to neocolonial control by imperialism, revolutions led by worker-peasant alliances against imperialism and local reaction have resulted in the establishment of socialist states. Unlike neocolonial bureaucratic authoritarianism or national state-capitalism, the socialist state has taken as its priority the redistribution of land, property, and income to elevate the living standard of the masses, without the exploitation of labor for private profits.[5]

These variants of the peripheral state have developed out of the complex relations within and between societies across the globe and between them and the imperial centers ever since the advent of colonialism and imperialism.

The development of capitalism and the capitalist state has been uneven chiefly because of variations in local precapitalist modes of production but also as a result of the nature and duration of contact with outside capitalist formations. This process took place during the period of Western colonialism and imperialism on a world scale, which began in the sixteenth century. The changes effected by this interaction yielded different results in different regions and led to alternative paths of development in Latin America, Asia, Africa, and the Middle East. This, in turn, gave way to the emergence and development of variants of the capitalist state throughout the less-developed world.

The State in Latin America

Prior to European expansion to the New World in the sixteenth century, the dominant mode of production in the Americas was tributary (i.e., the Asiatic mode of production) in some areas and tribal (i.e., the primitive communal mode) in others. In Mexico, much of Central America, and vast areas of South America, the Asiatic mode predominated in the Inca, Aztec, and Mayan empires. The central state, which had ultimate property rights, was the dominant force in society; peasants lived in villages and were obliged to pay tribute to the state. In North America, parts of the Caribbean, and some areas of South America, the primitive communal mode of production predominated among indigenous tribes. These societies were classless and stateless; they relied on hunting, fishing, gathering, and some early forms of horticulture for their subsistence. Lack of a substantial surplus and relative distance from aggressive empires prevented them from evolving toward a tributary mode through the emergence or imposition of a parasitic state. These formations remained intact until the arrival of the European colonizers in the early sixteenth century, which brought about major transformations in tributary and tribal societies throughout the New World.

The colonization of the Americas began at a time when Spain was in transition from feudalism to capitalism, with feudalism still dominant. Spanish expansion into the New World was characterized by plunder of the newly acquired colonies. The Spanish military leaders who conquered the native territories were granted the right to collect tribute or obtain labor services from the local populations. This system of labor relations throughout most of Spanish America came to be known as the *encomienda* system.[6] Essentially, it meant that the conquering state (Spain) replaced the empires previously dominant over the native territories, although it upheld the tributary mode that served the feudal (and increasingly capitalist) Spanish state in its worldwide mission to secure precious metals and luxury goods for the ruling classes of Europe. During the initial stage of plunder, the colonies became an appendage of Spain without undergoing a major transformation in their mode of production or social relations.

As the native population declined as a result of the plunder, and Spain accelerated its acquisition of new land, it became necessary to secure indigenous labor to work the land. The system of *repartimiento* (corvée labor), which allocated Indian workers to Spanish estates (*haciendas*), came to supplant the *encomienda*: Under the new system, Indians were required to work on the *haciendas* on a rotational basis for specific periods of time. Gradually, European forms of feudal relations were introduced as Indians became permanently bound serfs on the *haciendas*. This was facilitated by the destruction of native irrigation systems, the incorporation of native land into Spanish estates, and the forced evacuation of Indians from their land.[7] The subservience of the natives to the new landowning class ushered in a period of lord-serf relations similar to those practiced in Spain. Feudal relations of production were dominant throughout much of Spanish America until the early nineteenth century.[8]

Elsewhere, in Brazil, an insufficient number of natives necessitated the importation of slaves from Africa. Thus, feudal Portugal set up slavery as the dominant mode of production in its Brazilian colony in order to facilitate the extraction of precious metals and other raw materials for sale on the world market. Slaves were used first in sugarcane fields and later in mining gold and diamonds. This continued until the late eighteenth century when slavery was abolished and the ex-slaves were turned into "semi-serfs"—they still worked their masters' land but had some rights granted to them. Sharecropping developed alongside these feudal relations and, with the expansion of an export sector and later capitalist agriculture, wage labor as well.

In the Caribbean and along the Atlantic coast of North America, a similar pattern was established. Black slaves from Africa worked the sugar and cotton plantations, while the indigenous of these areas were displaced or physically eliminated, thus transforming local social structures.[9] In these regions, the British colonialists became the dominant force.

The colonial expansion of Europe not only transformed the mode of production in the New World through the introduction of slavery and feudalism, but also facilitated the development of capitalism in Europe and led to its later spread to the colonies. With the development of European capitalism in the eighteenth century, trade with the colonies increasingly took on a capitalist character. As a result, alongside the feudal landowning class in the colonies, a class of merchants developed, tied to the world market controlled by European commercial interests. In time, some of these merchants expanded into industrial pursuits and set the basis for capitalist development. Small-scale manufacturing, based on wage labor, began to take root in the colonies and provided an outlet for capital accumulation among a section of the propertied elite. Nevertheless, the feudal landowners and their political ally, the commercial capitalists, remained the dominant economic and political forces in the colonies even after independence.

In the early nineteenth century, while the main sources of wealth in Latin America were controlled by the local propertied classes, political power was monopolized by the Spanish crown. This division of economic and political control of Latin colonies served as the principal source of conflict between the Creole[10] bourgeoisie and Spain.

The independence movement of the nineteenth century was an attempt to obtain political autonomy from Spain. From 1830 to 1880, most of the newly formed nations of Latin America underwent a series of brutal civil wars. Federalists, provincialists, nationalists (both economic and political), and manufacturers stood on one side; unitarists, Latin American free traders, exporters and importers, landowners, and British or French imperialism were on the other side.[11] These groups opposed one another in a seemingly perpetual battle that lasted for decades. In the end, the latter group emerged victorious. The victory, first a political and military one and subsequently an economic one, subjugated the industrial and internally oriented national bourgeoisie. It was the beginning of an intimate relationship between British imperialism and the externally oriented

Latin American commercial capitalists, which implemented policies that would promote their interests. The end result of these policies was the concentration of wealth in the hands of compradors tied to the world economy, dominated by British imperialism.

During the period of British imperialism, Latin American economies, especially those of Brazil and Argentina, were thoroughly penetrated by British finance capital. Such penetration manifested itself in the direct control of raw materials by British interests. The investment of foreign capital in the Latin economy consequently integrated the local capitalists into the global system in such a way that most Latin American countries became semicolonies of the expanding British Empire.

The outbreak of major global crises during the first half of the twentieth century brought about important changes in the external relations and internal structures of the majority of Latin American countries. The disruption of world trade during World War I was to be intensified by the Great Depression of the 1930s and by World War II. The decline in foreign trade and foreign capital substantially weakened Latin America's economic ties with Britain. These changes in the structure of the global economy created economic conditions and allowed political changes in Latin America that were to begin the region's strongest nationalist policy and largest independent industrialization drive since the 1830s. The drive subsequently opened for the Latin American industrial capitalists the period of import-substituting industrialization directed toward the diversification of the production structure in manufactures. Global crises thus freed Latin America from outright subordination to imperial centers and accelerated its growth toward independent capitalist development. During this period, the state came under the control of the national bourgeoisie, whose interests dictated the development of a strong capitalist state.

The ascendancy of the United States in the Western hemisphere after World War II, a result of Britain's declining economic power and near defeat during the war, effected the inter-imperialist transfer of control over Latin America from Britain to the United States. U.S. economic expansion into Latin America accelerated during the 1950s, as the United States began to rely increasingly on strategic raw materials from abroad. The need for metals and minerals brought about a rapid expansion of U.S. investment in Latin America in subsequent decades. While extractive industries (e.g., petroleum and mining) continued throughout the 1950s and 1960s to constitute an important part of U.S. investment in Latin America, by the mid 1960s, the pattern of U.S. economic penetration in the hemisphere had taken on new forms. From this point onward, U.S.-based transnational corporations began to penetrate the national industries of Latin

America and to control the manufacturing sector developed by the local industrial capitalists.[12] As a result, the independent industrialization process initiated by the national bourgeoisie in the more advanced countries of the region in the 1930s was gradually transformed, and their economies became an appendage of the global capitalist economy dominated by U.S. transnational corporations. Moving them in the direction of export-oriented satellites as they fulfilled their role in the new international division of labor, the economic changes effected by this new relationship required the introduction of political changes as well. Repressive military rule was needed to stabilize the dependent social order.[13] The "democratic" capitalist state of an earlier period—in Brazil, Argentina, Chile, Peru, and elsewhere—gave way to the authoritarian and repressive neocolonial state, followed by a transition to civilian rule orchestrated by the military. Capitalist development in Latin America in the postwar period thus brought about a transformation in the balance of class forces and transferred state power into the hands of comprador elements tied to the transnationals and the U.S. imperial state.[14] And in the post–Cold War unipolar world of globalization, this linkage to the current center of world imperialism was further strengthened through renewed integration of the Latin economies into the structure of the new global political economy through neoliberal economic policies up through the 1990s.[15]

As the policies and practices of neoliberal globalization resulted in immense inequalities throughout Latin America and led to the crisis of the capitalist state by the turn of the twenty-first century, social movements of broad segments of the population (including workers, dispossessed farmers, the unemployed, indigenous peoples, and other marginalized sectors of the population) across the hemisphere mobilized to struggle against neoliberalism and imperialism and the local collaborating state to force changes in the political economy of countries most affected by these policies (e.g., Argentina, Chile, Bolivia, Brazil, Ecuador, and others) by mounting a mass political movement that swept into power center-left political parties and leaders to change the course of development in a progressive direction. These changes in the politics of a growing number of Latin American states have been the outcome of the mass political mobilization of the affected populations across Latin America, which is now spreading to other parts of the globe.

The State in Asia

Vast areas of Asia were colonized by Western powers until the middle of the twentieth century. British and European imperialism mercilessly plundered these regions at the height of their empires. Through their presence in the area, they effected major changes in the social and economic structures of the societies of Asia they came to dominate.

As in Latin America, feudal relations of production were introduced in Spain's Asian colony, the Philippines; the slave mode was introduced and despotic rule was reinforced in Java and other parts of colonial Indonesia by the Dutch; and capitalism made headway in British India and British-controlled parts of Southeast Asia. Although not formally colonized, China too came under the influence and control of the Western powers, as traditional forms of exploitation were reinforced through the link to Europe and other centers of Western imperialism.

Before the arrival of colonial and imperial powers, many Asian societies evolved within the framework of an Oriental despotic system where the Asiatic mode of production was dominant. With the expansion of Europe to remote corners of Asia, these societies came into contact with and were transformed by different colonizers. Thus, the results were different in British colonies from those in colonies held by Spain, Holland, France, or other colonial powers. While today the remnants of semifeudal relations are the product of an earlier phase of colonial transformation, capitalism and capitalist relations were introduced in later periods of imperial expansion.

Before the arrival of the British in India, the dominant mode of production there was the Asiatic mode. Unlike European feudalism, land in India did not belong to any private landlord; the state was the supreme owner of the soil. The central authority, the king, delegated to some persons the right of *zamin,* or the right to collect revenues for the state. The *zamindars* were intermediaries between the communal villages and the state, and had no rights over the land. In return for their function as tax collectors, the *zamindars* were given a share of the taxes they collected. The absence of proprietary rights in land thus hindered the accumulation of wealth and the development of social classes on the basis of ownership of the means of production.[16] From the late sixteenth century onward, however, the *zamindars* had the right to sell their *zamindari* with the approval of the state, but were unable to acquire proprietary rights over the land.[17] Such prescriptions for the mode of surplus extraction made the nobility in pre-British India a class dependent on the state.[18]

Britain assumed political sovereignty in India late in the eighteenth century, and the *zamindars* emerged as an independent class with full rights in the ownership of land. In some parts of India, such as Bengal, the British decreed that the *zamindars* were to be considered landlords, thus creating a class of large landowners with inheritable ownership rights in the land. Elsewhere in India (e.g., in the south), the British considered the peasants to have ownership rights in the land

and collected taxes from them directly. As a result, this section of the country saw the development of the small landholding. During the course of the nineteenth century, market forces led to an increasing concentration of wealth and gave rise to a large landowning class on the one hand, and renters, sharecroppers, rural laborers, or urban proletarians on the other. British entry into India accelerated the activities of merchants as well; they were to become the intermediaries through whom the British would control the local economy. Engaged in import-export trade and incorporated into the global capitalist system, these merchants became the equivalent of the comprador capitalists. Through both the landlords and the compradors, who together constituted the local upper classes (tied to a weakened central state), the British were able to preserve the existing order and protect and advance their interests.[19]

Thus, while the domination of a class of landlords in the countryside ensured the development of feudal or semifeudal relations of production in agriculture in some parts of the country (and the emergence of capitalist relations through the use of wage labor in other parts), the growth of merchants' capital led to the development of an urban commercial economy tied to Britain through international trade.[20] As trade with Britain increased, and the demand for Indian goods grew, local capital expanded into crafts, textiles, and industrial production. This gave rise to a renewed expansion of local manufacturing industry and with it the development of a national capitalist class that came to be seen as a competitor of British imperialism. This prompted Britain to take steps to crush Indian industry and turn India into an appendage of Britain's colonial economy.[21] Antagonism between the British and local industrial capital led to a national alliance with the peasantry to throw off the British yoke through the independence movement.[22] Much as in North America, but unlike the situation in Latin America, the national capitalist interests were able to consolidate power and capture the leadership of the movement in a victory over the British. By the late 1940s, they installed a state committed to the development of local capitalism in India following independence. Given the relatively weak position of the national capitalists, the victorious national forces were able to utilize the powers of the state and establish a statecapitalist regime to assist the accumulation of capital by the Indian bourgeoisie.[23]

In the period following independence in 1947, the state played an important role in accelerating the development of capitalism in India. Industrial production grew at a rapid rate, as did total productive capital in large-scale industries. The most significant growth took place in capital goods industries. This growth in the first two decades following independence led to a steady increase in the share of industry in the gross domestic product (GDP). The development of private industry in the postindependence period, together with the expansion of state enterprises since the 1950s, accelerated the development of capitalism and the capitalist state, thus securing the domination of capitalism and capitalist relations of production. This process in turn gave rise to a large working class. The number of wage earners in India doubled between 1951 and 1971—reaching more than 23 million—and grew further during the 1970s and 1980s, to a total of 28 million in 1996.[24] Today, in 2012, this number has grown to such levels that wage-labor has become a formidable force in Indian society.

With the growth of the working class, conflict between labor and capital has intensified. The capitalist assault on workers' wages and democratic rights has met stiff resistance from organized labor and the trade union movement and led to the radicalization of large segments of the working class, whose demands have become increasingly political. Threatened with these developments and fearful of a general social explosion based on a revolutionary alliance of workers and peasants, the capitalist state has become more repressive; it has also opened its doors to transnational capital, thus seeking refuge in U.S. and European imperialism.

Over the years, the United States gradually replaced British control over India and emerged as a powerful force with the promotion of the "Green Revolution" in the 1960s. Thus, while the British share in total foreign investment in the private sector was roughly 80 percent in 1948, it fell to 48 percent by the mid 1960s; in contrast, the U.S. share in total private foreign investment increased from 4 percent in 1949 to 25 percent by the mid 1960s.[25] This trend continued during the 1970s and 1980s, and accelerated during the 1990s. Today, in the early twenty-first century, U.S. transnationals, along with the local capitalists, have a dominant position and control the "commanding heights" of the Indian economy.

A move from a state-capitalist to a neocolonial/neoliberal comprador capitalist path tied to foreign capital is the typical outcome of a state-capitalist formation developing within the parameters of the global capitalist system. India, as with many other state-capitalist regimes in the less-developed countries, has not been able to escape from this general rule of capitalist development in the age of globalization and imperialism. Its development within the context of the global economy has resulted in massive economic dislocations and crises over the past three decades and has led to further consolidation of the reactionary forces' grip over the state in more fully integrating India into the global capitalist system. This, in turn, has galvanized popular opposition forces in their struggle against the capitalist state and has given new impetus to their efforts to transform Indian society.

China's experience in state formation has been somewhat different from that of India. Until the nineteenth century, China was ruled by a series of despotic states under successive dynasties, but the imperial state was relatively weak and depended on private landlords who owned vast tracts of land.[26] The widespread presence of private property in the means of production in Imperial China meant that it was not dominated by the Asiatic mode of production (it is precisely the *absence* of private property that defines this mode). But the private landlords did not have such control of the state that they could turn it into an instrument of feudal rule; a fairly strong state bureaucracy maintained relative autonomy from the landlords and exercised its rule over society as a whole. Thus, it would be erroneous to characterize Chinese society at this time as feudal. During the imperial epoch, China possessed a despotic state, within the boundaries of which existed a landed nobility, a merchant class, petty commodity producers (consisting of peasants and artisans), and hired laborers. The economic strength of an already developed landed gentry, by way of its access to and control over a significant portion of the means of production, compelled the state to share power with the landlords over the peasants and landless laborers from whom they extracted a share of the surplus in the form of taxes, produce, or rent. Within this framework of domination in a semi-Asiatic, semi-feudal society, a merchant class tied to overseas trade flourished. The capital accumulated from trade was gradually invested in crafts and manufacturing production and, together with a merger with expanding artisan elements in basic home industries, led to the development of a national capitalist class. At the same time, some peasants were able to improve their lot and accumulate sufficient wealth to constitute a rich peasant class (similar to *kulaks*). Others lost their land to large landowners, ending up either working for them as rural laborers or migrating to the cities and becoming wage earners. These parallel developments in city and countryside strengthened the development of feudalism and capitalism throughout China and laid the basis for the transformation of Chinese society following the disintegration of the central state. With the landlords allied with commercial interests in firm control of the state, China entered a period of feudal rule and later evolved toward capitalism.

By the end of the eighteenth and beginning of the nineteenth centuries, Western powers had begun to intervene in China and attempted to incorporate it into the global capitalist orbit.[27] A protracted struggle against Western imperialism followed, and ushered in a period of intense nationalism that paved the way for the national capitalist forces that captured state power by the early twentieth century. Remaining within the global capitalist system and unable to suppress internal reaction, the nationalist government of Sun Yat Sen was considerably weakened. Taking advantage of the situation, the reactionary anticommunist forces within the Kuomintang, under the leadership of Chiang Kai-shek, captured power and imposed an iron rule over China that led to a long and bloody civil war during which thousands of communists and revolutionaries were executed. The betrayal of the national-democratic, anti-imperialist revolution by the rightists in the Kuomintang, who embraced imperialism to crush the growing working-class and communist movements, led to the reemergence of an independent communist movement based on a worker-peasant alliance under the leadership of the Chinese Communist Party (CCP) headed by Mao Zedong. After a long struggle against Japanese and U.S. imperialism, and internal reaction and the mobilization of millions of workers and peasants during the 1930s and 1940s, the Chinese masses triumphed in a communist-led revolution in 1949 that brought to an end feudalist-capitalist exploitation and imperialist plunder and launched a new people's democracy through the institution of a socialist state. Thus was born the People's Republic of China.

In the post-revolutionary period, China went through several stages in its development and matured into a highly developed state. From the Great Leap Forward of the 1950s to the Cultural Revolution of the late 1960s to the transformations in the 1980s to the present, China built the foundations of an advanced industrial society with high rates of economic growth and development that has become the envy of the world. While the nature of the Chinese state, the developments of the past three decades, and the implications of the recent transformations that China has gone through are not very clear, the fact that China has become a major player in the global political economy and is now the second largest economic power in the world is not in dispute. It has, in fact, become a source of intense discussion and debate, as the global economy struggles to recover from its deepest and longest crisis since the Great Depression.

Elsewhere in East and Southeast Asia, a number of states emerged as appendages of the global capitalist system following World War II. Evolving as neocolonies of the expanding U.S. empire in the postwar period, these states came to serve the economic and strategic interests of U.S. transnationals and the state in providing cheap labor, raw materials, new markets, new investment outlets, and a military foothold throughout the area to protect capitalist interests and encircle and contain socialist states in the region. South Korea, Taiwan, the Philippines, Indonesia, Thailand, Malaysia, Hong Kong, Singapore, Cambodia, and South Vietnam (until 1975) served one or more of the above functions and provided the material base for U.S. transnational expansion in the region after the fall of Japan. By the early 1950s, South Korea, Taiwan, and the Philippines, together with defeated Japan, came under the U.S. military umbrella in the Pacific Basin and provided a foundation for the expansion of U.S. transnational corporations in these countries. A similar stance was taken toward South Vietnam, Cambodia, Laos, and Thailand in the aftermath of the British and French defeat in the region, which brought the United States into the conflict there during the late

1950s and early 1960s. The U.S. military escalation in Southeast Asia expanded the conflict into one of the biggest wars in the region's recent history—one that lasted over three decades. By the mid 1970s, U.S. efforts at domination over the region collapsed, as the Indochinese drove the U.S. forces out of their territories. With Vietnam, Cambodia, and Laos out of the U.S. grip, Thailand, Indonesia, and especially the Philippines took on the role of regional policemen to protect U.S. interests in Southeast Asia and provide security for regional operations of U.S. transnationals. Thus, while U.S. military presence in or economic aid to these countries turned them into de facto neocolonial states, their subsequent economic integration into the global capitalist system transformed their social and economic structures to suit the needs of U.S. and other transnational corporations. They advanced along the capitalist path—with high growth rates and profits for foreign and local capitalists on the one hand, and the exploitation of workers and peasants on the other.[28]

With the expansion of U.S. capital in East and Southeast Asia in the 1960s and 1970s, these regions became more fully integrated into the global economy dominated by the United States. Through such investments, and other economic arrangements, these states were to fulfill their special role in the international division of labor controlled by the United States.[29] This prompted a rapid expansion of capitalism in these countries through increased foreign investment and subcontracting with local firms to fill transnational orders destined for markets in advanced capitalist countries.[30]

But this transnational-directed industrialization process exacerbated larger social and economic problems confronting these countries while creating employment at very low wages, depleting local resources, maintaining control over the technology transferred to the recipient countries, and draining the profits made from the sale of exported goods. Additionally, it resulted in, one, the destruction of an integrated national economy and the installation of enclave export processing zones controlled by transnational firms; two, the bankruptcy of small and medium-size businesses and the monopolization of the local economy by foreign capital; three, wealth and income inequalities based on an internal market dependent on no more than 5 percent of the population; four, low wages leading to a decline in the standard of living of the majority of the population with its attendant consequences on diet, housing, health care, education, and other needs; five, rising unemployment, poverty, malnutrition, and related ills; and six, social and political repression through the installation of brutal (often military) dictatorships that violated basic human rights. These effects of export-oriented industrialization in states under the grip of foreign capital are the outcome of a system of relations imposed on the working people of the less-developed countries by imperialism—a system that is based on the exploitation of the working class and the peasantry by foreign capital.[31] The social significance of global capitalist expansion in these regions lies in the transformation of local relations of production in a capitalist direction and the consolidation of a capitalist state that is subservient to imperialism, with all its inherent class contradictions.

The increase in number of workers in the manufacturing sector and, more broadly, in all major branches of industry, accompanied by below-subsistence wages and antilabor legislation enacted by repressive neocolonial states, has led to the intensification of the class struggle in these countries, with some of them (e.g., South Korea, the Philippines, and Indonesia) reaching a near-revolutionary stage, as the masses come to challenge the rule of the capitalist state.

The State in Africa

Prior to European intervention, Africa had a diverse social structure based on various modes of production in different regions of the continent. The primitive communal mode was dominant in some areas, and the Asiatic and feudal modes were paramount in others. Although slavery was practiced in various parts of the continent before the European-initiated slave trade, it never became a dominant mode of production in precolonial Africa. Primitive communal relations of production were prevalent in central and parts of southern Africa, while the Asiatic mode dominated much of North Africa until the end of the nineteenth century. Feudalism in various forms was practiced in parts of East and West Africa.[32]

Despite the prevalence of these diverse modes in various parts of the continent, precolonial Africa consisted in large part of self-sufficient village communities engaged in subsistence agriculture. Where feudalism or a despotic state existed, villagers provided a surplus to the ruling classes in the form of tribute or a part of their produce. With the widespread introduction of the slave trade by European imperialism, greater stratification was induced in the continent, and many newly created tribal chiefs were corrupted by European conquerors and turned into tyrants serving the interests of Western imperialism. The artificial creation of "district chiefs" in the French colonies and of "headmen" in the English colonies was done for this purpose.[33] After the sixteenth century, when the world economy facilitated the spread of the slave trade in Africa, slaves became Africa's major export. They were bought and sold to masters in various parts of the world, especially in the Americas.

The slave trade inhibited indigenous capital accumulation and thus the development of local capitalism, as it deprived Africa of able-bodied workers, undermined local artisan production because of the cheap European goods received for the slaves, and reinforced slavery as a mode of production. The economic development that did take place during this period was highly dependent on the European colonial economy tied to the slave trade.[34] With the end of the slave trade in the first half of the nineteenth century, African economies shifted to commercial export crops. Commodities such as cocoa, peanuts, palm oil, coffee, and rubber became the principle exports. As a result, the previously dominant ruling classes, whose wealth and power were based on the slave trade, transformed themselves into planters who imposed semifeudal production relations on their ex-slaves, who now labored on vast plantations in serf-like conditions. The wealth and power of the local ruling class declined during the course of the nineteenth century as European colonialism gained a more direct foothold in the continent and became involved in production and trade throughout the area. By the end of the nineteenth century, the European powers had moved in with full force against local states and chiefdoms and set up colonial regimes. Labor migration became the main mechanism to secure a labor force in the mining sector, as well as in commercial crop production. Africans engaged in subsistence production on communal lands were manipulated into providing labor to the Europeans, who introduced taxes payable in money. In this way, they were able to force Africans to work in European-owned enterprises to secure the means to pay their taxes. At the same time, labor services (corvée) were introduced, although they could often be avoided in exchange for a cash payment. To avoid corvée, one had to prove gainful employment. Either way, the European colonialists were the only ones to gain from these practices.

In time, the notion of private property was introduced, which undermined traditional subsistence agriculture and led to increased demands for commercial goods. This provided sufficient incentive to get Africans to sell their labor power for a wage. Over time, the African economies became increasingly commercial, wage labor became more prevalent, raw material exports grew, and the demand for European industrial imports increased. As a result, Africa evolved along the capitalist path tied to the European-dominated world economy, which at the end of the nineteenth and beginning of the twentieth century had transformed Africa by introducing capitalist relations of production into the continent through colonial rule.

The different forms of exploitation and the different class structures that developed during the colonial era in Latin America, Asia, and Africa can thus be explained in terms of the different modes of production prevailing in Europe and in the colonies, as well as the interaction between the two at different points in history. In this sense, the precapitalist colonialism of Spain in Latin America and elsewhere produced a legacy of feudalism that lingers today, while the capitalist imperialism of a more developed industrial Europe in transition to monopoly capital at a later period produced a qualitatively different result in Africa, as well as in parts of Asia, where capitalist relations of production began to take root.[35]

Until the middle of the twentieth century, when most African countries won their formal independence, the local economies were a direct appendage of the colonial center, which directed development in the colonies. The pattern was based on the logic of the capitalist mode of production that dominated the economies of the center states and evolved according to its needs of accumulation, resulting in uneven development between the imperial center and the colonies, and within the colonies. In general, most African colonies specialized in one or a few raw materials for export and depended on the importation of finished manufactured goods from the imperial center.

This classic colonial relationship prevailed in a number of African countries after the granting of formal independence, and led to the restructuring of social-economic relations on a neocolonial basis—that is, the continuation of colonial relations through the intermediary of a local ruling class dependent on and nourished by imperialism. This has been the case in various parts of the continent, from Kenya in the east to Nigeria and the Ivory Coast in the west, to Zaire, Uganda, and other countries in Africa.[36] As in the colonial period, the main characteristic of these neocolonial states is their heavy reliance on the export of raw materials to the advanced capitalist countries and the importation of finished manufactured goods from them—a condition that has become an impediment to industrialization and held back the development of the industrial sector in these countries.[37]

Within this broader framework of the neocolonial structure, there has nevertheless occurred a parallel development of transnational corporate expansion into the manufacturing sector of some of these countries in order to utilize cheap labor in a variety of manufacturing and industrial undertakings. This has contributed to the growth of the industrial sector. As a result, the share of industry relative to agriculture has increased over time. This is most evident in western and northern Africa, notably in Nigeria, Liberia, Ivory Coast, Tunisia, and Egypt.

Despite the fact that the pace of industrialization in these countries is considerably slower than in Latin America and East and Southeast Asia, the move in the direction of investments in industry has brought about a significant change in the economic and labor force structure of these countries and placed them on the road to further capitalist development within the bounds of the global economy. Thus, while neocolonial African states continue to remain primarily agricultural or raw-material-exporting countries, the relative growth of manufacturing and other industry vis-à-vis agriculture indicates an overall trend toward industrialization within a neocolonial framework tied to imperialism.[38]

In other countries of Africa, such as the Sudan, Uganda, and Zaire, semifeudal relations based on raw material production continue with little progress on the industrial front. This shows the dual nature of imperialist penetration in different regions and countries of the continent where traditional colonial relations are reinforced in some areas, while comprador-capitalist neocolonial relations are developed and strengthened in others under the guise of neoliberalism. However, looking at the experience of a number of countries following the state-capitalist path, we find that independent capitalist development through state aid has failed to achieve its stated goals because these countries have remained within the global capitalist system.

On the other hand, in countries in which workers and peasants have played an active role in the struggle for liberation against colonialism and imperialism (such as in Angola and Mozambique), strides have been made toward genuine economic and political independence, accompanied by deep social transformations. With political power in the hands of workers, peasants, and intellectuals committed to advancing the interests of the masses, these countries have progressed in all facets of social-economic life, despite the enormous international (imperialist) and regional South African (colonial/racist) encroachments into their territories.

Historically, the presence of a racist apartheid regime in South Africa has been a great impediment to the development of revolutionary forces in the southern cone of Africa and has had a major impact on the scope and pace of development on the continent in a progressive direction. With the abolition of the apartheid regime in South Africa in the 1990s, however, the last vestiges of racist colonial and neocolonial oppression have been removed, so that an open political struggle could be waged by the masses to take control of their destiny and build a new society free of the oppression and exploitation that they have suffered for so long. And this has started to happen with the Arab Spring of 2011, which started in Tunisia, in North Africa, and quickly spread to other countries in the region, including Morocco, Egypt, and Libya, and much of the rest of the Middle East. Whether this wave of uprisings will move southward to sub-Saharan Africa, time will tell. But having been enslaved for so long, it is clear that the people of Africa will stand up and fight for their liberation.

The State in the Middle East

Until the beginning of the twentieth century, the Ottoman Empire was the major political force in the Middle East. For seven centuries, the predominant mode of production in Ottoman society had been the Asiatic mode of production.

Although it came in contact with many different modes of production and exchange, Ottoman Empire retained its powerful despotic state.

Interaction between Ottoman and Byzantine society developed after the invasion of Constantinople by Ottoman forces in 1453. This, along with other European societies following the Ottoman expansion into Europe in the fifteenth and sixteenth centuries, plus the state's land-allocation system (*timar*),[39] eventually led to feudal forms in Ottoman agriculture (*iltizam*, or tax farming) where, over time, large-scale private property in land (*çiftlik*) acquired increasing importance, transferring a higher proportion of the land to a few owners.[40] This transformation of the agrarian structure took place during the seventeenth and eighteenth centuries; as a result, a landed gentry (*ayan*) developed, displacing the *sipahis* as intermediaries between the state and producers. By the end of the eighteenth and beginning of the nineteenth centuries, the *ayan* was a fully developed feudal landowning class that began to challenge the authority of the central state by equipping its own armies. But the *ayan* never became powerful enough to overthrow the central state.[41]

While the position of landlords was strengthened as a result of the introduction of tax farming initiated by the state, interaction with Europe also facilitated the expansion of European commercial capital into the empire, leading to the development of a comprador class tied to European imperialism. Nevertheless, the development of feudalism in agriculture and, later, capitalism in commerce and industry, took place within the confines of a society dominated by the Asiatic state, which permitted the coexistence of these diverse modes.

The collapse of the Ottoman Empire came gradually. After centuries of expansion and conquest, the Ottoman state began to lose ground to rival forces in Europe during the eighteenth and nineteenth centuries and became vulnerable to pressures from the West. European powers, taking advantage of the endless wars in the empire's various provinces, found their way in through direct economic controls and military occupation of large parts of Ottoman territory at the end of the nineteenth and beginning of the twentieth century, which culminated in the occupation of virtually every corner of the empire during World War I. Following the collapse of the empire at the end of the war, Britain, France, Italy, Greece, and other European countries colonized its territories and remained in control of its various provinces for several decades. The region from the Persian Gulf to Palestine, to the Suez Canal, down to the Arabian Peninsula, and across North Africa came under the jurisdiction primarily of Britain and France, who divided up these territories to secure trade routes, raw materials, and new markets for the expanding European-controlled global economy.

In time, local populations resented foreign domination and attempted to oust the Europeans from their lands. After long struggles for national liberation, some regions of the empire occupied by the imperialist powers gained political independence and set up a series of nation-states. To understand the nature and dynamics of contemporary Middle Eastern societies, we will briefly look at the evolution of three of the region's most important states—Egypt, Iraq, and Iran.

The state played an important role in directing the course of events in the various provinces of the Ottoman Empire tied to the Ottoman central state. In Egypt, a distant and semiautonomous province of the empire, the governor maintained his title as long as the province met its tributary obligations to the Ottoman central state. This relationship continued until 1893 when Governor Mehmet Ali Paşa and his provincial army rebelled and marched on Kütahya in central Anatolia, defeating the imperial army not far from the Ottoman capital, Istanbul. One of the strongest *ayans* of the time, Mehmet Ali attempted to free Egypt from ties to the Ottoman state and acquire direct control over the region. But Mehmet Ali's forces were soon driven back by Britain and France, which intervened on behalf of the Ottoman throne.

After the collapse of the Ottoman Empire at the end of World War I, Britain occupied Egypt, as it did other parts of the empire, and remained in the Middle East through the first half of the twentieth century. It was during this period that Britain, France, and lesser imperial powers set up a series of colonial states—Egypt, Jordan, Iraq, Syria, Lebanon, Palestine (later Israel), Kuwait, Saudi Arabia, Libya, Tunisia, Algeria, Morocco, Cyprus—and a chain of dependencies in the Gulf region. Local rulers stayed on as figureheads, but the occupied territories served the economic and strategic interests of the imperialist forces by securing access to oil and other raw materials; a passage to India, China, and the rest of the Far East; and military domination of a region joining three continents. Egypt played an important role in this regard by allowing the imperialist powers to use the Suez Canal, linking the Mediterranean with the Indian Ocean through the Red Sea.

However, nationalist sentiment ran deep in Egypt. The Egyptian intelligentsia, youth, and junior army officers resented the foreign occupation and the dictates of European powers over the social, economic, and political life of the nation. Supported by a series of revolts of poor peasants and agricultural workers, and by industrial strikes in Shubra El Khaima, Kafr El Dawwar, and Elmahalla Elkubra in the late 1940s and early 1950s, the petty-bourgeois nationalist forces within the army led a coup in 1952, under the leadership of Gamal Abdel Nasser, and overthrew the monarchy.

Nasser's victory ushered in a period of anti-imperialism and state centered capitalist development:[42] The Nasser regime rallied the support of broad segments of the propertyless masses and used the state as an instrument of national development under petty-bourgeois technocratic bureaucratic rule. Although a desire to elevate the masses to a higher standard of living led them to improve education, working conditions, health care, and other social programs, as well as the national economy, the nationalist perspective of the officers prevented them from having a clear understanding of Egyptian society and its class divisions. Without a class analysis of the prevailing social structure, the new rulers ended up supporting and enhancing capitalist relations of production in a new state-sanctioned setting.[43]

In time, this led to conflict between the public and private sectors, and by the mid 1960s, the state-capitalist economy entered a period of crisis. The private capitalist sector challenged the economics of Nasserism from which it had itself emerged in an earlier period.[44] The gradual integration of Egypt into the global capitalist economy during the 1960s also contributed to this development and paved the way for the disintegration of state-capitalism and the emergence of Anwar Sadat and a new capitalist class allied with the largest interests in the private sector, as a ruling coalition of class forces dependent on imperialism.[45]

The transition to a neocolonial capitalist economy further enhanced the penetration of foreign capital into Egypt during the 1970s and 1980s and reversed the trends set in motion in the two previous decades. With the shift in the balance of forces in the postwar global economy in favor of the United States, U.S. investment and interest in Egypt became more pronounced. By the late 1990s, foreign and joint-venture investments totaled over $12 billion, the overwhelming majority from the United States. Foreign investment in Egypt is concentrated most heavily in petroleum, banking, chemicals, pharmaceuticals, and other branches of manufacturing industry, notably electronics and transportation equipment.[46]

The trend away from state-capitalism and toward a neocolonial "open door" policy evolved during the Sadat regime. This development was the logical outcome of the evolution of state-capitalism that became subordinated to foreign interests. Thus, state-capitalism in Egypt facilitated the transition to a neocolonial capitalism dependent on imperialism. Class conflict and struggles between contending class forces in Egyptian society contributed to the unfolding crisis of the Egyptian state and led to the assassination of Anwar Sadat in 1981. Despite these events, the government of Hosni Mubarak throughout the 1990s and 2000s represented a further evolution along Sadat's path that later evolved into neoliberal capitalist integration into the global economy with greater ties to the United States. And it is this integration into the global economy and the neoliberal policies that were pursued in Egypt during the past three decades, as well as the corruption and the iron-fisted dictatorship with which Mubarak reigned over the country, that finally toppled him during the Arab Spring of 2011 that swept through the Middle East. While the mass rebellion and revolution in Egypt in 2011 succeeded in driving Mubarak out of power, the military and police apparatuses of the Egyptian state were brutally unleashed to suppress the people's movement to prevent them from taking state power, but to no avail. The people of Egypt are now in the process of constructing a new society and a state that is democratic and responsive to their needs. The final outcome of this struggle to build their society anew is a difficult task that is yet to be achieved.

In Iraq, a similar colonial history under British rule yielded comparable results in the formation and transformation of the state. Prior to World War I, Basra, Baghdad, and Mosul were provinces of the Ottoman Empire. After the war, Britain took control of this territory. The motive forces behind British colonization were oil and access to the Persian Gulf. The British installed a monarchy including pro-British local officers from the Ottoman army, wealthy merchants, and local bureaucrats with ties to the sheikhs and landlords in the countryside. The colonial regime in Iraq shored up the large sheikh and comprador elements and turned the state into an instrument of imperial rule designed to fulfill the dictates of the British-controlled global economy. The monarchy installed by Britain carried out the British mandate over the colony and safeguarded British interests in the region.

The onset of the Great Depression and the sharp fall in world prices for Iraq's chief exports (barley and wheat) brought about an economic and political crisis that led to limited independence in 1932. The expansion of industrial and commercial activity during the 1930s and 1940s brought into being newer social forces, including a small proletariat and a more numerous petty bourgeoisie. Excluded from centers of political and economic power, and subordinated to a monarchy propped up by British imperialism, these sectors came to articulate widespread resentment of foreign control and local ruling-class collaboration with imperialism. This led to numerous clashes between the state and popular sectors of Iraqi society, including a series of tribal rebellions from 1936 to 1941.[47]

The outbreak of World War II gave Britain an opportunity to intervene in the simmering political climate, but doing so only intensified anti-British sentiment and sparked a series of strikes, demonstrations, and clashes. By 1948, the political situation in Iraq had reached crisis proportions. Mass repression quelled efforts to overthrow the colonial puppet regime, but the oil boom in the 1950s began to transform the economic structure of the country through increased trade, construction, and manufacturing, thus moving the economy in a capitalist direction. Such expansion led to the emergence and growth of a capitalist class whose interests were distinct from those of the old power block of comprador merchants and landlords that formed the power base of the monarchy.

At the same time, industrial activity expanded the number of workers in industry and led to further labor organizing by trade unions and other workers' organizations, such as the Iraqi Communist Party (ICP). The ICP became an influential political force, organizing strategic concentrations of workers, those working on the state railway and at the port of Basra and the oil fields.[48]

The growth of national capital and the aspiration of middle layers of society to nationhood and independence on the one hand, and the growth and development of an increasingly organized and class-conscious working class on the other, coupled with the massive dislocation of peasants forced to migrate to large cities, led to unrest in the army and resulted in a coup by the Free Officers, led by Colonel Abdul-Karim Qasim, in 1958. Representing the interests of the rising national and petty bourgeoisies, the Qasim regime set out to restructure the economy on a state-capitalist basis that protected and advanced the interests of these two classes while providing social services, government programs, and benefits directed at workers and poorer sectors of society in order to maintain a mass support base for the regime. The revenues accrued from oil provided the funds to achieve these goals without disturbing the prevailing urban class structure.

The transformation of the class structure in Iraq involved the dismantling of the power of both the landowning class and foreign capital, and the transfer of this power to the national and petty bourgeoisies. In line with this development, the 1960s saw an agrarian reform program and the nationalization of oil. Soon, the largest manufacturing, trading, and financial firms were transferred to the public sector.[49] Despite a crisis in the mid 1960s—largely the result of a drop in oil revenues, which precipitated the coup of 1968 by right-wing military officers allied with the Ba'th party, bringing to power Saddam Hussein—Iraq continued to develop along the state-capitalist road, further strengthening the power of the state.

The industrial and commercial expansion of the 1960s and 1970s led to the development of a local capitalist class tied to state-directed national industry. As in Egypt, the maturing local industrial bourgeoisie asserted itself in Iraq by the late 1970s and opened up ventures with foreign capital in both the Arab world and the West, integrating itself even more into the global economy, thus undermining the state-capitalist project. The repression of popular forces, the attack on the communists, and the exercise of authoritarian rule over the people in Iraq have coincided with the crisis of state-capitalism and the gradual transition to a neocolonial state allied with imperialism.

The Gulf War of 1991, directed at Iraq to settle the question of which imperialist power would rule over the region, was a serious blow to Iraq's own designs as an emerging sub-imperialist power in alliance with one or another of the leading imperialist forces engaged in rivalry for control over sources of oil in the Middle East.[50] The showdown between the United States and Iraq, which culminated in a major catastrophe for the latter, derailed Iraq's efforts in this direction and led to the re-exertion of U.S. power over the entire region to the end of the twentieth century.

A decade after the Gulf War, the September 11, 2001, attacks on the twin towers of the World Trade Center, which led the U.S. to pursue al-Qaeda by invading and occupying Afghanistan in October 2001, provided the impetus for the United States to launch a massive assault against Iraq by invading, bombing, and occupying Baghdad and the rest of Iraq in March 2003 by alleging links between Iraq and al-Qaeda, thus implicating the Iraqi state in the September 11 attacks. The war on Iraq, by some 150,000 U.S. troops invading the country to disarm it of its "weapons of mass destruction" to prevent another terrorist attack against the United States, resulted in the biggest U.S. military operation against another country since the war in Vietnam.

The March 2003 "shock and awe" campaign of mass bombings launched several thousand tomahawk and cruise missiles against Iraqi targets, especially in Baghdad, including several presidential palaces, the Ministry of Information, command and control centers, and numerous other government buildings and bunkers. The bombings set the city ablaze for more than two weeks, causing much destruction and death. The U.S. and British troops engaged in bloody battles and met with stiff resistance from the Iraqi army, the Republican Guard, and irregulars, including the fedayeen and the paramilitary forces, who fought to defend Umm Qasr, Basra, An Nasiriyah, An Najaf, and Karbala, as well as Baghdad and other cities across Iraq. But by early April 2003, the U.S. forces succeeded in entering Baghdad, taking control of much of Iraq, and toppling the regime of Saddam Hussein, who later was captured and, following a show trial, was executed by hanging.

The war against Iraq waged by the sole global superpower, the United States (and its junior coalition partner, Britain, and an assortment of secondary sources), which started with the unleashing of thousands of missiles and threatening the region with nuclear war, was designed to lay claim to the oil resources of Iraq and the Middle East and thus expand to include Syria and Iran to redraw the map of the entire region in favor of the United States. After nearly a decade of war and occupation, which cost thousands of U.S. lives and left nearly a million Iraqis dead, with tens of thousands more wounded and maimed on both sides, at a cost of over a trillion dollars for U.S. taxpayers, the situation in Iraq and the rest of the Middle East has become worse, not better. After nearly a decade of occupation and devastation, the departure of tens of thousands of U.S. troops from the country that held rival factions in check may now signal the start of a new civil war in Iraq.

Having deposed the regime of Saddam Hussein and siphoned off billions of barrels of oil from Iraqi soil, U.S. imperialism is now bent on destroying Iran on similarly bogus charges of possession of "weapons of mass destruction" by targeting its nuclear power program to actually regain access to Iranian oil that the United States lost after the downfall of the shah. Carrying a $15 trillion debt, Uncle Sam might think taking possession of Iranian oil is one sure way of reducing its enormous debt burden, though such action might drag the empire into a long quagmire that may lead to its final collapse in the coming years.

Unlike most Middle Eastern states, Iran was never formally colonized by the Western powers. Although its economic and strategic importance to the West was apparent by the turn of the century, it became paramount during and following World War II. The transfer of power in the region from Britain to the United States at the conclusion of the war set the stage for the restructuring of the Iranian state along lines complementary to the interests of U.S. oil companies and the Pentagon's geopolitical interests in the region. This transformation of the Iranian state into an appendage of U.S. imperialism came following the CIA-engineered overthrow of the Mossadeq regime in the early 1950s, which brought to a halt a brief experiment in state-capitalism and reinstalled the discredited Pahlavi dynasty. The regime of Shah Reza Pahlavi was thus set up as an arm of the U.S. state, as a strategic outpost of the United States in the Middle East.[51]

During the shah's reign, from 1953 until his overthrow in 1979, the Iranian state began to bear the classic characteristics of a neocolonial state dependent on imperialism. From the so-called White Revolution of the early 1960s, which implemented a U.S.-initiated capitalist transformation of the agrarian sector, to the agro-mineral enclave of the transnationals in the 1970s, Iran became a well-financed sub-imperialist power with a 300,000-man army and U.S. military purchases in excess of $20 billion.[52] Iran's close economic, political, and military relationship with the United States, combined with its bureaucratic corruption, the economic disaster faced by small farmers and *bazaari* merchants, and the repression of the working class and other progressive sectors of society (which included torture, imprisonment, and executions), gave the necessary opening to the clerics to launch an attack on the shah's regime. Joined by workers, students, and the masses in general (through prolonged strikes and mass demonstrations), the clerics overthrew the shah in February 1979, bringing to an end twenty-five years of U.S.-sponsored authoritarian rule.[53]

Although a popular uprising ushered in the 1979 Iranian revolution, ended the shah's rule, and expelled the United States from the country, bringing with it hopes of a democratic transition to popular rule and social justice for the laboring masses, what actually resulted from the revolutionary turmoil was an organized political takeover by clerical elements.[54] The *mullahs* and *imams*, allied with reactionary landed interests able to mobilize a critical mass of the dispossessed peasantry and marginalized sectors of the urban population, gained a mass base with which to take the seats of power.[55] Strikes in the oil fields, in public services and utilities, in communication, and in related sectors of the economy thus provided the necessary political momentum to topple the shah and place power in the hands of the Islamic clergy and their reactionary allies. In this sense, and to the extent that no major social transformation took place following the uprising, the Iranian revolution *cannot* be seen as a social revolution; it was in fact a political rebellion that consolidated power in the hands of a reactionary coalition of class forces—landlords, merchants, and an assortment of small and medium-sized propertied interests—led by Islamic fundamentalist clerics. Thus the February revolution transferred power from one propertied ruling class to another, in the name of the people, with Islam as the organizing ideology directed at the dispossessed.[56] Islam, in essence, was used as a mobilizing force by traditional class forces that wanted to prevent a socialist revolution in the wake of the shah's downfall. What they succeeded in installing was a reactionary landlord-clerical dictatorship.[57]

Today, after more than three decades of Islamic rule and continued exploitation and repression (including the torture and execution of thousands of progressives and revolutionaries),[58] after a decade-long war with Iraq that cost thousands of Iranians their lives, and after continuing crises in the Iranian economy have so deteriorated living standards as to force the masses into desperation, the Islamic Republic faces an imminent social explosion. How soon the crisis-ridden conditions will reach a revolutionary stage and trigger an uprising against the regime, only time will tell. What is certain is that signs of such an outcome are becoming increasingly clear. Now, as ever, how well organized the popular forces are, and will become in the months and years ahead, in order to topple the regime, remains largely a *political* question.

Class, State, and Social Transformation

The historical development of states in the less-developed countries illustrates the varied nature and dynamics of the capitalist state that has evolved out of the interaction between local, precapitalist modes of production and capitalism originating in Europe and other colonial and imperial centers of the global economy and the responses to colonial and imperial domination through struggles for national liberation.

In some regions, such as Latin America and parts of Asia, Africa, and the Middle East, the Oriental despotic state was overrun by European colonialism. Feudal land-tenure practices were introduced, together with merchant's capital tied to the colonial center. Despite revolts against the European colonial empires, the local introduction of feudal and commercial practices had a profound effect on the later development of capitalism and the capitalist state in these areas. Although formally independent of center states, the local ruling classes developed as appendages of European colonialism and imperialism. This relationship continued despite shifts in power in the colonial and imperial centers, so that the transition from colonial status did not alter the underlying relationship between the ruling classes in the ex-colonies and the colonial centers. Remnants of feudal landed and commercial moneyed interests lingered on in the context of an emerging local capitalist class in a changing global economy that accommodated all three class segments. Within this framework of the colonial and neocolonial states in these regions, there resulted the development of two variants of the neocolonial capitalist state: the semifeudal or semicapitalist, and the more developed comprador-capitalist. While they have a similar political relationship with the colonial and imperial centers, these two variants of the capitalist state were nevertheless ruled by classes that occupied different positions in the social and economic structure.

Prevailing in much of the less-developed capitalist world, the comprador-capitalist states were the main variant of the capitalist state across the less-developed world for decades. The dominant mode of production in comprador-capitalist states, such as Brazil, Mexico, Argentina, South Korea, and the Philippines, was capitalist, with precapitalist (i.e., feudal or transitional petty commodity) modes surviving in the countryside and sometimes having considerable influence within their domain. The expansion of foreign investment in manufacturing, agriculture, and raw materials in these countries since the early 1960s accelerated the process of capitalist development so that previously precapitalist production and commercial relations have been transformed into capitalist ones. With the spread of capitalism and capitalist relations in these societies, state power has increasingly come under the influence and later control of the local capitalists, as the traditional alliance of landlords and compradors has proven to be an obstacle to the further expansion of the economic interests of local capitalists collaborating with imperialism. The change in relations between imperialism and the local ruling classes came in the 1960s in many parts of the less-developed world: In Latin America, it coincided with and was reinforced by the so-called Alliance for Progress; in Asia, it came with the Green Revolution in India; in the Middle East, it was facilitated by the White Revolution in Iran; and in Africa, it came with the transition from colonial rule to independence.

In these and other capitalist societies, state power is no longer shared between landlords and compradors, but it is in the hands of an emergent capitalist class tied to imperialism. At the current stage of development of these local capitalist forces emerging under conditions of globalization, this new alliance with imperialism is directed against the precapitalist landowning class for the transformation of the countryside into capitalist agriculture. Mechanization and wage labor, introduced and expanded by transnational agricultural corporations, are important components of the ongoing integration of these states into the global capitalist economy dominated and controlled by the transnational corporations of the advanced capitalist countries.

The transformation of the internal social structure of less-developed capitalist states has been most visible in countries receiving the greatest amount of foreign (primarily U.S.) manufacturing investments since the early 1960s. Largely as a result of these investments, there has occurred a high rate of growth in the manufacturing sector of these countries, signifying the new relationship between local capitalists and imperialism as these countries have come to serve the special needs of the transnationals, especially the need for cheap labor.

Nevertheless, the expansion of foreign capital into the local economy through the intermediary of these emergent capitalists has increasingly become a threat to the national interest, giving rise to growing nationalist sentiments among various affected sectors of society. More fundamentally, the unfolding process of capitalist development, which has accelerated the spread of capitalist production relations in these societies, has given rise to the growth of an increasingly class-conscious working class that is beginning to challenge the prevailing capitalist power structure across the less-developed world.

Such challenge had developed in an earlier period in parts of Asia, Africa, and the Middle East when successful national liberation movements struggling against imperialism and the local collaborating states, led by the national or petty bourgeoisies, had resulted in the establishment of an independent nationalist state. With petty-bourgeois forces in control of the state machine, these states adopted various measures to advance the class interests of the petty bourgeoisie as well as its closest ally, the national bourgeoisie.

The main objective of the petty-bourgeois states, such as Turkey and Mexico in the 1930s, India in the 1950s, Egypt in the 1950s and 1960s, and Iraq in the 1960s and 1970s, was to provide the necessary capital to develop and expand the national economy where a national bourgeoisie had not developed sufficiently to assume leadership in the major sectors of the economy. Hence, the state in these countries played a major role in the realization of the long-term interests of the agent of capital accumulation in the less-developed countries (i.e., the national bourgeoisie). In addition to its active role in the development of the productive forces, the state in these countries attempted to eliminate the remnants of pre-capitalist relations of production in the countryside through a series of agrarian reforms that included expropriation of large tracts of land controlled by the big landlords. It also nationalized the major means of production and restricted or expelled foreign capital. Parallel to these developments were the planning and implementation of a broad-based industrialization program with high levels of state investment in heavy industry, the regulation of commerce by the state, and the creation of special organs such as state banks and development corporations.

While such state intervention in the economy has had a positive impact on development in some less-developed countries, the historical experience of peripheral social formations following a state-capitalist path shows that the struggle between the national- or petty-bourgeois state and various antagonistic classes (landlords and compradors on the one hand, workers and peasants on the other, as well as pressure from imperialist powers) significantly weakens these nationalist regimes and makes them politically vulnerable. Moreover, because of the highly unstable nature of this form of capitalist accumulation in the periphery, state-capitalist regimes have ultimately been overpowered by imperialism and local reaction and transformed into neocolonial dependent states or have been overthrown by the working class through a socialist revolution.

As we have seen from the above analysis of the nature and dynamics of the state in the less-developed countries, the internal and external forces at work in defining the role of the state and the process of development in Latin America, Asia, Africa, and the Middle East has been a complex one over the long history of societies in these regions. The outcome of power relations within and between states in the process of state formation has been a formidable one characterized by social, political, and economic inequalities that have led to strife and struggle to transform the state and establish an egalitarian and just society that meets the needs of broad segments of the population. To this end, the masses the world over have waged a protracted struggle to bring about a state and society that is in line with their interests. The Arab Spring across North Africa and the Middle East is but the latest manifestation of this effort that is bound to spread around the world and become a viable force for social change and transformation in the twenty-first century.

Notes

1. This chapter draws heavily from my earlier study of class-state relations in the less-developed countries. See Berch Berberoglu, *The Internationalization of Capital* (New York: Praeger, 1987), Part 2. See also Berch Berberoglu, *The Political Economy of Development:*

Development Theory and the Prospects for Change in the Third World (Albany: State University of New York Press, 1992), Part 3.

2. Leo Panitch and Colin Leys, eds., *Global Capitalism Versus Democracy* (New York: Monthly Review Press, 1999).

3. On corporatist interpretations of the peripheral state, see Alfred Stepan, *The State and Society: Peru in Comparative Perspective* (Princeton: Princeton University Press, 1978). On bureaucratic authoritarianism, see Guillermo O'Donnell, *Modernization and Bureaucratic Authoritarianism: Studies in South American Politics* (Berkeley: Institute of International Studies, University of California at Berkeley, 1973) and O'Donnell, "Tensions in the Bureaucratic Authoritarian State and the Question of Democracy," in *The New Authoritarianism in Latin America,* ed. David Collier (Princeton: Princeton University Press, 1979). On the neofascist character of dependent states ruled by military dictatorships, see James Petras, *Class, State and Power in the Third World* (Montclair, NJ: Allanheld, Osmun, 1981), Chap. 7. For a discussion on the nature of the bureaucratic authoritarian and other forms of the dependent state, see Berch Berberoglu, *The Internationalization of Capital,* Chap. 7, and Berberoglu, "The Contradictions of Export-Oriented Development in the Third World," *Social and Economic Studies* 36, no. 4 (December 1987). Also see Martin Carnoy, *The State and Political Theory* (Princeton: Princeton University Press, 1984), Chap. 7.

4. On state-capitalism in the less-developed countries, see Berch Berberoglu, "The Nature and Contradictions of State Capitalism in the Third World," *Social and Economic Studies* 28, no. 2 (1980).

5. See Berch Berberoglu, *The Internationalization of Capital,* Chap. 7.

6. Stanley J. Stein and Barbara H. Stein, *The Colonial Heritage of Latin America* (New York: Oxford University Press, 1970).

7. Ibid.

8. Ernesto Laclau, "Feudalism and Capitalism in Latin America," *New Left Review,* no. 67 (May–June 1971).

9. Eric Williams, *Capitalism and Slavery* (New York: Capricorn, 1966).

10. This term refers to native-born Latin Americans of Spanish descent.

11. Andre Gunder Frank, *Capitalism and Underdevelopment in Latin America* (New York: Monthly Review Press, 1967).

12. Analysis of the evolution of U.S. direct investment in Latin American manufacturing industries reveals that capital held by parent companies rose from $780 million in 1950 to $4.2 billion in 1970 to $17.9 billion in 1988 to $46.1 billion in 1997 to $78.4 billion in 2010. U.S. Department of Commerce, *Survey of Current Business* (August 1989), 62; (July 1999), 56; and (July 2011), 139.

13. Atilio Boron, *State, Capitalism, and Democracy in Latin America* (Boulder, CO: Lynne Rienner Publishers, 1995).

14. See Sander Halebsky and Richard L. Harris, eds., *Capital, Power, and Inequality in Latin America* (Boulder, CO: Westview Press, 1995).

15. Ash Narain Roy, *The Third World in the Age of Globalization* (London: Zed Books, 1999).

16. See Anupam Sen, *The State, Industrialization, and Class Formations in India* (London: Routledge & Kegan Paul, 1982).

17. See Wan Habib, *The Agrarian System of Mughal India* (London: Asia Publishing House, 1963), 115.

18. Sen, *The State, Industrialization, and Class Formation in India,* 28.

19. Berch Berberoglu, ed., *India: National Liberation and Class Struggles* (Meerut: Sarup & Sons, 1985). See also Berch Berberoglu, ed., *Class, State, and Development in India* (Delhi: Sage Publications, 1992).

20. Sen, *The State, Industrialization, and Class Formation in India*.

21. Hamza Alavi, "India and the Colonial Mode of Production," *Economic and Political Weekly* (August 1975).

22. See Bipan Chandra, "The Indian Capitalist Class and Imperialism Before 1947," *Journal of Contemporary Asia* 5, no. 3 (1975).

23. A. L. Levkovsky, *Capitalism in India* (Delhi: People's Publishing House, 1966). See also Berberoglu, *Class, State, and Development in India*.

24. International Labour Office, Table 2E, *Yearbook of Labour Statistics, 1998* (Geneva: ILO, 1998), 311.

25. Paresh Chattopadhyay, "Some Trends in India's Capitalist Industrialization," in *Class, State and Development in India,* ed. Berch Berberoglu (New Delhi: Sage Publications, 1992).

26. Frances V. Moulder, *Japan, China and the Modern World Economy* (Cambridge: Cambridge University Press, 1977), 60–62.

27. Ibid., 98–127.

28. See Sam Wynn, "The Taiwanese 'Economic Miracle,'" *Monthly Review* 33, no. 11 (April 1982); Clive Hamilton, "Capitalist Industrialization in East Asia's Four Little Tigers," *Journal of Contemporary Asia* 13, no. 1 (1983); Charles W. Lindsey, "The Philippine Economy," *Monthly Review* 36, no. 11 (April 1985).

29. Thus, while large investments were made in the Indonesian oil industry, countries such as South Korea, Taiwan, Hong Kong, Singapore, and the Philippines came to serve as cheap labor reserves, and Hong Kong and Singapore took on additional roles as important financial and trade centers for the transnational corporations and banks. Moreover, South Korea, the Philippines, and Thailand took up the further strategic role of providing a military shield in the area for the expansion of the newly established export-oriented economies.

30. See Martin Landsberg, "Export-Led Industrialization in the Third World: Manufacturing Imperialism," *Review of Radical Political Economics* 11, no. 4 (Winter 1979). See also Bill Warren, *Imperialism, Pioneer of Capitalism* (London: Verso, 1980). Warren argues that imperialism, in the form of overseas investments, promotes the development of capitalism and capitalist relations, regardless of its point of origin and deformed character.

31. Berch Berberoglu, "The Contradictions of Export-Oriented Development in the Third World," *Social and Economic Studies* 36, no. 4 (December 1987).

32. Feudalism practiced in these regions, especially in the East, however, was based mainly on control of cattle, rather than of land, as in Europe.

33. See Richard Harris, ed., *The Political Economy of Africa* (Cambridge, MA: Schenkman, 1975).

34. Basil Davidson, *The African Slave Trade* (Boston: Little, Brown, 1961).

35. See Berch Berberoglu, "Pre-Capitalist Modes of Production: Their Origins, Contradictions, and Transformation," *Quarterly Review of Historical Studies* 19, nos. 1–2 (1980).

36. Colin Leys, *Underdevelopment in Kenya* (Berkeley: University of California Press, 1975); Mahmood Mamdani, *Politics and Class Formation in Uganda* (New York: Monthly Review Press, 1976).

37. For a fuller discussion on this, see Berberoglu, "The Contradictions of Export-Oriented Development in the Third World," 106–110.

38. Berberoglu, *The Internationalization of Capital*, Chap. 5.

39. This was the allocation of parcels of conquered lands to *sipahis* (rural cavalry with military and administrative functions in the provinces) and to the civilian sector of the *devşirmes* (top officials of the central bureaucracy) in the form of fiefs (*timar*). The *sipahis* and the civilian *devşirmes* were given these lands for the purpose of administering them in the name of the state. This system of land allocation was put into effect during the reign of Süleyman I and continued for quite some time.

40. As the central state began gradually to lose its authority in the countryside, however, the *sipahis* and other fief holders increasingly evaded their obligations to the state and attempted to take over the ownership of state lands. In reaction to these developments, realizing that the old rural military-administrative system had outlived its usefulness, the state moved against the *sipahis* and displaced them. This was done, above all, by the introduction of tax farming (*iltizam*).

41. Although private property in land and feudal relations of production began to develop in the Ottoman formation in the seventeenth century and rapidly expanded and surpassed that owned by the state in many parts of the empire by the eighteenth century, the feudal lords were never able to overthrow the central state and exert political domination over the empire's affairs. Nevertheless, in one instance at least, a rebellion by the landlords led by Mehmet Ali Paşa, the governor of Egypt, in the late nineteenth century nearly succeeded, but the rebellion was put down with the aid of the French and British armies. The *ayans* nevertheless continued to exercise economic control over vast areas of the empire.

42. Samir Amin, *The Arab Nation: Nationalism and Class Struggles* (London: Zed Press, 1978).

43. Mahmoud Hussain, *Class Conflict in Egypt, 1945–1970* (New York: Monthly Review Press, 1973).

44. See Mark Cooper, "Egyptian State Capitalism in Crisis," in *The Middle East*, eds. Talal Asad and Roger Owen (New York: Monthly Review Press, 1983).

45. Joel Beinin, "Egypt's Transition under Nasser," *MERIP Reports*, no. 107 (July–August 1982).

46. Jim Paul, "Foreign Investment in Egypt," *MERIP Reports*, no. 107 (July–August 1982); U.S. Department of Commerce, StatUSA, *Country Commerce Guide: Egypt*, FY 2000 (available online).

47. See Joe Stork, "Iraq and the War in the Gulf," *MERIP Reports*, no. 97 (June 1981): 5.

48. Ibid.; Hanna Batatu, *The Old Social Classes and the Revolutionary Movements of Iraq* (Princeton: Princeton University Press, 1978).

49. Majid Khadduri, *Republican Iraq* (London, 1969); Patrick Clawson, "The Internationalization of Capital and Capital Accumulation in Iran and Iraq," *Insurgent Sociologist* 7, no. 2 (Spring 1977).

50. Berch Berberoglu, *Turmoil in the Middle East: Imperialism, War, and Political Instability* (Albany: State University of New York Press, 1999), Chap. 7.

51. See Fred Halliday, *Iran: Dictatorship and Development* (New York: Penguin, 1979).

52. Ervand Abrahamian, *Iran: Between Two Revolutions* (Princeton: Princeton University Press, 1982). See also Eric *Hooglund, Land and Revolution in Iran, 1960–1980* (Austin: University of Texas Press, 1982).

53. Farideh Farhi, "Class Struggles, the State, and Revolution in Iran," in *Power and Stability in the Middle East*, ed. Berch Berberoglu (London: Zed Books, 1989), 90–113. See also

John Foran, ed., *A Century of Revolution: Social Movements in Iran* (Minneapolis: University of Minnesota Press, 1994).

54. See Mansoor Moaddel, *Class, Politics, and Ideology in the Iranian Revolution* (New York: Columbia University Press, 1993).

55. See *MERIP Reports*, no. 98 (July–August 1981).

56. See Saeed Rahnema and Sohrab Behdad, eds., *Iran After the Revolution: Crisis of an Islamic State* (London: I.B. Tauris, 1995).

57. Ahmad Ashraf, "Bazaar and Mosque in Iran's Revolution," *MERIP Reports,* no. 113 (March–April, 1983): 16–18.

58. Ervand Abrahamian, *Tortured Confessions: Prisons and Public Recantations in Modern Iran* (Berkeley: University of California, 1999).

Chapter 7

The State, Social Movements, and Revolution on a Global Scale

SOCIAL MOVEMENTS HAVE EMERGED and struggled against authoritarian and despotic states long before the Arab Spring of 2011 succeeded in overthrowing a series of dictatorships across North Africa and the Middle East. But the determined struggle of the masses in this otherwise socially conservative region of the world has inspired the oppressed across the globe to such an extent that even traditionally apolitical countries like the United States, as well as politically advanced ones like Greece, have erupted in social protests and uprisings threatening the foundations of capitalist states to an extent that it has led to the unleashing of the powers of the state—the police and the military—to crush these movements in the name of law and order—that is, the established social order—to cripple the will of the masses. Movements struggling against repressive states that advance the interests of the wealthy owners of capital over the interests of the great majority have become empowered to rise up in revolution to bring about social transformations across the globe.[1]

This chapter provides an analysis of the conditions that lead to the emergence and development of social movements struggling to bring about transformation of the global capitalist system. It examines the origins, nature, dynamics, and challenges of social movements as they struggle to transform the prevailing social, economic, and political system. After a brief theoretical discussion on the conditions leading to the development of social movements, the chapter explores the dynamics of movement organization and mobilization with examples of concrete cases of social movements that have succeeded in taking state power through a revolution. Likewise, similar recent mobilization, protests, and uprisings by various social movements are leading to protracted struggles to topple entrenched ruling classes that have held on to state power for decades. The significance of the success of the Arab Spring is more for its inspirational value across the globe than the simple replacement of dictatorships in favor of elections to secure civilian, multi-party rule. It is for this reason that the rebellions across North Africa and the Middle East have had a ripple effect in triggering similar uprisings in other countries when millions across the world have shed their fears and found their way to express their will through collective political action.

Historical Background

Many diverse social movements have emerged and developed in different societies throughout history. Some of these movements have developed spontaneously and without any prior preparation in terms of organization, strategy, and tactics, such as slave rebellions in Ancient Rome and peasant revolts in medieval Germany. Uprisings have occurred in despotic empires, just as they have under slavery, feudalism, and other exploitative systems, where states ruled by despots, slave masters, and landlords have often crushed such attempts against the existing order and prevented the oppressed and exploited from coming to power. But they have not always succeeded in keeping the masses down. There have been instances when the oppressed have risen and put up a determined fight, and occasionally won, through a series of rebellions and revolutions that have brought about social transformations across the globe.

In the transition from feudalism to capitalism in Europe and elsewhere, a variety of social movements have come to challenge existing states and have transformed them to serve the interests of the victorious classes that have succeeded in taking state power. Among these we find the bourgeois revolutions of the seventeenth and eighteenth centuries, when the nascent national bourgeoisies of Europe rose up in arms to smash the old (feudal) system and to rule over society by unfurling the great industrial capitalist revolutions across the continent, facilitating the accumulation of private capital through the exploitation of wage labor.[2] The surplus value generated by wage-labor translating into profits, assured the domination of moneyed wealth of the capitalist class that now came to hold state power to advance its own interests against that of the landlords, peasants, and workers. Thus, the rule of capital and the capitalist state was established in Europe, followed by a similar development in North America, where slavery and the rule of the slaveowners were replaced by that of the capitalists after the victory of the latter in the Civil War that brought them to power in the United States in the late nineteenth century.[3]

The domination of society by the new ruling classes in Europe and North America under conditions of capitalist production and exchange that rested on the exploitation of wage labor meant that this fundamental contradiction of the capitalist system on which the entire system was based would sooner or later lead to rebellions and revolutions by the working class against the capitalist state, to liberate the workers through a socialist revolution that would overthrow capitalism and replace it with an egalitarian socialist system. The history of the labor movement in Europe and the United States is replete with struggles to organize and mobilize workers to wage a determined fight against the capitalist system.[4] Many of the benefits that organized labor has secured from the system have been the result of such struggles over many decades. While the balance of class forces in the class struggle under capitalism came close to (but did not quite result in) workers taking state power to transform society during the Great Depression in Europe and the United States; they did succeed, however, in Russia earlier in the twentieth century through the Great October Socialist Revolution in 1917, and in China in the mid twentieth century through the October Revolution in 1949, as well as elsewhere, including anti-imperialist national liberation movements in the third world in which labor played an important role (e.g., Cuba, Angola, Mozambique, Vietnam, and Nicaragua, to name a few) later in the twentieth century.[5]

Some of these movements succeeded to take state power despite the unrelenting imperialist onslaught to crush them, while others failed, facing the counter-revolutionary machinations of imperialist subversion (e.g., the Contra war in Nicaragua, the civil war in El Salvador, and the fascist military coups in Chile and Argentina, as well as the toppling of communism in the Soviet Union and Eastern Europe at century's end). Ironically, a few decades later, a number of these failed movements were able to regroup and retake state power and survive (as in Chile, Argentina, Nicaragua, and El Salvador), thanks in large part to the military entanglements of U.S. imperialism around the world. Others, such as Venezuela, Bolivia, Ecuador, Uruguay, and several other Latin American countries, as well as Brazil, led by grassroots people's movements, have taken a critical path and turned to the left, adopting policies that are contrary to neoliberalism and more in line with the interests of the great majority of the people in these countries. We will have more to say about some of these movements later in this chapter, but first we must examine the factors contributing to the formation of social movements in capitalist society under conditions of globalization.

Factors Leading to the Emergence of Social Movements

Much has been written on the factors contributing to the emergence and development of social movements and revolution. The conditions leading to the rise of social movements that challenge the established order are both objective and subjective. The objective conditions include the prevailing class structure of society (the prevalence of dominant and oppressed classes), the political structure and the nature of the state, and existing social and economic conditions. The subjective conditions include the level of class consciousness among the oppressed classes; the emergence of leading figures, organizations, and political parties of the oppressed; the response of the government and the ruling class; and the balance of class forces and mass mobilization. In considering the opposing forces engaged in class struggle, it is important to know the nature and composition of the dominant ruling class, including its various fractions, who (which fraction of the dominant class) the state represents, who the oppressed classes are that want to overthrow the established order, and what the class alliances are in the revolutionary movement poised to take state power.

Howard J. Sherman and James Wood provide a list of conditions required before a social movement can emerge:

(1) *Social structural conditions* must lead to certain stresses and strains between classes or other groups in society. This can occur as a result of economic and political crises in society, or as an outcome of general decline and decay of society and societal institutions that affect various classes, leading to conflict between them;

(2) Objective economic, political, or social *deprivation,* resulting from the structural conditions, must occur. This means that the unfolding crises in society are affecting an important segment of society in a negative way, leading to a decline in their standard of living;

(3) These objective deprivations must lead to *conscious feelings of deprivation,* which will crystallize into an ideology. Here, the increasing awareness of one's condition conveyed by the gravity of the situation transformed into consciousness leads to the formation of an ideology that shows the way out of the crisis;

(4) This ideology must lead to the *organization* and *mobilization* of the discontented group to become a powerful political force that can bring about change. As such, the mobilization necessary to take political action becomes a critical component of the class struggle being waged to transform society;

(5) The structural conditions must also include *weakened social control* by the ruling class. Here, the depth of the societal crisis weakens the ability and the will of the powers that be to effectively control society;

(6) Given these five conditions, many kinds of *precipitating events* can lead to the emergence of a social movement. Such events can trigger mass protests and demonstrations that quickly translate into action and serve as a catalyst to bring about change.[6]

Sherman and Wood go on to argue that the above list of six conditions for social movements to occur flows from the prevailing social structure: society is built on a certain economic base—including both technical forces of production and social relations of production within the productive process. On each particular economic base arises a different kind of social and political superstructure, which includes both particular institutions—such as the family, schools, the government, and so on—as well as ideologies, and that these institutions and ideologies play a vital role in supporting and justifying the present economic arrangements.[7]

Albert J. Szymanski in his book *The Capitalist State and the Politics of Class* provides additional insight into this process and argues that the material conditions necessary for the emergence of social movements and social revolution in capitalist society must include the following:

(1) *Felt oppression:* The oppression of the working class and the other non-privileged classes is increasingly felt to be unnecessary and intolerable (as the technological and social possibilities of living differently become more apparent).

(2) *Decline of the ruling class's ideological hegemony:* The ideological hegemony of the capitalist class spontaneously breaks down, as the masses become increasingly bitter and disillusioned with their present existence. The capitalist class itself becomes cynical about its ability and right to rule. It increasingly resorts to manipulation to preserve its rule. Internally, it becomes increasingly divided and demoralized, and hence incapable of adequately dealing with the movements of the oppressed.

(3) *The failure of non-revolutionary solutions to a social crisis:* The various alternative solutions being offered as solutions to the oppression of the working classes and other oppressed groups (such as nationalism, fascism, liberal reformism, social democracy, etc.) lose credibility among the oppressed as these solutions reveal themselves to be bankrupt (that is, incapable of actually relieving the oppression of the masses).

(4) *Decline of the ruling class's ability to solve a social crisis and counter the growth of revolutionary movements:* The ability of the ruling class to handle both a social crisis and a rising revolutionary movement is a product of its internal cohesion, the intensity of its belief in the legitimacy of its rule, and its willingness to use force when necessary. When a ruling class cannot unify around and implement a rational program to handle the crisis or the revolutionary movement,[8] it is likely to be overthrown.

(5) *Efficient organization and adoption of scientific strategy and theory by revolutionary movements:* In order to succeed, revolutionary movements create organizations that can mobilize the working class and other oppressed classes into a common united front, provide them with a realistic analysis of the causes of their oppression, a proposal about the historical alternatives, and a program to realize an alternative—that is, an organizational form, a strategy, and a set of tactics to make revolution.[9]

These five important conditions set the stage for the emergence and development of social movements under capitalism and facilitate the process that leads to revolution and social transformation, according to Szymanski. As these conditions stem from and are an outcome of capitalism, Szymanski concludes, "It is the contradictions of capitalism itself that generate the conditions for the development of movements designed to replace capitalism."[10]

Twentieth Century Social Revolutions

The twentieth century has seen the emergence and development of numerous social movements, and many of these movements have turned into full-blown social revolutions. The Mexican Revolution of 1910, as the first great peasant revolution of the twentieth century, had a major impact on all other subsequent rebellions and revolutions, as the peasants with the support of workers rose up to rid the feudal oligarchy that enslaved and oppressed them. The Russian Revolution of 1917—the first workers' revolution of the twentieth century—was not far behind, while Europe itself was embroiled in revolutionary fervor following the First World War. Whereas movements on the left came close to toppling some of the major capitalist states (e.g., Germany), the ruling capitalist classes were quick to respond with their own fascist regimes in Italy, Germany, and Spain, where civil wars across the continent divided states into rival forces that fought to impose their rule while crushing their enemies. This momentum of uprisings in various countries continued during the Great Depression and its aftermath, when ruling classes everywhere were challenged through the Second World War

We will in this section take up the Russian Revolution as a prime example of a socialist revolution in the twentieth century that succeeded in taking state power and had a great impact on all subsequent socialist revolutions in the twentieth century.

The Socialist Revolution in Russia

The Great October Socialist Revolution in Russia in 1917 marked the first successful proletarian revolution of the twentieth century that brought workers to state power. The socialist revolution in Russia, led by the Bolshevik Party under the leadership of Vladimir I. Lenin, was the most fundamental social upheaval of modern times. It brought about a complete social transformation of Russian society from a semifeudal-semicapitalist state to a socialist one, stretching across a vast territory from Europe in the West through Central Asia to the Pacific Ocean in the East. It swept away Tsar Nicolas II's reign over the Russian Empire and thus brought to an end some three hundred years of the Romanov Dynasty. The October 1917 socialist revolution marked the victory of the Russian proletariat and set the stage for a new era of social transformation ushered in by this first socialist revolution of the twentieth century.

Russia in the early twentieth century was a semifeudal-semicapitalist society with strong roots in an agrarian economy based on the labor of peasants who accounted for upward of 80 percent of the population. While serfdom was officially abolished in 1861, the condition of the peasantry did not improve in any real sense, and they continued to struggle to hold on to what little they possessed. Most of them lived in extreme poverty and were under the whims of the dominant semifeudal tsarist state. With little to show in material wealth, they were also repressed by the authoritarian state tied to the wealthy landowners who kept them in their place. However, this unbearable situation generated a high level of discontent among the peasantry and played a key role in the revolutionary turmoil that subsequently developed.[11]

The situation in the urban areas was not much better. While there was substantial development in commercial and industrial activity to move Russia along the capitalist path, the level of economic development was still quite low and the condition of the relatively small working class was no more than a notch above the impoverished peasantry. Workers were paid very low wages, had little protection in the factories and mines, and were under the constant watch of the repressive state and its police apparatus, especially in the repression of any trade union and organizing activity that would challenge the authority of the tsarist state.

While the formation of political parties was illegal through the end of the nineteenth century, a few managed to rally the support of workers and peasants into a strong political organization that became the driving force of the proletarian movement that later toppled the tsarist state. The Russian Social Democratic Party—which in 1903 split into the Bolshevik and Menshevik wings over strategy and tactics of the movement, its leadership, and views of the transition to a socialist society—played a central role in the developing revolutionary situation that moved Russia through the events of the first two decades of the twentieth century, most notably the political revolution of 1905 and the February and October revolutions of 1917.

The critical event that precipitated the developments surrounding the rebellion in 1905 occurred early in the year. On January 9, 1905, remembered in Russian history as Bloody Sunday, some fifty to sixty thousand workers marched to the Winter Palace to deliver a petition to Tsar Nicholas II, listing grievances regarding working conditions.[12] However, rather than meeting with the workers to address their grievances, "the tsar had his soldiers fire on the workers, killing thousands. This led to strikes and peasant protests throughout Russia."[13] Moreover, "The tsar sent the army into areas where rebellion was still occurring and had thousands of people shot; thousands of others were deported from the country."[14]

The period following the events of 1905 and the subsequent reforms, which failed to produce any lasting changes (in fact, most of these reforms were subverted by the government to prolong autocratic rule), can be characterized as a period of increasing political instability and crisis:

> Between 1905 and 1917, Russia remained a deeply divided and extremely contentious society. Unrest continued, as did revolutionary activism. Indeed, both intensified. In February of 1917 there were large-scale strikes by industrial workers in many cities. Troops were dispatched to Petrograd (formerly St. Petersburg) to disperse the large crowd that had assembled there, but the majority of soldiers refused to fire on the protesters, and, indeed, many joined forces with them. Lacking the military support it needed, the tsar's regime, already severely weakened through its involvement in World War I, lost its capacity to rule. Nicolas was forced to abdicate on March 16 and was put under house arrest.[15]

The Provisional Government that followed was made up of dominant class forces and could not reverse the deteriorating political situation. Led by Alexandr Kerensky, the Provisional Government failed to gain the legitimacy it needed to stay in power and thus was rejected by broad segments of the laboring population. In contrast, the Bolsheviks, led by Lenin, became more and more the key political organ that challenged Kerensky's bourgeois regime:

> Lenin ... saw the Provisional Government as representing the interests of the bourgeoisie and argued that another revolution was needed, a true Marxian proletarian revolution. In the months to follow, he was successful at pushing his fellow Bolsheviks into an increasingly hard-line position. Moreover, the Bolsheviks were attracting followers at an extraordinary rate. From at best 24,000 Bolsheviks at the time of the February Revolution, their numbers increased to over 100,000 by the end of April and to approximately 350,000 by October.[16]

With the decline in the ability of the Provisional Government to remain in control of the developing revolutionary situation on one hand, and the increasing ranks of the Bolsheviks, who succeeded in building a mass base to wage an all-out war to take state power, on the other, the fate of Russia was becoming more and more evident in the period leading to the events that were to come a few months later. "By the end of September," writes Sanderson, "the Bolsheviks had become a majority in the soviets of both Petrograd and Moscow, helping Lenin to reach the conclusion that it was time for the Bolsheviks to overthrow the Provisional Government and seize power themselves."[17]

This leads Tim McDaniel to conclude:

> Throughout 1917, confronted with deteriorating economic conditions and the continuation of the war, the urban working class increasingly came to regard class conflict irreconcilable. The workers therefore rejected compromise and opposed any government that sought to reconcile the interests of workers and industrialists. By October, in their overwhelming majority, they were willing to support the only party, the Bolsheviks, that advocated a workers' government to rule in their interests.[18]

The speed with which the revolutionary situation was unfolding gave the Bolsheviks the confidence that they were on the verge of a revolution in the making:

> On the evening of October 24, a group of soldiers, sailors, and workers followed the order of Trotsky—who had recently been released from prison and became the leader of the Bolsheviks in the absence of Lenin—to take control of several transportation and communication centers, as well as the Winter Palace of the tsar. The insurrectionists occupied the telegraph offices and railway stations,

and set up roadblocks on bridges. There was little resistance by military personnel, few of whom continued to recognize the legitimate authority of the Provisional Government, and thus little bloodshed. The Provisional Government was toppled by the next day, and its head, Kerensky, fled.[19]

A revolution had thus taken place, and the proletariat and its political organ, the Bolshevik Party, had taken state power to usher in the rule of the working class under communist leadership, a development that was to set the stage for post-revolutionary transformation of Russian society, but not before a three-year-long bloody civil war.

The socialist revolution in Russia provided an example and set the stage for all other socialist revolutions yet to come in the twentieth century. The Chinese, the Vietnamese, the Cuban, the Nicaraguan, and other great revolutions of the past century were inspired by the victory of the working class in Russia under the leadership of the Bolsheviks and their Marxist ideology to establish a socialist society. It is through this legacy of achieving socialism through a proletarian revolution that the memory and example of the Great October Socialist Revolution in Russia lives on for future generations of Marxist revolutionaries.

Social Movements of the Late Twentieth and Early Twenty-First Centuries

The emergence of the people's movements during the 1960s—when the civil rights, women's, antiwar, peace, student, environmental, and other related progressive movements coalesced—led to the many gains that these movements were able to secure through collective political action. The lull of the 1970s and 1980s reversed these trends, and a period of resignation set in under the right-wing, conservative forces in power led by Reaganism in the United States and Thatcherism in the United Kingdom, as well as right-wing dictatorships that came to power elsewhere during this period (e.g., in Chile and Argentina in the mid 1970s; in Egypt, Iran, Turkey, the Philippines, and others in the late 1970s or early 1980s; and across Eastern Europe at the end of the 1980s, when anticommunist counterrevolutions in Hungary, Poland, the Czech Republic, East Germany, Romania, Bulgaria, and later in the Soviet Union in the early 1990s shifted power away from communism and toward the capitalist West), which seemed to bring an end to the radical social movements of the previous periods. But, merely three years after the collapse of the Soviet Union in 1991, the first "postmodern rebellion"[20] erupted in Chiapas, in the hinterland of Mexico, led by the Zapatista National Liberation Army and its leader Subcommandante Marcos, in response to the signing of the North American Free Trade Agreement (NAFTA), which they argued would devastate the small impoverished peasantry. This unexpected people's rebellion signaled the rise of the first organized mass struggle against neoliberal globalization in Latin America, across the border from the United States.[21] This was followed by a series of protests and demonstrations against global capitalism that had by then come to dominate the policies and practices of many states around the world.[22]

The World Social Forum (WSF) and other similar organizations led efforts to build global solidarity focused on issues related to the effects of neoliberal globalization. The first meeting of the WSF took place in 2001 in Porto Alegre, Brazil, with some 15,000 participants from 117 countries; by the 2005 meetings, there were 155,000 participants from 135 countries. Since then, the WSF has met at various venues each year and engaged in movement activities that involve tens of thousands of activists at hundreds of grassroots organizations that are part of a global political network operating across the world.[23]

Neoliberalism was first practiced in Latin America, then in Indonesia and other Asian states, and finally in the Middle East (from its earlier beginnings in Turkey in the 1980s through its apex in the 1990s reinforced by the first Gulf War of 1991, and subsequently through the Bush doctrine of preemptive strike, unveiling the "vision" for the so-called New American Century, which prepared the ideological groundwork for the subsequent invasion of Afghanistan and Iraq). The right-wing offensive of the 1990s (even under a democratic president, Bill Clinton) included the NATO-led and U.S.-financed bombing of Yugoslavia and covert operations in Kosovo and Bosnia, in effect the partition and dismantling of former Yugoslavia.[24] Nevertheless, undeterred from the machinations of the powerful imperial states, especially that of the United States, the people's movements around the world once again went into action to protest against capitalist globalization—from Seattle to Prague, Quebec City, Genoa, Barcelona, Washington, DC, and other cities around the globe—to counter capitalist domination of the world under the auspices of the transnational corporations, the World Trade Organization (WTO), the World Bank (WB), the International Monetary Fund (IMF), and other supportive institutions of the advanced capitalist states.[25]

These protests, which were quite successful in disrupting the WTO meetings and derailing corporate efforts to impose their policies on the people, reached new heights when over 15 million people across the globe protested against the planned U.S. invasion of Iraq. Despite these efforts, the United States went ahead and invaded Iraq anyway, unleashing a reign of terror through its savage attack to destroy both Afghanistan and Iraq with its "shock and awe" assault using tomahawk and cruise missiles and bombs backed by some 150,000 troops—against

Afghanistan to overthrow the government of the Taliban and pursue Osama Bin Laden and al-Qaeda, and against Iraq for its alleged "weapons of mass destruction" and links to al-Qaeda.[26] While it succeeded in leveling both countries and killing their leaders (including Saddam Hussein and other high-ranking government officials in Iraq, and some of the top leadership of al-Qaeda, including Osama bin Laden) in retaliation for the 9/11 attacks on the World Trade Center, the U.S. response ended up costing the American people more than five thousand U.S. troops' lives, tens of thousands of wounded and injured soldiers, and over a trillion dollars spent in an imperial occupation lasting nearly a decade in Iraq and continuing into its twelfth year in Afghanistan, with the death toll in Iraq alone more than a million (mostly civilians), with tens of thousands more dead in Afghanistan.

The military misadventures of U.S. imperialism under the second Bush Administration (which continued under President Obama), leading to the biggest increase in the federal debt (over $16 trillion in 2012), together with the mortgage crisis and the collapse of big banks and financial institutions on Wall Street, were a major contributor of the great recession that sank the U.S. economy—and with it the global economy—into the deepest and most severe recession since the Great Depression of the 1930s.[27] This "Rambo imperialism" of the declining American Empire, coupled with the corrupt practices of high finance, has devastated the people of the United States while enriching the defense contractors, oil companies, and the big banks and their cronies at an enormous cost to the American people, who will carry the burden of a declining and collapsing empire for generations to come.[28]

The global capitalist crisis of 2008, which entered its fifth year in 2012, has devastated the economies and societies of many countries across the globe, especially those most severely affected by the sovereign debt crisis in Europe (Greece, Spain, Portugal, Ireland, and Italy). And this has led to a crisis of the Euro-zone, affecting the very stability of the European Union (E.U.) itself. The deepening recession in the E.U. and the depression in Greece, Spain, and other countries in Europe's periphery have led to the mobilization of millions of working people who are fighting back against the austerity measures that are being imposed on them. And the expanding mass protests and struggles of working people in these countries are galvanizing the popular social movements to wage battle against the capitalist state—a development that has immense political implications for the situation in Europe.[29]

Elsewhere across the globe, most notably in North Africa and the Middle East, the people are fighting back to regain their lost power and are determined to take back their countries from the ruling classes that have used despots to maintain power and keep the people in check. In Tunisia, Egypt, Yemen, Bahrain, Libya, and Syria, the people have risen up and are in the midst of a revolutionary situation, and have toppled, or are in the process of toppling, regimes and rulers across this region, an unprecedented scenario in the history of the Middle East.[30] The Arab Spring of 2011 across the Middle East has ushered in a period of mass rebellion and revolution that will have major political repercussions across many regions of the world in the coming years.

In North America, the anti-WTO and anticorporate globalization demonstrations in Seattle in 1999 and Toronto in 2010 became the training grounds for the Occupy Wall Street movement of 2011, which mobilized hundreds of thousands of people across twenty states and hundreds of cities throughout the United States and in eighty countries around the world. The biggest and most vocal protest movement of recent times, the Occupy Wall Street movement was no doubt inspired by the Arab Spring and the people's struggles across the globe and became a symbol of the struggle against the big banks, corporations, and the capitalist class (the top 1 percent of the population) who raked in billions of dollars in profits, while a large segment of the 99 percent struggles to survive in the midst of a capitalist crisis that has devastated the lives of millions of people across the globe. Clearly, the millionaires and billionaires have seen their wealth and income grow and expand during these depressionary times, while millions of working people have lost their jobs, foreclosed and been thrown out of their homes, are without health care, and are in desperate conditions. It is this tragic situation that has finally forced people to the streets to fight back and reclaim their communities, their government, and their country.

As social movements emerge, develop, and expand, the necessity for organized collective political action becomes more and more evident. And as the material conditions of life under capitalism deteriorate and the situation becomes unbearable, more and more people are bound to come together to express their frustration and anger to force the state to meet their needs—a demand that the state cannot meet as long as it remains dominated and controlled by big business (the capitalists). Therein one faces both the problem *and* the solution to the crisis of capitalist society and the capitalist state: The capitalist crisis that has affected millions of working people in the United States and the rest of the world cannot be resolved without a thorough transformation of capitalist society. And this transformation requires the full democratic participation of working people, who must gain control of the state so that the government can become a people's government—a "government of the people, by the people, and for the people"!

Notes

1. Valentine M. Moghadam, *Globalization and Social Movements* (Lanham, MD: Rowman & Littlefield, 2009).

2. Rodney Hilton, *The Transition From Feudalism to Capitalism* (London: New Left Books, 1976). See also Kenneth Neill Cameron, *Humanity and Society: A World History* (New York: Monthly Review Press, 1977).

3. Herbert Aptheker, *The Unfolding Drama: Studies in U.S. History* (New York: International Publishers, 1978). See also Charles Beard and Mary Beard, *The Rise of American Civilization* (New York: Macmillan, 1930).

4. Richard Boyer and Herbert Morais, *Labor's Untold Story*, 3rd ed. (New York: United Electrical, Radio, and Machine Workers of America, 1980).

5. Berch Berberoglu, *The State and Revolution in the Twentieth Century: Major Social Transformations of Our Time* (Lanham, MD: Rowman & Littlefield, 2007), esp. Chap. 3.

6. Howard Sherman and James Wood, *Sociology* (New York: Harper Collins, 1989), Chap. 18.

7. Ibid.

8. This could occur because of a loss at war, the disaffection of many upper-class youth and their rejection of upper-class traditions, widespread corruption, encroaching decadence and loss of will, or demoralizing internal antagonisms that cannot be contained by a strong sense of class solidarity.

9. Albert J. Szymanski, *The Capitalist State and the Politics of Class* (Cambridge, MA: Winthrop, 1978), 293–318.

10. Ibid., 294.

11. Stephen K. Sanderson, *Revolutions: A Worldwide Introduction to Political and Social Change* (Boulder, CO: Paradigm Publishers, 2005), 26–27.

12. Tim McDaniel, "The Russian Revolution of 1917: Autocracy and Modernization" in *Revolutions: Theoretical, Historical, and Comparative Studies*, 3rd ed., ed. Jack A. Goldstone (Belmont, CA: Wadsworth/Thomson Learning, 2003), 187.

13. Sanderson, *Revolutions*, 29.

14. Ibid., 30.

15. Ibid.

16. Ibid., 31.

17. Ibid., 32.

18. McDaniel, "The Russian Revolution of 1917," 188.

19. Sanderson, *Revolutions*, 32.

20. R. Burbach, "Roots of the Postmodern Rebellion in Chiapas," *New Left Review* 1, no. 205 (May–June 1994).

21. Neil Harvey, *The Chiapas Rebellion: The Struggle for Land and Democracy* (Durham: Duke University Press, 1998).

22. James Petras and Henry Veltmeyer, *Social Movements in Latin America* (New York: Palgrave-Macmillan, 2011).

23. See Jackie Smith, et al., *Global Democracy and the World Social Forums* (Boulder, CO: Paradigm, 2008), xi–xii, 3–4; and Moghadam, *Globalization and Social Movements*, 106.

24. Michael Parenti, *To Kill A Nation: The Attack on Yugoslavia* (London: Verso, 2002).

25. Martin Orr, "The Struggle Against Capitalist Globalization: The Worldwide Protests Against the WTO" in *Globalization and Change: The Transformation of Global Capitalism*, ed. Berch Berberoglu (Lanham, MD: Lexington Books, 2005). See also Jackie Smith, "Globalizing Resistance: The Battle of Seattle and the Future of Social Movements," in *Globalizing Resistance: Transnational Dimensions of Social Movements*, eds. Jackie Smith and H. Johnston (Lanham, MD: Rowman & Littlefield, 2002).

26. Berch Berberoglu, *Globalization of Capital and the Nation-State: Imperialism, Class Struggle, and the State in the Age of Global Capitalism* (Lanham, MD: Rowman & Littlefield, 2003), 75–82.

27. See Berch Berberoglu, ed., *Beyond the Global Capitalist Crisis: The World Economy in Transition* (Farnham, UK: Ashgate, 2012), 1–15.

28. See Scott Forsyth, "Evil Empire: Spectacle and Imperialism in Hollywood," in *The Socialist Register 1987* (New York: Monthly Review Press, 1987), 97–115. See also Steven Podovsky, "Rambo is a Big, Lumbering Metaphor for U.S. Imperialism," *Socialist Worker Online*, Issue 2090 (March 1, 2008). Available at www.socialistworker.co.uk/art.php?id=14250.

29. Mike-Frank Epitropoulos, "The Global Capitalist Crisis and the European Union, with Focus on Greece," in *Beyond the Global Capitalist Crisis: The World Economy in Transition*, ed. Berch Berberoglu (Farnham, UK: Ashgate Publishing, 2012), 83–101.

30. James Petras and Henry Veltmeyer, *Beyond Neoliberalism: A World to Win* (Farnham, UK: Ashgate, 2011), 175–197.

Chapter 8

Conclusion

WE CAN DRAW A NUMBER OF CONCLUSIONS from the analysis presented in this book. First, it is clear that the state has come to play an increasingly important role in a large number of societies around the world over an extended historical period that spans many centuries. Indeed, in class societies, the state has played a central role not only as the prime superstructural institution but also as the political organ reinforcing the class rule of the dominant class, hence the dominant mode of production. Moreover, its monopoly of force and violence has, in certain periods, given the state considerable independence, thus giving it extraordinary powers over society.

The major classical and contemporary conventional and critical theories in political sociology have provided alternative answers on the nature and role of the state and have attempted to develop a theory of the state and politics that would explain the form and content of the state as a key institution of modern society. We have in this book examined the central arguments of each perspective and their variants at length, and provided a critique of their formulations on the state.

We have shown that classical and contemporary conventional theories of the state fall far short of providing a complete and accurate analysis of the *real* nature of the state and its relation to class forces in society, although elements of their approach correspond to *appearances* of power relations in the bureaucratic organizations of society. In fact, the pronouncements of conventional theories are highly ideological and end up being not much more than an apologetic rationalization for varied forms of the capitalist state.

In contrast to these dominant theoretical positions in political sociology, we have counterposed classical and contemporary critical theories of the state and their variants, and have provided a critical analysis of the state based on the concepts and perspectives provided by the Marxist classics.

In line with this approach, we have argued that the state is a product of class divisions and class struggles lodged in the dominant mode of production, which, once articulated through the state, become politicized and take on the form of political struggles (i.e., struggles for state power). Moreover, under capitalism, the state as a rule remains the political organ of the dominant capitalist class and represents the interests of that class, except when such rule is challenged by forces whose interests run counter to the interests of this class and the state that it controls. Thus, short of a major shift in the balance of class forces and centers of political power effected through a social revolution, which would bring about a major restructuring of the state apparatus and dominant class linkages to the state, the actions of the state must be seen within the context of its ultimate control by the dominant capitalist class, which, by necessity, gives the state a degree of autonomy to serve capitalist class interests and capitalism in general. As such, the state in this context cannot be viewed as being free of dominant class sanctions; rather, the state must be seen as responding to (but not against) the prevailing social-economic order, which places the ultimate limits on the state's actions.[1]

Applying the Marxist approach to the study of the state, we have examined the origins and development of the state from its early beginnings to the most recent period—tracing its history through Oriental despotism, slavery, feudalism, and capitalism. We have found that the state has not always existed; its prevalence is a recent occurrence, going back only a few thousand years out of the tens of thousands of years in human history. In fact, only in the past few hundred years has the state, as the supreme superstructural institution in society, become prevalent throughout the world. A few societies still exist in isolated parts of the world that govern themselves without a state. But the growth and expansion of capitalism over the past two hundred years has led to the expansion of the capitalist state across national boundaries, claiming for itself the "exclusive right" to dictate its terms across the globe.

The origins of the capitalist state go back to the transition from feudalism to capitalism in Western Europe from the sixteenth to the eighteenth century, when a dual process of capital accumulation, aided by overseas trade, led to the establishment of the great commercial and manufacturing firms that gave rise to the industrial capitalist class throughout the Continent by the late eighteenth century. Evolving at a different pace in different parts of Europe and later in the United States, this class acquired state power to serve and expand its own class interests. Across the Continent and throughout the colonies, bourgeois revolutions took hold of the state machine and turned it into an instrument of capital accumulation that consolidated capitalist class rule over large portions of the world, in time giving rise to monopolies, cartels, and trusts. Thus was established the mass-scale exploitation of labor across continents that fostered the capital accumulation process—a process that could not have been fully realized without the active participation of the capitalist state.

We have seen this in our analysis of the formation of the U.S. state in the late eighteenth century, and the subsequent development and consolidation of capitalist rule nationwide following the Civil War. Since then, U.S. capitalism has developed beyond its territorial boundaries, and with it the U.S. state has extended its power and dominance throughout the world. As U.S. capitalism reached its postwar prominence and brought forth greater demands on the state, this led to increased conflicts and crises that have become ever more difficult to resolve within the framework of the prevailing economic and political structure. The increasing dominance of the monopoly fraction within the state has made matters worse, as the U.S. state has become a direct tool of big business to protect the latter's narrow interests.[2]

The crisis of the U.S. state in the early twenty-first century has in part emerged as a result of the challenge to its global dominance; revolts and revolutions around the world, together with a variety of protest movements in the heartland of imperialism, have set limits to U.S. capitalist domination of the global economy and polity, giving rise to countervailing forces in the global class struggle, leading to the establishment of various postcolonial and socialist states. This, in turn, has generated movements and struggles in the imperial centers, from antiwar to anti–corporate globalization, to the Occupy Wall Street movement in the United States, as the exploited and oppressed classes have put up a determined and protracted struggle against capital and the capitalist state, a struggle that continues to intensify as the crisis of capitalism enters a new stage.

Contradictions of the newly formed capitalist states in Asia, Africa, Latin America, and the Middle East during the twentieth century are being manifested in conflicts and crises across the world and are leading to an intensification of the class struggle between the dominant class forces and the state on one side and the exploited classes on the other. The working class, the peasantry, and other popular sectors across the globe are beginning to take things into their own hands and bring an end to capitalist exploitation and the rule of the capitalist state.

The protracted class struggles of the working class under advanced capitalism, whatever their temporal intensity or form, together with the struggles of the laboring masses around the globe, indicate the march of history that indeed one day will yield results in favor of the working class in capturing state power and establishing a democratic workers' state. They will make the monopoly of force and violence of the state over society obsolete, so society, organized "on the basis of free and equal association of the producers," as one champion of the working class has proclaimed, "will put the whole state machinery where it will then belong—into the museum of antiquities, next to the spinning wheel and the bronze ax."[3] Then, and only then, will humanity finally free itself from the class oppression it has suffered under the heavy hand of the dominant classes and the state. Hence, the decisive transformation of the state will thus be an inevitable outcome of the class struggle that will lead to the victory of the working class, who will be the agent of change to bring about a just and egalitarian society that promotes genuine freedom and equality.

Notes

1. Here, the state, as the supreme political institution of society, is dependent on (and reacts to reinforce) the interests of the dominant class(es) in society—interests that are lodged in the mode of production.

2. As Poulantzas has come to agree with Miliband over the course of their debate on the capitalist state, the rise of monopoly in the twentieth century has allowed the monopoly fraction of the capitalist class to completely control the state and turn it into its tool to advance big business interests, convincing the state that big business is "too big to fail"—thus forcing the state to champion, defend, and protect monopoly capitalist (big business) interests over other fractions of capital, let alone the people in general. See Nicos Poulantzas, "Political Crisis and the Crisis of the State," in *Critical Sociology: European Perspectives,* ed. J. W. Freiberg (New York: Irvington, 1979), 374–381.

3. Friedrich Engels, *The Origin of the Family, Private Property and the State* (New York: International Publishers, 1972), 232.

Bibliography

Alavi, Hamza. 1982. "State and Class under Peripheral Capitalism." In *An Introduction to the Sociology of "Developing Societies,"* edited by H. Alavi and T. Shanin. London: Macmillan.

Althusser, Louis. 1971. "Ideology and Ideological State Apparatuses." *Lenin and Philosophy and Other Essays.* London: New Left Books, 127–186.

Althusser, Louis, and Etienne Balibar. 1968. *Reading Capital.* London: New Left Books.

Amin, Samir. 1974. *Accumulation on a World Scale.* New York: Monthly Review Press.

———. 1976. *Unequal Development: An Essay on the Social Formations of Peripheral Capitalism.* New York: Monthly Review Press.

———. 1997. *Capitalism in the Age of Globalization.* London: Zed Books.

Anderson, Perry. 1974. *Lineages of the Absolutist State.* London: New Left Books.

Angrist, Michelle Penner, ed. 2010. *Politics and Society in the Middle East.* Boulder, CO: Lynne Rienner Publishers.

———. 1974. *Passages from Antiquity to Feudalism.* London: New Left Books.

Aptheker, Herbert. 1960. *The American Revolution, 1763–1783.* New York: International Publishers.

———. 1976. *Early Years of the Republic.* New York: International Publishers.

Avineri, Shlomo. 1972. *Hegel's Theory of the Modern State.* Cambridge: Cambridge University Press.

Bacevic, Andrew. 2006. *The New American Militarism: How Americans Are Seduced by War.* New York: Oxford University Press.

———. 2008. *The Limits of Power.* New York: Metropolitan Books.

———. 2010. *Washington Rules: America's Path to Permanent War.* New York: Metropolitan Books.

Balibar, Etienne. 1977. *On the Dictatorship of the Proletariat.* London: New Left Books.

Baran, Paul, and Paul M. Sweezy. 1966. *Monopoly Capital.* New York: Monthly Review Press.

Barrow, C. W. 1993. *Critical Theories of the State: Marxist, Neo-Marxist, Post-Marxist.* Madison: University of Wisconsin Press.

Batatu, Hanna. 1978. *The Old Social Classes and the Revolutionary Movements of Iraq.* Princeton: Princeton University Press.

Beard, Charles. 1962. *An Economic Interpretation of the Constitution of the United States.* New York: Macmillan.

Beard, Charles, and Mary Beard. 1930. *The Rise of American Civilization.* New York: Macmillan.

Beinin, Joel. 1982. "Egypt's Transition under Nasser." *MERIP Reports,* no. 107 (July–August): 23–26.

Belov, Gennady. 1986. *What Is the State?* Moscow: Progress Publishers.

Bentley, Arthur. 1967. *The Process of Government*. Cambridge, MA: Belknap Press of Harvard University.

Berberoglu, Berch. 1977. "The Transition from Feudalism to Capitalism: The Sweezy-Dobb Debate." *Revista Mexicana de Sociologia* 39, no. 4 (October–December): 1323–1334.

———. 1980. "Pre-Capitalist Modes of Production: Their Origins, Contradictions, and Transformation." *Quarterly Review of Historical Studies* 19, nos. 1–2: 7–19.

———. 1986. *India: National Liberation and Class Struggles*. Meerut: Sarup & Sons.

———. 1987. *The Internationalization of Capital: Imperialism and Capitalist Development on a World Scale*. New York: Praeger.

———. 1989. *Power and Stability in the Middle East*. London: Zed Books.

———. 1992. *The Legacy of Empire: Economic Decline and Class Polarization in the United States*. New York: Praeger.

———. 1992. *Class, State, and Development in India*. Delhi: Sage Publications.

———. 1992. *The Political Economy of Development: Development Theory and the Prospects for Change in the Third World*. Albany: State University of New York Press.

———. 1992. *The Labor Process and Control of Labor*. New York: Praeger Publishers.

———. 1994. *Class Structure and Social Transformation*. Westport, CT: Praeger Publishers.

———. 1995. *The National Question: Nationalism, Ethnic Conflict, and Self-Determination*. Philadelphia: Temple University Press.

———. 1999. *Turmoil in the Middle East: Imperialism, War, and Political Instability*. Albany: State University of New York Press.

———. 2001. *Political Sociology: A Comparative/Historical Approach*, 2nd ed. Dix Hills, NY: General Hall.

———. 2002. *Labor and Capital in the Age of Globalization: The Labor Process and the Changing Nature of Work in the Global Economy*. Lanham, MD: Rowman & Littlefield.

———. 2003. *Globalization of Capital and the Nation-State: Imperialism, Class Struggle, and the State in the Age of Global Capitalism*. Lanham, MD: Rowman & Littlefield.

———. 2004. *Nationalism and Ethnic Conflict: Class, State, and Nation in the Age of Globalization*. Lanham, MD: Rowman & Littlefield.

———. 2005. *Globalization and Change: The Transformation of Global Capitalism*. Lanham, MD: Lexington Books.

———. 2007. *The State and Revolution in the Twentieth Century: Major Social Transformations of Our Time*. Lanham, MD: Rowman & Littlefield.

———. 2009. *Class and Class Conflict in the Age of Globalization*. Lanham, MD: Rowman & Littlefield.

———. 2010. *Globalization in the 21st Century: Labor, Capital, and the State on a World Scale*. New York: Palgrave Macmillan.

———. 2012. *Beyond the Global Capitalist Crisis: The World Economy in Transition*. Burlington, VT: Ashgate.

Bertramsen, Rene Brugge, J. P. F. Thomsen, and J. Torfing. 1991. *State, Economy, and Society*. London: Unwin Hyman.

Bivens, Josh. 2011. *Failure by Design: The Story Behind America's Broken Economy*. Ithaca, NY: ILR Press.

Block, Fred. 1977. "The Ruling Class Does Not Rule: Notes on the Marxist Theory of the State." *Socialist Review* 33 (May–June): 6–28.

———. 1978. "Class Consciousness and Capitalist Rationalization: A Reply to Critics." *Socialist Review*, no. 40–41 (July–October): 212–220.

———. 1996. *The Vampire State*. New York: The New Press.

Blum, William. 2000. *Rogue State: A Guide to the World's Only Superpower*. Monroe: Common Courage Press.

Boggs, Carl. 2010. *The Crimes of Empire*. London: Pluto Press.

Bookman, Ann, and Sandra Morgen, eds. 1987. *Women and Politics of Empowerment*. Philadelphia: Temple University Press.

Borkenau, Franz. 1937. "State and Revolution in the Paris Commune, the Russian Revolution, and the Spanish Civil War." *Sociological Review* 29, no. 41: 41–75.

Bonefeld, W. 1987. "Reformulation of State Theory." *Capital and Class* 33: 96–128.

Borón, Atilio. 1995. *State, Capitalism, and Democracy in Latin America*. Boulder, CO: Lynne Rienner Publishers.

Bose, Sugata, and Ayesha Jalal, eds. 1997. *Nationalism, Democracy, and Development*. New York: Oxford University Press.

Bottomore, T. B. 1966. *Elites and Society*. Baltimore: Penguin.

Boyer, Richard O., and Herbert M. Morais. 1980. *Labor's Untold Story*, 3rd ed. New York: United Electrical, Radio and Machine Workers of America.

Brass, Tom. 2005. "Late Antiquity as Early Capitalism?" *The Journal of Peasant Studies* 32, no. 1: 118–150.

Brenner, Johanna. 2000. *Women and the Politics of Class*. New York: Monthly Review Press.

Bromley, Simon. 2003. "Reflections on Empire, Imperialism and United States Hegemony." *Historical Materialism* 11, no. 3: 17–68.

Buechler, Steven M. 1999. *Social Movements in Advanced Capitalism*. New York: Oxford University Press.

Byres, Terence J. 2005. "Neoliberalism and Primitive Accumulation in Less Developed Countries." In *Neoliberalism*, edited by Alfredo Saad-Filho and Deborah Johnston. London: Pluto, 83–90.

Cameron, Kenneth Neill. 1977. *Humanity and Society: A World History*. New York: Monthly Review Press.

Camilleri, Joseph A., et al., eds. 1995. *The State in Transition: Reimagining Political Space*. Boulder, CO: Lynne Rienner Publishers.

Carnoy, Martin. 1984. *The State and Political Theory*. Princeton: Princeton University Press.

Carroll, William K. 2010. *The Making of a Transnational Capitalist Class*. London: Zed Press.

Castells, Manuel. 1980. *The Economic Crisis and American Society*. Princeton: Princeton University Press.

Chatterjee, Partha, ed. 1997. *State and Politics in India*. New York: Oxford University Press.

Chattopadhyay, Paresh. 1992. "India's Capitalist Industrialization." In *Class, State and Development in India*, edited by Berch Berberoglu. Delhi: Sage Publications, 141–156.

Childe, V. Gordon. 1971. *What Happened in History*. Baltimore: Penguin.

Choueiri, Youssef M., ed. 1994. *State and Society in Syria and Lebanon*. New York: St. Martin's Press.

Clarke, Simon. 1977. "Marxism, Sociology and Poulantzas's Theory of the State." *Capital and Class* 2: 1–31.

———, ed. 1990. *The State Debate*. Basingstoke, UK: Macmillan.

Clawson, Dan, Alan Neustad, and Mark Weller. 1998. *Dollars and Votes: How Business Campaign Contributions Subvert Democracy*. Philadelphia: Temple University Press.

Cockcroft, James D. 1999. *Mexico's Hope: An Encounter with Politics and History*. New York: Monthly Review Press.

Cooper, Mark. 1983. "Egyptian State Capitalism in Crisis." In *The Middle East,* edited by Talal Asad and Roger Owen. New York: Monthly Review Press, 77–90.

Cox, Ronald W., and Daniel Skidmore-Hess. 1999. *U.S. Politics and the Global Economy: Corporate Power, Conservative Shift.* Boulder, CO: Lynne Rienner Publishers.

Croetau, David. 1994. *Politics and the Class Divide: Working People and the Middle Class Left.* Philadelphia: Temple University Press.

Dahl, Robert. 1961. *Who Governs?* New Haven: Yale University Press.

———. 1967. *Pluralist Democracy in the United States: Conflict and Consensus.* Chicago: Rand McNally.

Dahms, Harry F., ed. 2000. *Transformations of Capitalism: Economy, Society, and the State in Modern Times.* New York: New York University Press.

Davenport, John. 2007. *The Age of Feudalism.* San Diego, CA: Lucent.

Davidson, Basil. 1961. *The African Slave Trade.* Boston: Little, Brown.

Devine, Jim. 1982. "The Structural Crisis of U.S. Capitalism." *Southwest Economy and Society* 6, no. 1 (Fall): 49–64.

Domhoff, G. William. 1967. *Who Rules America?* Englewood Cliffs, NJ: Prentice-Hall.

———. 1970. *The Higher Circles.* New York: Vintage.

———. 1979. *The Powers That Be.* New York: Random House.

———. 2010. *Who Rules America? Challenges to Corporate and Class Dominance,* 6th ed. New York: McGraw-Hill.

Doogan, Kevin. 2009. *New Capitalism? The Transformation of Work.* Cambridge: Polity.

Drake, Michael S. 2010. *Political Sociology for a Globalizing World.* London: Polity.

Draper, Hal. 1977. *Karl Marx's Theory of Revolution: State and Bureaucracy.* Parts 1 and 2. New York: Monthly Review Press.

Earle, E. M. 1966. *Turkey, The Great Powers, and the Baghdad Railway: A Study in Imperialism.* New York: Russell and Russell.

Easton, David. 1971. *The Political System.* New York: Knopf.

Eldersveld, Samuel J., and Hanes Walton Jr. 1999. *Political Parties in American Society.* New York: St. Martin's Press.

Eliasoph, Nina. 1998. *Avoiding Politics: How Americans Produce Apathy in Everyday Life.* Cambridge: Cambridge University Press.

Engels, Friedrich. 1972. *The Origin of the Family, Private Property and the State.* New York: International Publishers.

———. 1976. *Anti-Duhring.* New York: International Publishers.

Ersson, Svante O. 1998. *Politics and Society in Western Europe.* Thousand Oaks, CA: Sage Publications.

Esping-Andersen, Gosta, Roger Friedland, and Erik Olin Wright. 1976. "Modes of Class Struggle and the Capitalist State." *Kapitalistate,* nos. 4–5 (Summer): 186–220.

Evans, Geoffrey, ed. 1999. *The End of Class Politics?* New York: Oxford University Press.

Ewen, Lynda Ann. 1998. *Social Stratification and Power in America.* New York: General Hall.

Faulks, Keith. 2000. *Political Sociology: A Critical Introduction.* New York: New York University Press.

Faux, Jeff. 2006. *The Global Class War.* Hoboken, NJ: Wiley.

Flammang, Janet A. 1997. *Women's Political Voice: How Women Are Transforming the Practice and Study of Politics.* Philadelphia: Temple University Press.

Foran, John, ed. 1994. *A Century of Revolution: Social Movements in Iran.* Minneapolis: University of Minnesota Press.

Foster, John Bellamy, and Fred Magdoff. 2009. *The Great Financial Crisis: Causes and Consequences.* New York: Monthly Review Press.

Frank, Andre Gunder. 1967. *Capitalism and Underdevelopment in Latin America.* New York: Monthly Review Press.

Friedman, Gerald, Fred Moseley, and Chris Sturr, eds. 2009. *The Economic Crisis Reader.* Boston: Economic Affairs Bureau, Inc.

Gandy, D. R. 1979. *Marx and History.* Austin: University of Texas Press.

Genschel, P. 2004. "Globalization and the Welfare State: A Retrospective." *Journal of European Public Policy* 11, no. 4: 613–636.

Glasberg, Davita Silfen, and Deric Shannon. 2010. *Political Sociology: Oppression, Resistance, and the State.* Newbury Park, CA: Pine Forge.

Gledhill, J., B. Bender, and M. T. Larsen, eds. 1995. *State and Society: The Emergence and Development of Social Hierarchy and Political Centralization.* London: Routledge.

Gold, David, Clarence Y. H. Lo, and Erik Olin Wright. 1975. "Some Recent Developments in Marxist Theories of the Capitalist State." Parts 1 and 2. *Monthly Review* 27, nos. 5 and 6 (October and November).

Goldstone, Jack. 2003. *States, Parties, and Social Movements.* New York: Cambridge University Press.

Gramsci, Antonio. 1971. *Prison Notebooks.* New York: International Publishers.

———. 1978. *Selections from Political Writings 1921–26.* London: Lawrence & Wishart.

Grillo, R. D. 1999. *Pluralism and the Politics of Difference.* New York: Oxford University Press.

Gurley, John G. 1976. *Challengers to Capitalism.* San Francisco: San Francisco Book Company.

Halebsky, Sandor, and Richard L. Harris, eds. 1995. *Capital, Power, and Inequality in Latin America.* Boulder, CO: Westview Press.

Hamilton, Clive. 1983. "Capitalist Industrialization in East Asia's Four Little Tigers." *Journal of Contemporary Asia* 13, no. 1.

Hamilton, Richard. 1972. *Class and Politics in the United States.* New York: Wiley.

Harris, Nigel. 2003. *The Return of Cosmopolitan Capital: Globalization, the State and War.* London: I. B. Tauris.

Harris, Richard, ed. 1975. *The Political Economy of Africa.* Cambridge, MA: Schenkman.

Harrison, Bennett, and Barry Bluestone. 1988. *The Great U-Turn: Corporate Restructuring and the Polarizing of America.* New York: Basic Books.

Harvey, David. 2003. *The New Imperialism.* London: Oxford University Press.

———. 2007. "Neoliberalism as Creative Destruction." *The Annals of the American Academy of Political and Social Science* 160, no. 1: 21–44.

Hersh, Seymour M. 1983. *The Price of Power.* New York: Summitt Books.

Hilton, Rodney, ed. 1976. *The Transition from Feudalism to Capitalism.* London: New Left Books.

Hirsh, Joachim. 1979. "The State Apparatus and Social Reproduction: Elements of a Theory of the Bourgeois State." In *State and Capital: A Marxist Debate,* edited by John Holloway and Sol Picciotto. Austin: University of Texas Press, 57–107.

Holloway, John, and Sol Picciotto. 1977. "Capital, Crisis and the State." *Capital and Class,* no. 2: 76–101.

——. 1979. "Introduction: Towards a Marxist Theory of the State." In *State and Capital*, edited by John Holloway and Sol Picciotto. London: Edward Arnold, 1–31.

Hooglund, Eric J. 1982. *Land and Revolution in Iran, 1960–1980*. Austin: University of Texas Press.

Hoogvelt, Ankie. 1997. *Globalization and the Postcolonial World*. Baltimore: The Johns Hopkins University Press.

Houtart, Francois, and Francois Polet, eds. 2001. *The Other Davos Summit: The Globalization of Resistance to the World Economic System*. London: Zed Books.

Hunter, Floyd. 1953. *Community Power Structure*. Chapel Hill: University of North Carolina Press.

——. 1959. *Top Leadership U.S.A.* Chapel Hill: University of North Carolina Press.

Hurrell, Andrew, and Ngaire Woods, eds. 1999. *Inequality, Globalization, and World Politics*. New York: Oxford University Press.

Hussain, Mahmoud. 1973. *Class Conflict in Egypt, 1945–1970*. New York: Monthly Review Press.

Hytrek, Gary, and Kristine M. Zentgraf. 2008. *America Transformed: Globalization, Inequality, and Power*. New York: Oxford University Press.

Ismael, Tareq Y., and Jacqueline S. Ismael, eds. 1994. *The Gulf War and the New World Order: International Relations in the Middle East*. Gainesville: University Press of Florida.

Janoski, Thomas, Robert R. Alford, Alexander M. Hicks, and Mildred A. Schwartz, eds. 2005. *The Handbook of Political Sociology: States, Civil Societies, and Globalization*. Cambridge: Cambridge University Press.

Jayal, Niraja Gopal. 1999. *Democracy and the State*. New York: Oxford University Press.

Jenkins, J. Craig, and Bert Klandermans, eds. 1995. *The Politics of Social Protest: Comparative Perspectives on States and Social Movements*. Minneapolis: University of Minnesota Press.

Jessop, Bob. 1982. *The Capitalist State*. New York: New York University Press.

——. 2002. *The Future of the Capitalist State*. Cambridge: Polity.

——. 2008. *State Power: A Strategic-Relational Approach*. London: Polity.

Johnson, Chalmers. 2004. *Blowback: The Costs and Consequences of American Empire*. New York: Holt.

——. 2005. *The Sorrows of Empire*. New York: Holt.

——. 2007. *Nemesis: The Last Days of the American Republic*. New York: Metropolitan Books.

——. 2010. *Dismantling the Empire: America's Last Best Hope*. New York: Metropolitan Books.

Katz, Richard S. 1997. *Democracy and Elections*. New York: Oxford University Press.

Kaufman, Michael, and Haroldo Dilla Alfonso, eds. 1997. *Community Power and Grassroots Democracy*. London: Zed Books.

Kennedy, Paul. 1987. *The Rise and Fall of the Great Powers*. New York: Random House.

Kidron, Michael. 1970. *Western Capitalism Since the War*. Harmondsworth, UK: Penguin.

Kimmel, Michael S., and Charles Stephen. 1998. *Social and Political Theory*. Boston: Allyn and Bacon.

King, Roger. 1986. *The State in Modern Society*. Chatham, NJ: Chatham House.

Kloby, Jerry. 2003. *Inequality, Power, and Development: Issues in Political Sociology*. Amherst, NY: Humanity.

Knapp, Peter, and Alan J. Spector. 2011. *Crisis and Change Today: Basic Questions of Marxist Sociology*. Lanham, MD: Rowman & Littlefield.

Kourvetaris, George A. 1997. *Political Sociology: Structure and Process*. Boston: Allyn and Bacon.

Krader, Lawrence. 1975. *The Asiatic Mode of Production*. Assem: Van Gorcum.

Laclau, Ernesto. 1971. "Feudalism and Capitalism in Latin America." *New Left Review,* no. 67 (May–June): 19–38.

Lachman, Richard. 2010. *States and Power.* London: Polity.

Leicht, Kevin T., and J. Craig Jenkins, eds. 2011. *Handbook of Politics: State and Society in Global Perspective.* New York: Springer.

Lenin, V. I. 1947. *Works.* Vol. 31. Moscow: Foreign Languages Publishing House.

———. 1971. *The State and Revolution.* In *Selected Works,* by V. I. Lenin. New York: International Publishers.

———. 1974. *The State.* In *On Historical Materialism,* by Karl Marx, Friedrich Engels, and V. I. Lenin. New York: International Publishers.

———. 1975. *Selected Works in Three Volumes.* Vol. 2. Moscow: Progress Publishers.

Levine, Rhonda F., ed. 1998. *Social Class and Stratification.* Boulder, CO: Rowman & Littlefield.

Levkovsky, A. I. 1966. *Capitalism in India.* Delhi: People's Publishing House.

Lewis, Cleona. 1938. *America's Stake in International Investments.* Washington, DC: Brookings Institution.

Leys, Colin. 1976. "The 'Overdeveloped' Post-Colonial State: A Reevaluation." *Review of African Political Economy* 5: 39–48.

Lindholm, Charles, and Jose Pedro Zuquete. 2010. *The Struggle for the World: Liberation Movements for the 21st Century.* Palo Alto, CA: Stanford University Press.

Linklater, Andrew. 1998. *The Transformation of Political Community.* Columbia: University of South Carolina Press.

Lipset, Seymour Martin. 1960. *Political Man.* Garden City, NY: Doubleday Anchor.

Lloyd, David, and Paul Thomas. 1998. *Culture and the State.* New York: Routledge.

Longuenesse, Elizabeth. 1979. "The Class Nature of the State in Syria." *MERIP Reports* 9, no. 4 (May): 3–11.

Luger, Stan. 2000. *Corporate Power, American Democracy, and the Automobile Industry.* Cambridge: Cambridge University Press.

Lutz, Catherine. 2009. *The Bases of Empire.* New York: New York University Press.

MacEwan, Arthur. 1999. *Neo-Liberalism or Democracy?* London: Zed Books.

Mandel, Ernest. 1975. *Late Capitalism.* London: New Left Books.

———. 1979. *From Class Society to Communism.* London: Ink Links.

Manza, Jeff, and Clem Brooks. 1999. *Social Cleavages and Political Change.* New York: Oxford University Press.

Marger, Martin N. 1987. *Elites and Masses: An Introduction to Political Sociology,* 2nd ed. Belmont, CA: Wadsworth.

Markoff, John. 1996. *Waves of Democracy: Social Movements and Political Change.* Thousand Oaks, CA: Pine Forge.

Martin, William G., et al. 2008. *Making Waves: Worldwide Social Movements, 1750–2005.* Boulder, CO: Paradigm.

Martinussen, John. 1997. *State, Society and Market.* London: Zed Books.

Marx, Karl. 1972. *The Eighteenth Brumaire of Louis Bonaparte.* In *Selected Works,* by Karl Marx and Friedrich Engels. New York: International Publishers.

———. 1972. *The Civil War in France.* In *Selected Works,* by Karl Marx and Friedrich Engels. New York: International Publishers.

———. 1972. *Critique of the Gotha Program.* In *Selected Works,* by Karl Marx and Friedrich Engels. New York: International Publishers.

———. 1972. *Preface to a Contribution to the Critique of Political Economy.* In *Selected Works,* by Karl Marx and Friedrich Engels. New York: International Publishers.

Marx, Karl, and Friedrich Engels. 1969. *The German Ideology.* New York: International Publishers.

———. 1972. *Manifesto of the Communist Party.* In *Selected Works,* by Karl Marx and Friedrich Engels. New York: International Publishers.

McConnell, Grant. 1966. *Private Power and American Democracy.* New York: Knopf.

McCrone, David. 1998. *The Sociology of Nationalism: Tomorrow's Ancestors.* London: Routledge.

McDonough, Terrence, Michael Reich, and David M. Kotz, eds. 2010. *Contemporary Capitalism and Its Crises.* New York: Cambridge University Press.

McNeely, Connie L., ed. 1998. *Public Rights, Public Rules: Constituting Citizens in the World Polity and National Policy.* New York: Garland Publishers.

Michels, Robert. 1968. *Political Parties.* New York: Free Press.

Migdal, Joel S. 2001. *State in Society: Studying How States and Societies Transform and Constitute One Another.* Cambridge: Cambridge University Press.

Miliband, Ralph. 1969. *The State in Capitalist Society.* New York: Basic Books.

———. 1970. "The Capitalist State—Reply to Nicos Poulantzas." *New Left Review,* no. 59: 53–60.

———. 1973. "Poulantzas and the Capitalist State." *New Left Review,* no. 82: 83–92.

———. 1975. "Political Forms and Historical Materialism." In *Socialist Register, 1975,* edited by R. Miliband and J. Saville. London: Merlin Press, 308–318.

———. 1977. *Marxism and Politics.* London: Oxford University Press.

———. 1982. *Capitalist Democracy in Britain.* London: Oxford University Press.

Mills, C. Wright. 1956. *The Power Elite.* New York: Oxford University Press.

Moaddel, Mansoor. 1993. *Class, Politics, and Ideology in the Iranian Revolution.* New York: Columbia University Press.

Moghadam, Valentine. 2009. *Globalization and Social Movements.* Lanham, MD: Rowman & Littlefield.

Mollenkopf, John. 1975. "Theories of the State and Power Structure Research." *Insurgent Sociologist* 5, no. 3: 245–264.

Moore, Barrington, Jr. 1968. *The Social Origins of Democracy and Dictatorship.* London: Penguin.

Mosca, Gaetano. 1939. *The Ruling Class.* New York: McGraw-Hill.

Nash, Kate. 2010. *Contemporary Political Sociology: Globalization, Politics, and Power.* Hoboken, NJ: Wiley-Blackwell.

Neuman, William Lawrence. 2004. *Power, State, and Society: An Introduction to Political Sociology.* New York: McGraw-Hill.

Newman, Bruce I. 1999. *The Mass Marketing of Politics.* Thousand Oaks, CA: Sage Publications.

Nikolas, Rose S. 1999. *Powers of Freedom: Reframing Political Thought.* Cambridge: Cambridge University Press.

O'Connor, James. 1973. *The Fiscal Crisis of the State.* New York: St. Martin's.

———. 1984. *Accumulation Crisis.* New York: Basil Blackwell.

O'Donnell, Guillermo. 1973. *Modernization and Bureaucratic Authoritarianism: Studies in South American Politics.* Berkeley: Institute of International Studies, University of California at Berkeley.

———. 1979. "Tensions in the Bureaucratic-Authoritarian State and the Questions of Democracy." In *The New Authoritarianism in Latin America,* edited by David Collier. Princeton: Princeton University Press, 285–318.

Offe, Claus. 1974. "Structural Problems of the Capitalist State." In *German Political Studies,* edited by K. Von Beyme. Vol. 1. London: Sage.

———. 1975. "The Theory of the Capitalist State and the Problem of Policy Formation." In *Stress and Contradiction in Modern Capitalism,* edited by L. Lindberg, et al. Lexington, MA: Heath, 125–144.

———. 1980. "The Separation of Form and Content in Liberal Democratic Politics." *Studies in Political Economy* 3: 5–16.

———. 1981. "Some Contradictions of the Modern Welfare State." *International Praxis* 1, no. 3: 219–229.

Olsen, Marvin E., and Martin N. Marger, eds. 1993. *Power in Societies.* Boulder, CO: Westview Press.

Opello Jr., Walter C., and Stephen J. Rosow. 1999. *The Nation-State and Global Order.* Boulder, CO: Lynne Rienner Publishers.

Oppenheimer, Martin. 2000. *The State in Modern Society.* Amherst, NY: Humanity Books.

Orum, Anthony M., and John G. Dale. 2008. *Political Sociology: Power and Participation in the Modern World.* New York: Oxford University Press.

Owen, Roger. 1992. *State, Power, and Politics in the Making of the Modern Middle East.* London: Routledge.

Panitch, Leo, and Colin Leys, eds. 1999. *Global Capitalism Versus Democracy.* New York: Monthly Review Press.

Parenti, Michael. 1970. "Power and Pluralism: The View from the Bottom." *Journal of Politics* 32 (August): 501–530.

———. 1994. *Land of Idols: Political Mythology in America.* New York: St. Martin's Press.

———. 1995. *Against Empire.* San Francisco: City Lights Books.

———. 1997. *America Besieged.* San Francisco: City Lights Books.

———. 2010. *Democracy for the Few,* 9th ed. Florence, KY: Wadsworth.

———. 2011. *The Face of Imperialism.* Boulder, CO: Paradigm.

Pareto, Vilfredo. 1935. *The Mind and Society.* 4 vols. London: Jonathan Cape.

———. 1969. "Elites and Their Circulation." In *Structured Social Inequality,* edited by C. S. Heller. New York: Macmillan, 34–39.

Parsons, Talcott. 1960. *Structure and Process in Modern Societies.* New York: Free Press.

———. 1967. "On the Concept of Political Power." In *Sociological Theory and Modern Society.* New York: Free Press, 297–354.

Paul, T. V., and John A. Hall, eds. 1999. *International Order and the Future of World Politics.* Cambridge: Cambridge University Press.

Perlo, Victor. 1984. *Super Profits and Crises: Modern U.S. Capitalism.* New York: International Publishers.

Petras, James F. 1981. *Class, State and Power in the Third World.* Montclair, NJ: Allanheld, Osmun.

———. 1983. *Capitalist and Socialist Crises in the Late Twentieth Century.* Totowa, NJ: Rowman & Allanheld.

———. 2007. *Rulers and Ruled in the U.S. Empire.* Atlanta: Clarity Press.

————. 2009. *Global Depression and Regional Wars.* Atlanta: Clarity Press.

Petras, James, and Henry Veltmeyer. 2004. *System in Crisis: The Dynamics of Free Market Capitalism.* London: Zed Books.

————. 2005. *Social Movements and State Power.* London: Pluto Press.

————. 2007. *Multinationals on Trial.* Aldershot, UK: Ashgate.

————. 2009. *What's Left in Latin America.* Aldershot, UK: Ashgate.

————. 2011. *Social Movements in Latin America: Neoliberalism and Popular Resistance.* New York: Palgrave Macmillan.

————. 2012. *Beyond Neoliberalism.* Aldershot, UK: Ashgate.

Petras, James, with Todd Cavaluzzi, Morris Morely, and Steve Vieux. 1999. *The Left Strikes Back: Class Conflict in Latin America in the Age of Neoliberalism.* Boulder, CO: Westview Press.

Petras, James, and Henry Veltmeyer, with Luciano Vasapollo and Mauro Casadio. 2006. *Empire with Imperialism: The Globalizing Dynamics of Neoliberal Capitalism.* London: Zed Books.

Picciotto, Sol. 1979. "The Theory of the State, Class Struggle, and the Rule of Law." In *Capitalism and the Rule of Law,* edited by Ben Fine, et al. London: Hutchinson, 164–177.

Polsby, Nelson. 1963. *Community Power and Political Theory.* New Haven: Yale University Press.

Poulantzas, Nicos. 1969. "The Problem of the Capitalist State." *New Left Review,* no. 58: 67–78.

————. 1973. *Political Power and Social Classes.* London: Verso.

————. 1974. *Fascism and Dictatorship.* London: New Left Books.

————. 1975. *Classes in Contemporary Capitalism.* London: New Left Books.

————. 1976. *The Crisis of the Dictatorships.* London: New Left Books.

————. 1976. "The Capitalist State: A Reply to Miliband and Laclau." *New Left Review,* no. 95: 63–83.

————. 1978. *State, Power, Socialism.* London: Verso.

————. 1979. "The Political Crisis and the Crisis of the State." In *Critical Sociology: European Perspectives,* edited by J. W. Freiberg. New York: Irvington Publishers, 357–393.

Przeworski, Adam, and Michael Wallerstein. 1982. "The Structure of Class Conflict in Democratic Capitalist Societies." *American Political Science Review* 76, no. 2: 215–238.

Rahnema, Saeed, and Sohrab Behdad, eds. 1995. *Iran After the Revolution: Crisis of an Islamic State.* London: I. B. Tauris.

Reed, Adolph L. 1997. *W. E. B. Du Bois and American Political Thought.* New York: Oxford University Press.

Robinson, William I. 1996. *Promoting Polyarchy: Globalization, U.S. Intervention and Hegemony.* Cambridge: Cambridge University Press.

Robinson, William I. 2004. *A Theory of Global Capitalism: Production, Class, and State in a Transnational World.* Baltimore: The Johns Hopkins University Press.

————. 2008. *Latin America and Globalization.* Baltimore: Johns Hopkins University Press.

————. 2010. "The Crisis of Global Capitalism: Cyclical, Structural or Systemic?" In *The Great Credit Crash,* edited by Martijn Konings. London: Verso, 289–310.

Roelofs, H. Mark. 1998. *The Poverty of American Politics: A Theoretical Interpretation,* 2nd ed. Philadelphia: Temple University Press.

Rose, Arnold. 1967. *The Power Structure.* New York: Oxford University Press.

Rose, Nikolas. 1999. *Powers of Freedom: Reframing Political Thought.* Cambridge: Cambridge University Press.

Roy, Ash Narain. 1999. *The Third World in the Age of Globalization.* London: Zed Books.

Saville, John. 1995. *The Consolidation of the Capitalist State, 1800–1850.* London: Pluto Press.

Sassen, Saskia. 1998. *Globalization and Its Discontents.* New York: The New Press.

Schatzki, Theodore R., and Wolfgang Natter, eds. 1996. *The Social and Political Body.* New York: Guilford Press.

Schmitter, Phillippe. 1974. "Still the Century of Corporatism?" In *The New Corporatism,* edited by Frederick Pike and Thomas Stritch. Notre Dame, IN: University of Notre Dame Press, 85–131.

Sen, Anupam. 1982. *The State, Industrialization, and Class Formations in India.* London: Routledge & Kegan Paul.

Sherman, Howard J. 2006. *How Society Makes Itself: The Evolution of Political and Economic Institutions.* Armonk, NY: M. E. Sharpe.

———. 2010. *The Roller Coaster Economy: Financial Crisis, Great Recession, and the Public Option.* Armonk, NY: M. E. Sharpe.

Shivji, Issa G. 1976. *Class Struggles in Tanzania.* New York: Monthly Review Press.

Shklar, Judith N. 1998. *Political Thought and Political Thinkers.* Chicago: University of Chicago Press.

———. 1998. *Redeeming American Political Thought.* Chicago: University of Chicago Press.

Silver, Beverly J. 2003. *Forces of Labor: Workers Movements and Globalization Since 1870.* Cambridge: Cambridge University Press.

Skocpol, Theda. 1979. *States and Revolutions: A Comparative Analysis of France, Russia and China.* Cambridge: Cambridge University Press.

Smith, M. J. 2000. *Rethinking State Theory.* London: Routledge.

Stalin, J. V. 1934. *Marxism and the National Question.* New York: International Publishers.

———. 1939. *Questions of Leninism.* Moscow: Foreign Languages Publishing House.

Stein, Stanley J., and Barbara H. Stein. 1970. *The Colonial Heritage of Latin America.* New York: Oxford University Press.

Stepan, Alfred. 1978. *The State and Society: Peru in Comparative Perspective.* Princeton: Princeton University Press.

Stork, Joe. 1981. "Iraq and the War in the Gulf." *MERIP Reports,* no. 97 (June): 3–18.

Street, John. 1998. *Politics and Popular Culture.* Philadelphia: Temple University Press.

Suri, Jeremi. 2005. *Power and Protest: Global Revolution and the Rise of Détente.* Cambridge, MA: Harvard University Press.

Sweezy, Paul M., and Charles Bettelheim, eds. 1971. *On the Transition to Socialism.* New York: Monthly Review Press.

Szymanski, Albeit. 1978. *The Capitalist State and the Politics of Class.* Cambridge, MA: Winthrop.

———. 1981. *The Logic of Imperialism.* New York: Praeger.

———. 1983. *Class Structure: A Critical Perspective.* New York: Praeger.

Therborn, Goran. 1976. *Science, Class and Society.* London: New Left Books.

———. 1977. "The Rule of Capital and the Rise of Democracy." *New Left Review,* no. 103: 3–41.

———. 1978. *What Does the Ruling Class Do When It Rules?* London: New Left Books.

———. 1980. *The Ideology of Power and the Power of Ideology.* London: New Left Books.

———. 1986. "Neo-Marxist, Pluralist, Corporatist, Statist Theories and the Welfare State." In *The State in Global Perspective,* edited by A. Kazancigil. Aldershot, UK: Gower and UNESCO, 204–231.

Thompson, E. P. 1963. *The Making of the English Working Class.* New York: Vintage.

Tigar, Michael. 2000. *Law and the Rise of Capitalism.* New York: Monthly Review Press.

Tillman, Ray M., and Michael S. Cummings, eds. 1999. *The Transformation of U.S. Unions.* Boulder, CO: Lynne Rienner Publishers.

Tocqueville, Alexis de. 1945. *Democracy in America.* New York: Knopf.

Tornquist, Olle. 1998. *Politics and Development.* Thousand Oaks, CA: Sage Publications.

Townsend, Janet, et al. 1999. *Women and Power.* London: Zed Books.

Trimberger, E. K. 1978. *Revolution from Above: Military Bureaucrats and Development in Japan, Turkey and Peru.* New Brunswick, NJ: Transaction Books.

Truman, David. 1964. *The Government Process.* New York: Knopf.

Turam, Berna, ed. 2012. *Secular State and Religious Society: Two Forces in Play in Turkey.* London: Palgrave Macmillan.

Turner, Bryan S. 2011. *Religion and Modern Society: Citizenship, Secularization, and the State.* New York: Cambridge University Press.

Veltmeyer, Henry, ed. 2008. *New Perspectives on Globalization and Antiglobalization.* Aldershot, UK: Ashgate.

———. 2010. *Imperialism, Crisis, and Class Struggle.* Leiden: E. J. Brill.

Wallerstein, Immanuel. 1974. *The Modern World System.* New York: Academic Press.

———. 1979. *The Capitalist World Economy.* Cambridge: Cambridge University Press.

———. 1984. *The Politics of the World-Economy: The States, the Movements and the Civilizations.* Cambridge: Cambridge University Press.

———. 2003. *The Decline of American Power.* New York: New Press.

Warren, Bill. 1980. *Imperialism, Pioneer of Capitalism.* London: Verso.

Weber, Max. 1967. *From Max Weber: Essays in Sociology.* Translated, edited, and with an introduction by H. H. Gerth and C. Wright Mills. New York: Oxford University Press.

———. 1968. *Economy and Society.* New York: Bedminster Press.

Weiss, Linda. 1998. *The Myth of the Powerless State, Governing the Economy in a Global Era.* Cambridge: Polity.

———, ed. 2003. *States in the Global Economy.* Cambridge: Cambridge University Press.

Williams, Eric. 1944. *Capitalism and Slavery.* Reprint. New York: Capricorn.

Wolfe, Alan. 1977. *The Limits of Legitimacy: Political Contradictions of Late Capitalism.* New York: Free Press.

Wolff, Jonathan, and Michael Rosen, eds. 1999. *Political Thought.* New York: Oxford University Press.

Wright, Erik Olin. 1974–1975. "To Control or To Smash Bureaucracy: Weber and Lenin on Politics, the State, and Bureaucracy." *Berkeley Journal of Sociology* 19: 69–108.

———. 1978. *Class, Crisis and the State.* London: New Left Books.

———. 1985. *Classes.* London: Verso.

———. 1994. *Interrogating Inequality.* London: Verso.

———. 1997. *Class Counts.* London: Verso.

———. 2005. *Approaches to Class Analysis.* Cambridge: Cambridge University Press.

Zeitlin, Maurice. 1980. *Classes, Class Conflict, and the State.* Cambridge, MA: Winthrop.

Index

About the Author

Dr. Berch Berberoglu is Foundation Professor of Sociology and Director of Graduate Studies in the Department of Sociology at the University of Nevada, Reno, where he has been teaching and conducting research for the past thirty-five years.

Dr. Berberoglu has written and edited twenty-eight books and many articles on topics related to political sociology, the state, globalization, and the political economy of class and class conflict on a global scale. His most recent books include *The Globalization of Capital and the Nation-State*; *Nationalism and Ethnic Conflict: Class, State, and Nation in the Age of Globalization*; *Globalization and Change: The Transformation of Global Capitalism*; *The State and Revolution in the Twentieth Century: Major Social Transformations of Our Time*; *Class and Class Conflict in the Age of Globalization*; and *Globalization in the 21st Century: Labor, Capital, and the State on a World Scale*.

Dr. Berberoglu's areas of specialization include political sociology, political economy, globalization, class analysis, development, and comparative historical sociology. His most recent book, *Beyond the Global Capitalist Crisis: The World Economy in Transition*, was published in 2012. He is currently working on a new book, *America Beyond Empire: The Promise and the Vision for a New America in the 21st Century*, which will be published by Paradigm in 2013.

Dr. Berberoglu received his PhD in Sociology from the University of Oregon in 1977 and his BA and MA from Central Michigan University in 1972 and 1974, respectively. He also did graduate studies at the State University of New York at Binghamton in the early 1970s.